THE 1998
Crime & Disorder Act
explained RICHARD POWER

2

1 2

London: The Stationery Office

A CIP catalogue record for this book is available from the British Library
A Library of Congress CIP catalogue record has been applied for

First published 1999

ISBN 0 11 702685 9

About the author

Richard Power is a barrister practising from the Chambers of Kieran Coonan QC at 6 Pump Court, Temple, London, EC4Y LAR

Disclaimer

This publication is intended to be a brief commentary on the Crime and Disorder Act 1998 and should not be relied upon by any party without taking further legal advice.

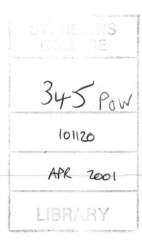
Printed in the United Kingdom for the Stationery Office by Albert Gait Ltd, Grimsby
J69893 C10 3/99 9385 9692

Contents

PART IV DEALING WITH OFFENDERS

CHAPTER I ENGLAND AND WALES

Sexual or violent offenders

Offenders dependent etc. on drugs

Young offenders: reprimands and warnings

Young offenders: non-custodial orders

Young offenders: detention and training orders

Sentencing: general

Miscellaneous and supplemental

CHAPTER II SCOTLAND

Sexual or violent offenders

Offenders dependent etc. on drugs

Racial aggravation

PART V MISCELLANEOUS AND SUPPLEMENTAL

Remands and committals

Release and recall of prisoners

INTRODUCTION

PART I PREVENTION OF CRIME AND DISORDER

Part I of the Crime and Disorder Act 1998 grants the criminal courts the power to make a number of orders which operate very like civil injunctions. Failure to comply with these orders is a criminal offence in its own right. The power to make anti-social behaviour orders, sex offender orders and parenting orders in each case allows the court either to prohibit certain particular actions or to require certain positive action with criminal sanctions. The courts have in effect a power to make a personalised criminal law. An action by a person who is the subject of an order may therefore be criminal, when the same action by anyone else may not even be a tort, or illegal in any sense.

Part I of the Act also creates a system whereby the local authority, the police, probation committees and other local bodies are to cooperate in considering how crime can be reduced in the local area.

Local child curfew schemes are introduced by which a local authority may ban all children under the age of 10 from particular public areas between 9pm and 6am. The police have power to take any child, who is in breach of the order, home. That will trigger an investigation by social services as to whether other steps should be taken regarding the child under the Children Act 1989.

Measures are also included that are intended to deal with truanting children.

PART II CRIMINAL LAW

Part II of the Act seeks to address the racist element of crime by defining "racial aggravation" and providing stiffer penalties for racially aggravated offences.

This Part also abolishes the presumption of *doli incapax*, the rebuttable presumption that children aged 10 to 13 inclusive do not know the difference between right and wrong.

Various Acts dating from as early as 1542 are amended, abolishing the death penalty for piracy and treason, the last civilian offences for which it was still available.

PART III CRIMINAL JUSTICE SYSTEM

Part III reforms the youth justice system, introducing a system under which each local authority is to prepare a "youth justice plan" annually, setting out its strategy for dealing with offending by children and young persons. Youth offending teams are introduced to co-ordinate youth justice services and to perform the functions assigned to them in the youth justice plans. The whole youth justice system is in turn overseen by the new Youth Justice Board.

The Secretary of State is given power to make regulations limiting the time allowed for the preliminary stages of criminal proceedings, with additional time limits in respect of those under 18. Restrictions are imposed on the courts' power to extend the time limits. The intention is to speed up the criminal justice system and in particular the youth justice system. However, cases that fall foul of the time limits are stayed, and fresh proceedings may be instituted within 3 months.

Various court procedures are modified and in particular, committal proceedings for indictable-only offences are abandoned. Indictable-only offences are now to be sent direct to the Crown Court without any form of scrutiny by the magistrates' court.

The equivalent of a submission of no case to answer prior to trial can now be made to the Crown Court judge before arraignment (see Schedule 3 paragraph 2), provided written notice has been given to the court (see Schedule 3 paragraph 2(3)).

There is also provision in Schedule 3 for the taking of a deposition from an unwilling witness for the prosecution by a justice of the peace which can be used without further evidence at trial on indictment. There is no corresponding power to take depositions from unwilling witnesses for the defence.

PART IV DEALING WITH OFFENDERS

Part IV introduces extended sentences, which are custodial sentences followed by extended periods of supervision, allowing either sex offenders or violent offenders to be monitored after they have been released from prison.

Part IV also introduces drug treatment and testing orders which allow a court to prescribe treatment for offenders who abuse drugs and to monitor the success of the treatment, provided the offender is willing to comply.

The system of cautioning children or young offenders is replaced by a strictly controlled system of reprimands and warnings. A warning is more serious and involves referral to a youth offending team which may make arrangements for a rehabilitation programme.

Reparation orders and action plan orders are also introduced by this Part of the Act. A reparation order requires an offender to make reparation to the victim, if the victim is willing; and an action plan order requires a child or young offender for a period of 3 months to comply with a series of requirements concerning his actions and whereabouts, under the supervision of the responsible probation officer, social worker or member of the youth offending team.

Where a child or young person faces a custodial sentence, the sentence that is to be passed is now a detention and training order, which is a period of detention followed by a period of supervision. Detention in a young offender institute is still available as a sentence for those aged 18 to 21.

A Sentencing Advisory Panel is established to assist the Court of Appeal in considering guideline cases on sentence. The Court of Appeal is now obliged to consider issuing guidelines on sentence whenever it considers sentence in appropriate cases, and when the Sentencing Advisory Panel proposes it. The Sentencing Advisory Panel is obliged to provide the Court of Appeal with information, such as the cost effectiveness of particular sentences, when required.

PART V MISCELLANEOUS AND SUPPLEMENTAL

This Part of the Act deals with remands and committals of children and young persons to local authority accommodation, the responsibility of the Parole Board for both long and short term prisoners, and consequential amendments.

Commencement

The Act received the Royal Assent on the 31st July 1998. At the time of printing (February 1999) commencement orders have been made in respect of the following provisions:

Provisions	Date of commencement	S.I. No
Sections 41 and 49 (both partially), 114, 116 and 117	1.8.98	1998/1883
Section 84 and Schedules 2 and 9 (both partially)	7.8.98	1998/1883
Sections 5 to 9, 10 (partially), 11 and 12, 13 (partially), 14 and 15, 17 and 18, 28 to 37, 38 to 40 (all partially only), 41 and 42, 43 (partially), 46 (partially), 47 and 48, 49 (partially), 50, 52 (partially), 53 to 64, 65 and 66 (both partially), 67 to 70, 71 (partially), 72, 82 and 83, 85 to 96, 97 (partially), 100 (partially), 101 and 102, 104 to 108, 110 to 113, 115, 118, 119 and 120 and Schedules 2, 3 (partially), 4 to 7, and 8 to 10 (all partially only)	30.9.98	1998/2327
Sections 2 and 3, 4 (partially), 16, 20, 21 and 22 (both partially), 23, 24, 26 (partially) and Schedules 1 and 8 (partially)	1.12.98	1998/2327 (as amended)
Section 103, paragraphs 83 and 88 of Schedule 8 to the extent that they are not already in force, paragraph 12 of Schedule 9 and the entries in Schedule 10 relating to sections 37, 38 and 45 of the Criminal Justice Act 1991 that are not already in force.	1.1.99	1998/3263
Sections 51 and 52 and Schedules 3, 8 and 10 (both partially)	4.1.99	1998/2327
Sections 99, and 100 to the extent that it is not already in force, and paragraph 10 of Schedule 9	28.1.99	1998/3263
Sections 25, 26 (to the extent it is not already in force) and 27	1.3.99	1998/3236

Sections 1, 4, 19, 21, 22 and 71(4) to the extent that they are not already in force	1.4.99	1998/3263
Sections 80 and 81, and paragraph 7 of Schedule 9	1.7.99	1998/3263

1st April 1999 is the date appointed from which crime and disorder strategies (see section 6) must be formulated and implemented (S.I. No 1998/3236).

The Crime and Disorder Act 1998

1998 c. 37

An Act to make provision for preventing crime and disorder; to create certain racially-aggravated offences; to abolish the rebuttable presumption that a child is doli incapax and to make provision as to the effect of a child's failure to give evidence at his trial; to abolish the death penalty for treason and piracy; to make changes to the criminal justice system; to make further provision for dealing with offenders; to make further provision with respect to remands and committals for trial and the release and recall of prisoners; to amend Chapter I of Part II of the Crime (Sentences) Act 1997 and to repeal Chapter I of Part III of the Crime and Punishment (Scotland) Act 1997; to make amendments designed to facilitate, or otherwise desirable in connection with, the consolidation of certain enactments; and for connected purposes.

[31st July 1998]

Be it enacted by the Queen's most Excellent Majesty, by and with the advice and consent of the Lords Spiritual and Temporal, and Commons, in this present Parliament assembled, and by the authority of the same, as follows:-

PART I PREVENTION OF CRIME AND DISORDER

CHAPTER I ENGLAND AND WALES

Crime and disorder: general

1.– (1) An application for an order under this section may be made by a relevant authority if it appears to the authority that the following conditions are fulfilled with respect to any person aged 10 or over, namely-

(a) that the person has acted, since the commencement date, in an anti-social manner, that is to say, in a manner that caused or was likely to cause harassment, alarm or distress to one or more persons not of the same household as himself; and

(b) that such an order is necessary to protect persons in the local government area in which the harassment, alarm or distress was caused or was likely to be caused from further anti-social acts by him;

and in this section "relevant authority" means the council for the local government area or any chief officer of police any part of whose police area lies within that area.

(2) A relevant authority shall not make such an application without consulting each other relevant authority.

(3) Such an application shall be made by complaint to the magistrates' court whose commission area includes the place where it is alleged that the harassment, alarm or distress was caused or was likely to be caused.

(4) If, on such an application, it is proved that the conditions mentioned in subsection (1) above are fulfilled, the magistrates' court may make an order under this section (an "anti-social behaviour order") which prohibits the defendant from doing anything described in the order.

(5) For the purpose of determining whether the condition mentioned in subsection (1)(a) above is fulfilled, the court shall disregard any act of the defendant which he shows was reasonable in the circumstances.

(6) The prohibitions that may be imposed by an anti-social behaviour order are those necessary for the purpose of protecting from further anti-social acts by the defendant-

   (a) persons in the local government area; and
   (b) persons in any adjoining local government area specified in the application for the order;

and a relevant authority shall not specify an adjoining local government area in the application without consulting the council for that area and each chief officer of police any part of whose police area lies within that area.

(7) An anti-social behaviour order shall have effect for a period (not less than two years) specified in the order or until further order.

(8) Subject to subsection (9) below, the applicant or the defendant may apply by complaint to the court which made an anti-social behaviour order for it to be varied or discharged by a further order.

(9) Except with the consent of both parties, no anti-social behaviour order shall be discharged before the end of the period of two years beginning with the date of service of the order.

(10) If without reasonable excuse a person does anything which he is prohibited from doing by an anti-social behaviour order, he shall be liable-

   (a) on summary conviction, to imprisonment for a term not exceeding six months or to a fine not exceeding the statutory maximum, or to both; or
   (b) on conviction on indictment, to imprisonment for a term not exceeding five years or to a fine, or to both.

(11) Where a person is convicted of an offence under subsection (10) above, it shall not be open to the court by or before which he is so convicted to make an order under subsection (1)(b) (conditional discharge) of section 1A of the Powers of Criminal Courts Act 1973 ("the 1973 Act") in respect of the offence.

(12) In this section-

"the commencement date" means the date of the commencement of this section;

"local government area" means-

(a) in relation to England, a district or London borough, the City of London, the Isle of Wight and the Isles of Scilly;

(b) in relation to Wales, a county or county borough.

Section 1

1. *This section empowers a magistrates' court to make an "anti-social behaviour order" on the application of the local council or the police against an individual aged 10 or over. An anti-social behaviour order prohibits a named individual, the "defendant", from behaving in any manner specified by the order. It is akin to a civil injunction. Failure to comply with the order attracts a criminal sanction however. Thus, actions that may not be criminal or even tortious if committed by others will be criminal if committed by the defendant.*

2. *An application for an order may be made if it appears either to the council or to the chief officer of police, after consultation with the other, that an individual has acted in an anti-social manner, that is to say:*

1) *in a manner that caused or was likely to cause harassment, alarm or distress to one or more persons not of the same household as himself; and*

2) *that such an order is necessary to protect persons in that local government area from further anti-social acts by the individual.*

3. *If the magistrates' court is satisfied that both of those conditions are proved, it may impose any prohibitions necessary for the purpose of protecting persons in the local or adjoining government area from further anti-social acts by the defendant. There is power to prohibit <u>any</u> act or behaviour if the court is satisfied of the requisite conditions. In deciding whether to make an order, the magistrates' court must disregard behaviour that is shown by the defendant to be reasonable. The burden of proof is on him. Great care will clearly be needed to draft the order so that prohibitions are not ambiguous, unclear or otherwise unenforceable.*

4. *The standard of proving the conditions necessary before an anti-social order can be made is the civil standard of proof, that is, on the balance of probability. Applications for anti-social behaviour orders are made by complaint, a method of commencing civil rather than criminal proceedings in the magistrates' courts, hence the civil standard of proof. Breaches of anti-social behaviour orders must of course be proved to the criminal standard, beyond reasonable doubt.*

5. *An anti-social behaviour order will have effect for the period specified in the order, not being less than two years, or indefinitely until a further order. Either the applicant or the defendant may apply to vary or discharge the order. Except with the consent of both parties no anti-social behaviour order may be discharged before the expiry of two years.*

> 6. *On summary conviction for doing anything prohibited by the anti-social behaviour order without reasonable excuse, a person is liable to 6 months imprisonment or to a fine not exceeding the statutory maximum, or on conviction on indictment to 5 years imprisonment or to a fine, or both.*
>
> 7. *On conviction for breach of an anti-social behaviour order no court may order a conditional discharge, although there is no prohibition on granting an absolute discharge.*
>
> 8. *It is a defence for the defendant to show that he had a reasonable excuse for behaving in a prohibited manner. The onus of proof is on him.*

2.– (1) If it appears to a chief officer of police that the following conditions are fulfilled with respect to any person in his police area, namely-

  (a) that the person is a sex offender; and
  (b) that the person has acted, since the relevant date, in such a way as to give reasonable cause to believe that an order under this section is necessary to protect the public from serious harm from him,

the chief officer may apply for an order under this section to be made in respect of the person.

(2) Such an application shall be made by complaint to the magistrates' court whose commission area includes any place where it is alleged that the defendant acted in such a way as is mentioned in subsection (1)(b) above.

(3) If, on such an application, it is proved that the conditions mentioned in subsection (1) above are fulfilled, the magistrates' court may make an order under this section (a "sex offender order") which prohibits the defendant from doing anything described in the order.

(4) The prohibitions that may be imposed by a sex offender order are those necessary for the purpose of protecting the public from serious harm from the defendant.

(5) A sex offender order shall have effect for a period (not less than five years) specified in the order or until further order; and while such an order has effect, Part I of the Sex Offenders Act 1997 shall have effect as if-

  (a) the defendant were subject to the notification requirements of that Part; and
  (b) in relation to the defendant, the relevant date (within the meaning of that Part) were the date of service of the order.

(6) Subject to subsection (7) below, the applicant or the defendant may apply by complaint to the court which made a sex offender order for it to be varied or discharged by a further order.

(7) Except with the consent of both parties, no sex offender order shall be discharged before the end of the period of five years beginning with the date of service of the order.

(8) If without reasonable excuse a person does anything which he is prohibited from doing by a sex offender order, he shall be liable-

   (a) on summary conviction, to imprisonment for a term not exceeding six months or to a fine not exceeding the statutory maximum, or to both; or
   (b) on conviction on indictment, to imprisonment for a term not exceeding five years or to a fine, or to both.

(9) Where a person is convicted of an offence under subsection (8) above, it shall not be open to the court by or before which he is so convicted to make an order under subsection (1)(b) (conditional discharge) of section 1A of the 1973 Act in respect of the offence.

Section 2

1.   This section empowers a magistrates' court to make a "sex offender order" on the application of a chief officer of police. A "sex offender order" prohibits a named individual from any behaviour specified in the order. Again, like the anti-social behaviour order, the sex offender order is akin to a civil injunction.

2.   The magistrates' court may make an order if it is proved that the defendant:

1)   is a sex offender, that is (see section 3) that he has been convicted of an offence to which Part I of the Sex Offenders Act 1997 applies, or if he has admitted and been cautioned for such an offence, or been punished for a like offence abroad, or other specified categories; and

2)   that he has acted, since his conviction or caution, in such a way as to give reasonable cause for belief that an order under this section is necessary to protect the public from serious harm from him.

3.   The standard of proving the conditions necessary before a sex offender order can be made is the civil standard of proof, that is, on the balance of probability. Like applications for anti-social behaviour orders, applications for sex-offender orders must be made by complaint, a method of commencing civil proceedings in the magistrates' court, hence the civil standard of proof. Breaches of sex-offender orders must be proved to the criminal standard, beyond reasonable doubt.

4.   The magistrates' court may prohibit the defendant from doing anything necessary for the purpose of protecting the public.

5.   A sex offender order will have effect for a period specified in the order, not being less than five years, or indefinitely until a further order.

6. *During the currency of a sex offender order the notification provisions of Part I of the Sex Offenders Act 1997 will have effect once served.*

7. *Either the police or the defendant may apply for the order to be varied or discharged, but it may not be discharged without the consent of both parties before the expiry of five years.*

8. *On summary conviction for doing anything prohibited by a sex offender order without reasonable excuse, a defendant is liable to imprisonment for up to six months or to a fine not exceeding the statutory maximum, or to both; and on conviction on indictment, a defendant is liable to imprisonment for 5 years or a fine, or both.*

9. *On conviction for breach of a sex offender order no court may order a conditional discharge, although there is no prohibition on granting an absolute discharge.*

10. *It is a defence for the defendant to show that he had a reasonable excuse for behaving in a prohibited manner. The onus of proof is on him.*

3.– (1) In section 2 above and this section "sex offender" means a person who-

(a) has been convicted of a sexual offence to which Part I of the Sex Offenders Act 1997 applies;

(b) has been found not guilty of such an offence by reason of insanity, or found to be under a disability and to have done the act charged against him in respect of such an offence;

(c) has been cautioned by a constable, in England and Wales or Northern Ireland, in respect of such an offence which, at the time when the caution was given, he had admitted; or

(d) has been punished under the law in force in a country or territory outside the United Kingdom for an act which-

   (i) constituted an offence under that law; and

   (ii) would have constituted a sexual offence to which that Part applies if it had been done in any part of the United Kingdom.

(2) In subsection (1) of section 2 above "the relevant date", in relation to a sex offender, means-

(a) the date or, as the case may be, the latest date on which he has been convicted, found, cautioned or punished as mentioned in subsection (1) above; or

(b) if later, the date of the commencement of that section.

(3) Subsections (2) and (3) of section 6 of the (1997 c.51.)Sex Offenders Act 1997 apply for the construction of references in subsections (1) and (2) above as they apply for the construction of references in Part I of that Act.

(4) In subsections (1) and (2) above, any reference to a person having been cautioned shall be construed as including a reference to his having been reprimanded or warned (under section 65 below) as a child or young person.

(5) An act punishable under the law in force in any country or territory outside the United Kingdom constitutes an offence under that law for the purposes of subsection (1) above, however it is described in that law.

(6) Subject to subsection (7) below, the condition in subsection (1)(d)(i) above shall be taken to be satisfied unless, not later than rules of court may provide, the defendant serves on the applicant a notice-

    (a) stating that, on the facts as alleged with respect to the act in question, the condition is not in his opinion satisfied;

    (b) showing his grounds for that opinion; and

    (c) requiring the applicant to show that it is satisfied.

(7) The court, if it thinks fit, may permit the defendant to require the applicant to show that the condition is satisfied without the prior service of a notice under subsection (6) above.

Section 3
This section defines various terms concerning sex offenders, including "sex offender" and "relevant date". The "relevant date" is the date prior to which actions cannot be considered as giving cause to believe that a sex offender order is necessary. The Act is not retrospective. Before a sex offender order can be made, a sex offender will have to act in such a way as to give cause to believe that a sex offender order is necessary after the commencement of section 3. (1.12.98, see S.I. No 1998/2327)

4.– (1) An appeal shall lie to the Crown Court against the making by a magistrates' court of an anti-social behaviour order or sex offender order.

(2) On such an appeal the Crown Court-

    (a) may make such orders as may be necessary to give effect to its determination of the appeal; and

    (b) may also make such incidental or consequential orders as appear to it to be just.

(3) Any order of the Crown Court made on an appeal under this section (other than one directing that an application be re-heard by a magistrates' court) shall, for the purposes of section 1(8) or 2(6) above, be treated as if it were an order of the magistrates' court from which the appeal was brought and not an order of the Crown Court.

Section 4
This section provides the avenue of appeal from the magistrates' court to the Crown Court against the making of anti-social behaviour orders or sex offender orders.

Crime and disorder strategies

5.– (1) Subject to the provisions of this section, the functions conferred by section 6 below shall be exercisable in relation to each local government area by the responsible authorities, that is to say-

    (a) the council for the area and, where the area is a district and the council is not a unitary authority, the council for the county which includes the district; and

    (b) every chief officer of police any part of whose police area lies within the area.

(2) In exercising those functions, the responsible authorities shall act in co-operation with the following persons and bodies, namely-

    (a) every police authority any part of whose police area lies within the area;

    (b) every probation committee or health authority any part of whose area lies within the area; and

    (c) every person or body of a description which is for the time being prescribed by order of the Secretary of State under this subsection;

and it shall be the duty of those persons and bodies to co-operate in the exercise by the responsible authorities of those functions.

(3) The responsible authorities shall also invite the participation in their exercise of those functions of at least one person or body of each description which is for the time being prescribed by order of the Secretary of State under this subsection.

(4) In this section and sections 6 and 7 below "local government area" means-

    (a) in relation to England, each district or London borough, the City of London, the Isle of Wight and the Isles of Scilly;

    (b) in relation to Wales, each county or county borough.

Section 5
This section provides that certain bodies, namely the local council, the police, the probation committee, the health authority, and any other body that may be prescribed by the Secretary of State, are to cooperate when formulating and implementing the strategy (see section 6) for reducing crime and disorder in the area.

6.– (1) The responsible authorities for a local government area shall, in accordance with the provisions of section 5 above and this section, formulate and implement, for each relevant period, a strategy for the reduction of crime and disorder in the area.

(2) Before formulating a strategy, the responsible authorities shall-

(a) carry out a review of the levels and patterns of crime and disorder in the area (taking due account of the knowledge and experience of persons in the area);

(b) prepare an analysis of the results of that review;

(c) publish in the area a report of that analysis; and

(d) obtain the views on that report of persons or bodies in the area (including those of a description prescribed by order under section 5(3) above), whether by holding public meetings or otherwise.

(3) In formulating a strategy, the responsible authorities shall have regard to the analysis prepared under subsection (2)(b) above and the views obtained under subsection (2)(d) above.

(4) A strategy shall include-

(a) objectives to be pursued by the responsible authorities, by co-operating persons or bodies or, under agreements with the responsible authorities, by other persons or bodies; and

(b) long-term and short-term performance targets for measuring the extent to which such objectives are achieved.

(5) After formulating a strategy, the responsible authorities shall publish in the area a document which includes details of-

(a) co-operating persons and bodies;

(b) the review carried out under subsection (2)(a) above;

(c) the report published under subsection (2)(c) above; and

(d) the strategy, including in particular-

(i) the objectives mentioned in subsection (4)(a) above and, in each case, the authorities, persons or bodies by whom they are to be pursued; and

(ii) the performance targets mentioned in subsection (4)(b) above.

(6) While implementing a strategy, the responsible authorities shall keep it under review with a view to monitoring its effectiveness and making any changes to it that appear necessary or expedient.

(7) In this section-

"co-operating persons or bodies" means persons or bodies co-operating in the exercise of the responsible authorities' functions under this section;

"relevant period" means-

(a) the period of three years beginning with such day as the Secretary of State may by order appoint; and

(b) each subsequent period of three years.

Section 6

1. This section imposes the obligation on the bodies specified in section 5 to formulate and implement a strategy for the reduction of crime and disorder in their area.

2. Before formulating the strategy, the bodies concerned are to review the levels and patterns of crime in their area, prepare an analysis and publish a report, and obtain views on the report.

3. A strategy is to include objectives to be pursued by the council, the police and the other bodies concerned; and long-term and short-term performance targets.

4. The strategy is to be published.

7.– (1) The responsible authorities for a local government area shall, whenever so required by the Secretary of State, submit to the Secretary of State a report on such matters connected with the exercise of their functions under section 6 above as may be specified in the requirement.

(2) A requirement under subsection (1) above may specify the form in which a report is to be given.

(3) The Secretary of State may arrange, or require the responsible authorities to arrange, for a report under subsection (1) above to be published in such manner as appears to him to be appropriate.

Section 7

This section provides that the local authority and the police shall whenever so required submit a report to the Secretary of State concerning their obligations to formulate and implement a strategy for the reduction of crime and disorder. The Secretary of State may also require publication of the report.

Youth crime and disorder

8.– (1) This section applies where, in any court proceedings-

    (a) a child safety order is made in respect of a child;
    (b) an anti-social behaviour order or sex offender order is made in respect of a child or young person;
    (c) a child or young person is convicted of an offence; or

(d) a person is convicted of an offence under section 443 (failure to comply with school attendance order) or section 444 (failure to secure regular attendance at school of registered pupil) of the Education Act 1996.

(2) Subject to subsection (3) and section 9(1) below, if in the proceedings the court is satisfied that the relevant condition is fulfilled, it may make a parenting order in respect of a person who is a parent or guardian of the child or young person or, as the case may be, the person convicted of the offence under section 443 or 444 ("the parent").

(3) A court shall not make a parenting order unless it has been notified by the Secretary of State that arrangements for implementing such orders are available in the area in which it appears to the court that the parent resides or will reside and the notice has not been withdrawn.

(4) A parenting order is an order which requires the parent-

(a) to comply, for a period not exceeding twelve months, with such requirements as are specified in the order; and

(b) subject to subsection (5) below, to attend, for a concurrent period not exceeding three months and not more than once in any week, such counselling or guidance sessions as may be specified in directions given by the responsible officer;

and in this subsection "week" means a period of seven days beginning with a Sunday.

(5) A parenting order may, but need not, include such a requirement as is mentioned in subsection (4)(b) above in any case where such an order has been made in respect of the parent on a previous occasion.

(6) The relevant condition is that the parenting order would be desirable in the interests of preventing-

(a) in a case falling within paragraph (a) or (b) of subsection (1) above, any repetition of the kind of behaviour which led to the child safety order, anti-social behaviour order or sex offender order being made;

(b) in a case falling within paragraph (c) of that subsection, the commission of any further offence by the child or young person;

(c) in a case falling within paragraph (d) of that subsection, the commission of any further offence under section 443 or 444 of the Education Act 1996.

(7) The requirements that may be specified under subsection (4)(a) above are those which the court considers desirable in the interests of preventing any such repetition or, as the case may be, the commission of any such further offence.

(8) In this section and section 9 below "responsible officer", in relation to a parenting order, means one of the following who is specified in the order, namely-

(a) a probation officer;

(b) a social worker of a local authority social services department; and

(c) a member of a youth offending team.

Section 8

1.   This section deals with parenting orders. Whenever a child or young person is convicted of an offence or made the subject of a child safety order, an anti-social behaviour order or a sex offender order, the court may require a parent or guardian:

1)   to comply with requirements specified in the order for a period not exceeding twelve months; and

2)   to attend for counselling and guidance sessions not more than once a week for a period not exceeding three months as directed by a specified probation officer, social worker or member of a youth offending team.

2.   An order may also be made if a person is convicted under section 443 (failure to comply with a school attendance order) or section 444 (failure to secure regular attendance at school).

3.   The court may impose the requirements when it is satisfied that they are desirable in the interests of preventing repetition of the kind of behaviour that led to the commission of the offence or the making of the order.

4.   In order to achieve that aim the court may impose any requirements that it considers desirable.

5.   Failure to comply with a parenting order is a criminal offence: see section 9.

6.   A court cannot make a parenting order unless facilities exist for implementing it in the local area.

9.– (1) Where a person under the age of 16 is convicted of an offence, the court by or before which he is so convicted-

    (a) if it is satisfied that the relevant condition is fulfilled, shall make a parenting order; and

    (b) if it is not so satisfied, shall state in open court that it is not and why it is not.

(2) Before making a parenting order-

    (a) in a case falling within paragraph (a) of subsection (1) of section 8 above;

    (b) in a case falling within paragraph (b) or (c) of that subsection, where the person concerned is under the age of 16; or

    (c) in a case falling within paragraph (d) of that subsection, where the person to whom the offence related is under that age,

a court shall obtain and consider information about the person's family circumstances and the likely effect of the order on those circumstances.

(3) Before making a parenting order, a court shall explain to the parent in ordinary language-

    (a) the effect of the order and of the requirements proposed to be included in it;

(b) the consequences which may follow (under subsection (7) below) if he fails to comply with any of those requirements; and

(c) that the court has power (under subsection (5) below) to review the order on the application either of the parent or of the responsible officer.

(4) Requirements specified in, and directions given under, a parenting order shall, as far as practicable, be such as to avoid-

(a) any conflict with the parent's religious beliefs; and

(b) any interference with the times, if any, at which he normally works or attends an educational establishment.

(5) If while a parenting order is iwere exercising the power.

(6) Where an application under subsection (5) above for the discharge of a parenting order is dismissed, no further application for its discharge shall be made under that subsection by any person except with the consent of the court which made the order.

(7) If while a parenting order is in force the parent without reasonable excuse fails to comply with any requirement included in the order, or specified in directions given by the responsible officer, he shall be liable on summary conviction to a fine not exceeding level 3 on the standard scale.

Section 9

1.   On summary conviction for failing to comply with the requirements of a parenting order a person is liable to a fine not exceeding level 3.

2.   Where a person under the age of 16 is convicted of an offence, the court is obliged to consider whether a parenting order would be desirable in the interests of preventing the further commission of offences. If it is not, the court must state its reasons for considering that a parenting order would be undesirable.

3.   The court is obliged to obtain a report on the family's circumstances before making a parenting order and to explain its effect.

4.   Requirements imposed should not, so far as is practicable, conflict with the parent's religious beliefs or interfere with a parent's work or education.

5.   A parenting order may be varied on the application of the responsible probation officer, social worker or member of the youth offending team or the parent. If one application for discharge of the order is dismissed, no further application may be made without leave of the court which made the order.

10.– (1) An appeal shall lie-

(a) to the High Court against the making of a parenting order by virtue of paragraph (a) of subsection (1) of section 8 above; and

    (b) to the Crown Court against the making of a parenting order by virtue of paragraph (b) of that subsection.

(2) On an appeal under subsection (1) above the High Court or the Crown Court-

    (a) may make such orders as may be necessary to give effect to its determination of the appeal; and

    (b) may also make such incidental or consequential orders as appear to it to be just.

(3) Any order of the High Court or the Crown Court made on an appeal under subsection (1) above (other than one directing that an application be re-heard by a magistrates' court) shall, for the purposes of subsections (5) to (7) of section 9 above, be treated as if it were an order of the court from which the appeal was brought and not an order of the High Court or the Crown Court.

(4) A person in respect of whom a parenting order is made by virtue of section 8(1)(c) above shall have the same right of appeal against the making of the order as if-

    (a) the offence that led to the making of the order were an offence committed by him; and

    (b) the order were a sentence passed on him for the offence.

(5) A person in respect of whom a parenting order is made by virtue of section 8(1)(d) above shall have the same right of appeal against the making of the order as if the order were a sentence passed on him for the offence that led to the making of the order.

(6) The Lord Chancellor may by order make provision as to the circumstances in which appeals under subsection (1)(a) above may be made against decisions taken by courts on questions arising in connection with the transfer, or proposed transfer, of proceedings by virtue of any order under paragraph 2 of Schedule 11 (jurisdiction) to the Children Act 1989 ("the 1989 Act").

(7) Except to the extent provided for in any order made under subsection (6) above, no appeal may be made against any decision of a kind mentioned in that subsection.

Section 10

1.   This section provides that an appeal lies to the High Court if a parenting order is made in conjunction with a child safety order; and otherwise to the Crown Court.

2.   Both the High Court and the Crown Court have powers to make such orders as are necessary to give effect to the determination of the appeal.

11.– (1) Subject to subsection (2) below, if a magistrates' court, on the application of a local authority, is satisfied that one or more of the conditions specified in subsection (3) below are fulfilled with respect to a child under the age of 10, it may make an order (a "child safety order") which-

(a) places the child, for a period (not exceeding the permitted maximum) specified in the order, under the supervision of the responsible officer; and

(b) requires the child to comply with such requirements as are so specified.

(2) A court shall not make a child safety order unless it has been notified by the Secretary of State that arrangements for implementing such orders are available in the area in which it appears that the child resides or will reside and the notice has not been withdrawn.

(3) The conditions are-

(a) that the child has committed an act which, if he had been aged 10 or over, would have constituted an offence;

(b) that a child safety order is necessary for the purpose of preventing the commission by the child of such an act as is mentioned in paragraph (a) above;

(c) that the child has contravened a ban imposed by a curfew notice; and

(d) that the child has acted in a manner that caused or was likely to cause harassment, alarm or distress to one or more persons not of the same household as himself.

(4) The maximum period permitted for the purposes of subsection (1)(a) above is three months or, where the court is satisfied that the circumstances of the case are exceptional, 12 months.

(5) The requirements that may be specified under subsection (1)(b) above are those which the court considers desirable in the interests of-

(a) securing that the child receives appropriate care, protection and support and is subject to proper control; or

(b) preventing any repetition of the kind of behaviour which led to the child safety order being made.

(6) Proceedings under this section or section 12 below shall be family proceedings for the purposes of the 1989 Act or section 65 of the Magistrates' Courts Act 1980 ("the 1980 Act"); and the standard of proof applicable to such proceedings shall be that applicable to civil proceedings.

(7) In this section "local authority" has the same meaning as in the 1989 Act.

(8) In this section and section 12 below, "responsible officer", in relation to a child safety order, means one of the following who is specified in the order, namely-

(a) a social worker of a local authority social services department; and

(b) a member of a youth offending team.

Section 11

1.   This section deals with child safety orders. Where a child under the age of 10:

1)   commits an act that, but for the child's age, would have constituted a criminal offence, or

2)   the court considers it necessary for the purpose of preventing the commission of a further act of a similar nature by the child; or

3)   the child has contravened a curfew notice; or

4)   the child has acted in a manner that caused or was likely to cause harassment, distress or alarm to one or more persons not of the same household as himself;

a magistrates' court may, on the application of the local authority, place the child under the supervision of a probation officer or member of a youth offending team; or require the child to comply with whatever requirements the court considers desirable. Failure to comply may result in the making of a care order placing the child in the care of the local authority (see section 12).

2.   The requirements that may be imposed on the child are those considered desirable in the interests of securing that the child receives appropriate care, protection and support; or preventing repetition of the behaviour that led to the child safety order being made.

3.   Proceedings under this section are family proceedings for the purposes of the Children Act 1989 and section 65 of the Magistrates' Courts Act 1980; and the standard of proof applicable is the civil standard, on the balance of probability.

12.– (1) Before making a child safety order, a magistrates' court shall obtain and consider information about the child's family circumstances and the likely effect of the order on those circumstances.

(2) Before making a child safety order, a magistrates' court shall explain to the parent or guardian of the child in ordinary language-

   (a) the effect of the order and of the requirements proposed to be included in it;
   (b) the consequences which may follow (under subsection (6) below) if the child fails to comply with any of those requirements; and
   (c) that the court has power (under subsection (4) below) to review the order on the application either of the parent or guardian or of the responsible officer.

(3) Requirements included in a child safety order shall, as far as practicable, be such as to avoid-

   (a) any conflict with the parent's religious beliefs; and
   (b) any interference with the times, if any, at which the child normally attends school.

(4) If while a child safety order is in force in respect of a child it appears to the court which made it, on the application of the responsible officer or a parent or guardian of the child, that it is appropriate to make an order under this subsection, the court may make an order discharging the child safety order or varying it-

    (a) by cancelling any provision included in it; or

    (b) by inserting in it (either in addition to or in substitution for any of its provisions) any provision that could have been included in the order if the court had then had power to make it and were exercising the power.

(5) Where an application under subsection (4) above for the discharge of a child safety order is dismissed, no further application for its discharge shall be made under that subsection by any person except with the consent of the court which made the order.

(6) Where a child safety order is in force and it is proved to the satisfaction of the court which made it or another magistrates' court acting for the same petty sessions area, on the application of the responsible officer, that the child has failed to comply with any requirement included in the order, the court-

    (a) may discharge the order and make in respect of him a care order under subsection (1)(a) of section 31 of the 1989 Act; or

    (b) may make an order varying the order-

        (i) by cancelling any provision included in it; or

        (ii) by inserting in it (either in addition to or in substitution for any of its provisions) any provision that could have been included in the order if the court had then had power to make it and were exercising the power.

(7) Subsection (6)(a) above applies whether or not the court is satisfied that the conditions mentioned in section 31(2) of the 1989 Act are fulfilled.

Section 12

1.   Before a child safety order is made, a report on the family must be obtained, and the effect of the order properly explained. This section also provides that requirements should not conflict with the parent's religious beliefs or the child's schooling.

2.   In addition this section sets out the provisions for varying or discharging the order on the application of a parent, social worker or member of a youth offending team. If an application to discharge the order is dismissed, no further application may be made without the leave of the court making the original order.

3.   If the child fails to comply with the child safety order, the court may discharge the order and make a care order pursuant to section 31(1)(a) of the Children Act 1989 (placing a child in the care of a local authority), or vary the child safety order.

13.– (1) An appeal shall lie to the High Court against the making by a magistrates' court of a child safety order; and on such an appeal the High Court-

(a) may make such orders as may be necessary to give effect to its determination of the appeal; and

(b) may also make such incidental or consequential orders as appear to it to be just.

(2) Any order of the High Court made on an appeal under this section (other than one directing that an application be re-heard by a magistrates' court) shall, for the purposes of subsections (4) to (6) of section 12 above, be treated as if it were an order of the magistrates' court from which the appeal was brought and not an order of the High Court.

(3) Subsections (6) and (7) of section 10 above shall apply for the purposes of subsection (1) above as they apply for the purposes of subsection (1)(a) of that section.

> **Section 13**
> *An appeal against the making of a child safety order is to the High Court. This section sets out the provisions relating to appeals.*

14.– (1) A local authority may make a scheme (a "local child curfew scheme") for enabling the authority-

(a) subject to and in accordance with the provisions of the scheme; and

(b) if, after such consultation as is required by the scheme, the authority considers it necessary to do so for the purpose of maintaining order,

to give a notice imposing, for a specified period (not exceeding 90 days), a ban to which subsection (2) below applies.

(2) This subsection applies to a ban on children of specified ages (under 10) being in a public place within a specified area-

(a) during specified hours (between 9 pm and 6 am); and

(b) otherwise than under the effective control of a parent or a responsible person aged 18 or over.

(3) Before making a local child curfew scheme, a local authority shall consult-

(a) every chief officer of police any part of whose police area lies within its area; and

(b) such other persons or bodies as it considers appropriate.

(4) A local child curfew scheme shall be made under the common seal of the local authority and shall not have effect until it is confirmed by the Secretary of State.

(5) The Secretary of State-

   (a) may confirm, or refuse to confirm, a local child curfew scheme submitted under this section for confirmation; and
   (b) may fix the date on which such a scheme is to come into operation;

and if no date is so fixed, the scheme shall come into operation at the end of the period of one month beginning with the date of its confirmation.

(6) A notice given under a local child curfew scheme (a "curfew notice") may specify different hours in relation to children of different ages.

(7) A curfew notice shall be given-

   (a) by posting the notice in some conspicuous place or places within the specified area; and
   (b) in such other manner, if any, as appears to the local authority to be desirable for giving publicity to the notice.

(8) In this section-

   "local authority" means-

   (a) in relation to England, the council of a district or London borough, the Common Council of the City of London, the Council of the Isle of Wight and the Council of the Isles of Scilly;
   (b) in relation to Wales, the council of a county or county borough;

   "public place" has the same meaning as in Part II of the Public Order Act 1986.

Section 14

1.   The powers provided under this section enable a local authority to ban all children under the age of 10 from specified public areas between the hours of 9pm and 6am, unless they are under the effective control of a responsible person aged 18 or over. The ban cannot exceed 90 days.

2.   The local authority may exercise its powers by making a "local child curfew scheme", after consultation with the police and other bodies. A scheme shall not have effect until it is confirmed by the Secretary of State.

3.   A scheme is to be publicised by the posting of notices in conspicuous places and whatever other means the authority considers appropriate.

15.– (1) Subsections (2) and (3) below apply where a constable has reasonable cause to believe that a child is in contravention of a ban imposed by a curfew notice.

(2) The constable shall, as soon as practicable, inform the local authority for the area that the child has contravened the ban.

(3) The constable may remove the child to the child's place of residence unless he has reasonable cause to believe that the child would, if removed to that place, be likely to suffer significant harm.

(4) In subsection (1) of section 47 of the 1989 Act (local authority's duty to investigate)-

    (a) in paragraph (a), after sub-paragraph (ii) there shall be inserted the following sub-paragraph-

    "(iii) has contravened a ban imposed by a curfew notice within the meaning of Chapter I of Part I of the Crime and Disorder Act 1998; or "; and

    (b) at the end there shall be inserted the following paragraph-

    "In the case of a child falling within paragraph (a)(iii) above, the enquiries shall be commenced as soon as practicable and, in any event, within 48 hours of the authority receiving the information."

> **Section 15**
>
> *1.   This section sets out the means by which local child curfew schemes may be enforced.*
>
> *2.   A police officer may take a child breaching the curfew home, and must inform the local authority of the breach, whereupon the local authority is obliged to investigate whether it should take steps to safeguard or promote the child's welfare, pursuant to section 47 of the Children Act 1989.*
>
> *3.   The local authority must begin its investigation within 48 hours of being informed of the breach of the curfew.*

16.– (1) This section applies where a local authority-

    (a) designates premises in a police area ("designated premises") as premises to which children and young persons of compulsory school age may be removed under this section; and

    (b) notifies the chief officer of police for that area of the designation.

(2) A police officer of or above the rank of superintendent may direct that the powers conferred on a constable by subsection (3) below-

    (a) shall be exercisable as respects any area falling within the police area and specified in the direction; and

    (b) shall be so exercisable during a period so specified;

and references in that subsection to a specified area and a specified period shall be construed accordingly.

(3) If a constable has reasonable cause to believe that a child or young person found by him in a public place in a specified area during a specified period-

(a) is of compulsory school age; and

(b) is absent from a school without lawful authority,

the constable may remove the child or young person to designated premises, or to the school from which he is so absent.

(4) A child's or young person's absence from a school shall be taken to be without lawful authority unless it falls within subsection (3) (leave, sickness, unavoidable cause or day set apart for religious observance) of section 444 of the Education Act 1996.

(5) In this section-

"local authority" means-

(a) in relation to England, a county council, a district council whose district does not form part of an area that has a county council, a London borough council or the Common Council of the City of London;

(b) in relation to Wales, a county council or a county borough council;

"public place" has the same meaning as in section 14 above;

"school" has the same meaning as in the (1996 c.56.)Education Act 1996.

Section 16

1. This section allows a police constable to take school truants to areas designated for the purpose by the local authority.

2. If the constable has reasonable cause to believe that a child or young person of compulsory school age is absent from school without lawful authority in a public place, he may take them to a place designated by the local authority.

3. A child or young person's absence from school is taken to be without lawful authority unless it falls within section 444 of the Education Act 1996 (leave, sickness, unavoidable cause or day set apart for religious observance).

Miscellaneous and supplemental

17.– (1) Without prejudice to any other obligation imposed on it, it shall be the duty of each authority to which this section applies to exercise its various functions with due regard to the likely effect of the exercise of those functions on, and the need to do all that it reasonably can to prevent, crime and disorder in its area.

(2) This section applies to a local authority, a joint authority, a police authority, a National Park authority and the Broads Authority.

(3) In this section-

"local authority" means a local authority within the meaning given by section 270(1) of the Local Government Act 1972 or the Common Council of the City of London;

"joint authority" has the same meaning as in the Local Government Act 1985;

"National Park authority" means an authority established under section 63 of the Environment Act 1995.

Section 17
This section requires local, police and other specified authorities to consider the effect on crime and disorder, and the need to prevent it, whenever they exercise their functions.

18.– (1) In this Chapter-

"anti-social behaviour order" has the meaning given by section 1(4) above;

"chief officer of police" has the meaning given by section 101(1) of the Police Act 1996;

"child safety order" has the meaning given by section 11(1) above;

"curfew notice" has the meaning given by section 14(6) above;

"local child curfew scheme" has the meaning given by section 14(1) above;

"parenting order" has the meaning given by section 8(4) above;

"police area" has the meaning given by section 1(2) of the Police Act 1996;

"police authority" has the meaning given by section 101(1) of that Act;

"responsible officer"-

(a) in relation to a parenting order, has the meaning given by section 8(8) above;
(b) in relation to a child safety order, has the meaning given by section 11(8) above;

"sex offender order" has the meaning given by section 2(3) above.

(2) In this Chapter, unless the contrary intention appears, expressions which are also used in Part I of the Criminal Justice Act 1991 ("the 1991 Act") have the same meanings as in that Part.

(3) Where directions under a parenting order are to be given by a probation officer, the probation officer shall be an officer appointed for or assigned to the petty sessions area within which it appears to the court that the child or, as the case may be, the parent resides or will reside.

(4) Where the supervision under a child safety order is to be provided, or directions under a parenting order are to be given, by-

(a) a social worker of a local authority social services department; or
(b) a member of a youth offending team,

the social worker or member shall be a social worker of, or a member of a youth offending team established by, the local authority within whose area it appears to the court that the child or, as the case may be, the parent resides or will reside.

(5) For the purposes of this Chapter the Inner Temple and the Middle Temple form part of the City of London.

> **Section 18**
> *This section is an interpretation section.*

CHAPTER II SCOTLAND

19.– (1) A local authority may make an application for an order under this section if it appears to the authority that the following conditions are fulfilled with respect to any person of or over the age of 16, namely-

(a) that the person has-
   (i) acted in an anti-social manner, that is to say, in a manner that caused or was likely to cause alarm or distress; or
   (ii) pursued a course of anti-social conduct, that is to say, pursued a course of conduct that caused or was likely to cause alarm or distress,

to one or more persons not of the same household as himself in the authority's area (and in this section "anti-social acts" and "anti-social conduct" shall be construed accordingly); and

(b) that such an order is necessary to protect persons in the authority's area from further anti-social acts or conduct by him.

(2) An application under subsection (1) above shall be made by summary application to the sheriff within whose sheriffdom the alarm or distress was alleged to have been caused or to have been likely to be caused.

(3) On an application under subsection (1) above, the sheriff may, if he is satisfied that the conditions mentioned in that subsection are fulfilled, make an order under this section (an "anti-social behaviour order") which, for the purpose of protecting persons in the area of the local authority from further anti-social acts or conduct by the person against whom the order is sought, prohibits him from doing anything described in the order.

(4) For the purpose of determining whether the condition mentioned in subsection (1)(a) is fulfilled, the sheriff shall disregard any act of the person in respect of whom the application is made which that person shows was reasonable in the circumstances.

(5) This section does not apply in relation to anything done before the commencement of this section.

(6) Nothing in this section shall prevent a local authority from instituting any legal proceedings otherwise than under this section against any person in relation to any anti-social act or conduct.

(7) In this section "conduct" includes speech and a course of conduct must involve conduct on at least two occasions.

(8) In this section and section 21 below

"local authority" means a council constituted under section 2 of the Local Government etc. (Scotland) Act 1994 and any reference to the area of such an authority is a reference to the local government area within the meaning of that Act for which it is so constituted.

Section 19

1.   This section empowers a sheriff to make an anti-social behaviour order on the summary application of a local authority. It is the equivalent in Scotland of section 1.

2.   The grounds for making an order are largely the same as those set out in section 1, although there are minor differences in the definition of anti-social behaviour.

3.   A local authority may apply for an order if it appears to it that a person:

1)   has acted in a manner that caused or was likely to cause alarm or distress; or

2)   has pursued a course of conduct that caused or was likely to cause alarm or distress

to one or more persons not of the same household as himself in the local authority's area, and an order is necessary to protect persons in the authority's area from further anti-social acts by him. A sheriff may make the order if he is so satisfied.

4.   It is a defence to show that an act was reasonable, the onus being on the person against whom the order is sought.

5.   The procedural requirements are set out in section 21, and the criminal sanctions in section 22.

20.– (1) An application for an order under this section may be made by a chief constable if it appears to him that the conditions mentioned in subsection (2) below are fulfilled with respect to any person in the area of his police force.

(2) The conditions are-

    (a) that the person in respect of whom the application for the order is made is-
        (i) of or over the age of 16 years; and
        (ii) a sex offender; and
    (b) that the person has acted, since the relevant date, in such a way as to give reasonable cause to believe that an order under this section is necessary to protect the public from serious harm from him.

(3) An application under subsection (1) above shall be made by summary application to the sheriff within whose sheriffdom the person is alleged to have acted as mentioned in subsection (2)(b) above.

(4) On an application under subsection (1) above the sheriff may-

    (a) pending the determination of the application, make any such interim order as he considers appropriate; and
    (b) if he is satisfied that the conditions mentioned in subsection (2) above are fulfilled, make an order under this section ("a sex offender order") which prohibits the person in respect of whom it is made from doing anything described in the order.

(5) The prohibitions that may be imposed by an order made under subsection (4) above are those necessary for the purpose of protecting the public from serious harm from the person in respect of whom the order is made.

(6) While a sex offender order has effect, Part I of the Sex Offenders Act 1997 shall have effect as if-

    (a) the person in respect of whom the order has been obtained were subject to the notification requirements of that Part; and
    (b) in relation to that person, the relevant date (within the meaning of that Part) were the date on which the copy of the order was given or delivered to that person in accordance with subsections (8) and (9) of section 21 below.

(7) Section 3 above applies for the purposes of this section as it applies for the purposes of section 2 above with the following modifications-

    (a) any reference in that section to the defendant shall be construed as a reference to the person in respect of whom the order is sought; and
    (b) in subsection (2) of that section, the reference to subsection (1) of the said section 2 shall be construed as a reference to subsection (2)(b) of this section.

(8) A constable may arrest without warrant a person whom he reasonably suspects of doing, or having done, anything prohibited by an order under subsection (4)(a) above or a sex offender order.

Section 20

1.   This section empowers the sheriff to make a sex offender order on the summary application of the police.

2.   Whereas a magistrates' court in England and Wales can make a sex offender order in respect of a person under the age of 16, in Scotland the sheriff cannot. Otherwise, the requisite conditions for making sex offender orders are similar to the provisions set out in sections 2 and 3.

3.   The conditions are that the person is 16 or over, that he is a sex offender (defined in section 3), and that he has acted in such a way as to give reasonable cause to believe that an order is necessary to protect the public from serious harm from him.

4.   While a sex offender order has effect, the person against whom the order has been made is subject to the notification requirements of Part I of the Sex Offenders Act 1997.

5.   A constable may arrest without warrant anyone he reasonably suspects of breaching a sex offender order.

21.– (1) Before making an application under-

(a) section 19(1) above;
(b) subsection (7)(b)(i) below,

the local authority shall consult the relevant chief constable.

(2) Before making an application under section 20(1) above or subsection (7)(b)(i) below, the chief constable shall consult the local authority within whose area the person in respect of whom the order is sought is for the time being.

(3) In subsection (1) above "relevant chief constable" means the chief constable of the police force maintained under the Police (Scotland) Act 1967 the area of which includes the area of the local authority making the application.

(4) A failure to comply with subsection (1) or (2) above shall not affect the validity of an order made on any application to which either of those subsections applies.

(5) A record of evidence shall be kept on any summary application under section 19 or 20 above or subsection (7)(b) below.

(6) Subsections (7) to (9) below apply to anti-social behaviour orders and sex offender orders and subsections (8) and (9) below apply to an order made under section 20(4)(a) above.

(7) An order to which this subsection applies-

(a) shall have effect for a period specified in the order or indefinitely; and

(b) may at any time be varied or revoked on a summary application by-

  (i) the local authority or, as the case may be, chief constable who obtained the order; or

  (ii) the person subject to the order.

(8) The clerk of the court by which an order to which this subsection applies is made or varied shall cause a copy of the order as so made or varied to be-

(a) given to the person named in the order; or

(b) sent to the person so named by registered post or by the recorded delivery service.

(9) An acknowledgement or certificate of delivery of a letter sent under subsection (8)(b) above issued by the Post Office shall be sufficient evidence of the delivery of the letter on the day specified in such acknowledgement or certificate.

(10) Where an appeal is lodged against the determination of an application under section 19 or 20 above or subsection (7)(b) above, any order made on the application shall, without prejudice to the determination of an application under subsection (7)(b) above made after the lodging of the appeal, continue to have effect pending the disposal of the appeal.

Section 21

Section 21 sets out the procedural requirements for obtaining or varying anti-social behaviour orders or sex offender orders in Scotland. The main requirement is that the local authority and the police are required to consult each other before an application is made.

22.– (1) Subject to subsection (3) below, if without reasonable excuse a person breaches an anti-social behaviour order by doing anything which he is prohibited from doing by the order, he shall be guilty of an offence and shall be liable-

(a) on summary conviction, to a term of imprisonment not exceeding six months or to a fine not exceeding the statutory maximum or to both; or

(b) on conviction on indictment, to imprisonment for a term not exceeding five years or to a fine or to both.

(2) Subsection (3) applies where-

(a) the breach of the anti-social behaviour order referred to in subsection (1) above consists in the accused having acted in a manner prohibited by the order which constitutes a separate offence (in this section referred to as the "separate offence"); and

(b) the accused has been charged with that separate offence.

(3) Where this subsection applies, the accused shall not be liable to be proceeded against for an offence under subsection (1) above but, subject to subsection (4) below, the court which sentences him for that separate offence shall, in determining the appropriate sentence or disposal for that offence, have regard to-

(a) the fact that the offence was committed by him while subject to an anti-social behaviour order;

(b) the number of such orders to which he was subject at the time of the commission of the offence;

(c) any previous conviction of the accused of an offence under subsection (1) above; and

(d) the extent to which the sentence or disposal in respect of any such previous conviction of the accused differed, by virtue of this subsection, from that which the court would have imposed but for this subsection.

(4) The court shall not, under subsection (3) above, have regard to the fact that the separate offence was committed while the accused was subject to an anti-social behaviour order unless that fact is libelled in the indictment or, as the case may be, specified in the complaint.

(5) The fact that the separate offence was committed while the accused was subject to an anti-social behaviour order shall, unless challenged-

(a) in the case of proceedings on indictment, by giving notice of a preliminary objection under paragraph (b) of section 72 of the Criminal Procedure (Scotland) Act 1995 ("the 1995 Act") or under that paragraph as applied by section 71(2) of that Act; or

(b) in summary proceedings, by preliminary objection before his plea is recorded,

be held as admitted.

(6) Subject to subsection (7) below, subsections (1) to (5) above apply in relation to an order under section 20(4)(a) above and to a sex offender order as they apply in relation to an anti-social behaviour order.

(7) Subsection (2) above as applied for the purposes of subsection (6) above shall have effect with the substitution of the words "at the time at which he committed" for the words "which constitutes".

Section 22

1.   On summary conviction for breach of an anti-social behaviour order a person is liable to imprisonment for 6 months or a fine not exceeding the statutory maximum, or both; and on conviction on indictment to imprisonment for 5 years or a fine, or both.

2.   It is a defence to prove that there was a reasonable excuse for breaching the order, the onus being on the defendant.

3.   *Where breach of an anti-social behaviour order consists of an action that would itself amount to a criminal offence even if there had been no order, and the person has been charged with that offence, there can be no separate proceedings in respect of the breach of the anti-social behaviour order. However, when sentencing the offender for breach of the substantive offence, the court is to have regard to the fact that the action also amounted to a breach of an anti-social behaviour order, provided that that fact is libelled in the indictment or specified in the complaint. The court is also to have regard to the person's previous record relating to anti-social behaviour orders.*

23.– (1) Schedule 3 to the Housing (Scotland) Act 1987 (grounds of eviction in relation to secure tenancies) shall be amended in accordance with subsections (2) and (3) below.

(2) For paragraph 2 there shall be substituted the following paragraph-

"2.– (1) The tenant, a person residing or lodging in the house with the tenant or a person visiting the house has been convicted of-

(a) using or allowing the house to be used for immoral or illegal purposes; or
(b) an offence punishable by imprisonment committed in, or in the locality of, the house.

(2) In sub-paragraph (1) above "tenant" includes any one of joint tenants and any sub-tenant."

(3) For paragraph 7 there shall be substituted the following paragraph-

"7.– (1) The tenant, a person residing or lodging in the house with the tenant or a person visiting the house has-

(a) acted in an anti-social manner in relation to a person residing, visiting or otherwise engaging in lawful activity in the locality; or
(b) pursued a course of anti-social conduct in relation to such a person as is mentioned in head (a) above,

and it is not reasonable in all the circumstances that the landlord should be required to make other accommodation available to him.

(2) In sub-paragraph (1) above-

"anti-social", in relation to an action or course of conduct, means causing or likely to cause alarm, distress, nuisance or annoyance;

"conduct" includes speech and a course of conduct must involve conduct on at least two occasions; and

"tenant" includes any one of joint tenants and any sub-tenant."

(4) For Ground 15 in Schedule 5 to the Housing (Scotland) Act 1988 (eviction on ground of use of premises for immoral or illegal purposes etc.) there shall be substituted the following-

"Ground 15

The tenant, a person residing or lodging in the house with the tenant or a person visiting the house has-

(a) been convicted of-
    (i) using or allowing the house to be used for immoral or illegal purposes; or
    (ii) an offence punishable by imprisonment committed in, or in the locality of, the house; or
(b) acted in an anti-social manner in relation to a person residing, visiting or otherwise engaging in lawful activity in the locality; or
(c) pursued a course of anti-social conduct in relation to such a person as is mentioned in head (b) above.

In this Ground "anti-social", in relation to an action or course of conduct, means causing or likely to cause alarm, distress, nuisance or annoyance, "conduct" includes speech and a course of conduct must involve conduct on at least two occasions and "tenant" includes any one of joint tenants."

(5) No person shall be liable to eviction under paragraph 2 or 7 of Schedule 3 to the Housing (Scotland) Act 1987 or Ground 15 in Schedule 5 to the (1988 c.43.)Housing (Scotland) Act 1988 as substituted respectively by subsection (2), (3) and (4) above in respect of any act or conduct before the commencement of this section unless he would have been liable to be evicted under those paragraphs or, as the case may be, that Ground as they had effect before that substitution.

Section 23
1.   This section amends the Housing (Scotland) Act 1987 and the Housing (Scotland) Act 1988. The effect is that both a secure tenant and a tenant holding on an assured tenancy may be evicted on the grounds, not only that the tenant or a person residing or lodging with him has used the house for immoral or illegal purposes, but also that:

1)   a visitor has used or been allowed to use the premises for immoral or illegal purposes; or

2)   the tenant, or one of them, or any person residing or lodging with him, or a person visiting the house has committed an offence punishable with imprisonment in, or in the locality of the house; or

> 3) *the tenant, or one of them, or any person residing or lodging with him, or a person visiting the house has acted in a manner or pursued a course of conduct in the locality which is anti-social, and it is not reasonable that the landlord should be required to make other accommodation available.*
>
> 2. *"Anti-social" for the purposes of this section means causing or likely to cause alarm, distress, nuisance or annoyance.*

24.– (1) The Civic Government (Scotland) Act 1982 shall be amended in accordance with this section.

(2) In section 54 (offence of playing instruments, etc.), after subsection (2) there shall be inserted the following subsections-

"(2A) Where a constable reasonably suspects that an offence under subsection (1) above has been committed in relation to a musical instrument or in relation to such a device as is mentioned in paragraph (c) of that subsection, he may enter any premises on which he reasonably suspects that instrument or device to be and seize any such instrument or device he finds there.

(2B) A constable may use reasonable force in the exercise of the power conferred by subsection (2A) above.

(2C) Schedule 2A to this Act (which makes provision in relation to the retention and disposal of property seized under subsection (2A) above) shall have effect."

(3) In section 60 (powers of search and seizure)-

  (a) in subsection (5)-
    (i) after the words "Nothing in" there shall be inserted the words "section 54(2A) of this Act or"; and
    (ii) for the words from "which" to the end there shall be substituted the words "which is otherwise exercisable by a constable"; and
  (b) in subsection (6)-
    (i) in paragraph (a), for the words from "in pursuance" to the word "vessel" there shall be substituted the words-

"to enter and search-

    (i) any premises in pursuance of section 54(2A) of this Act or of subsection (1) above; or
    (ii) any vehicle or vessel in pursuance of the said subsection (1), "; and
    (ii) in paragraph (c), after "under" there shall be inserted the words "section 54(2A) of this Act or".

(4) After Schedule 2 there shall be inserted the Schedule set out in Schedule 1 to this Act.

Section 24
This section amends the Civic Government (Scotland) Act 1982:

1)   empowering a constable to enter premises and seize musical instruments or other devices playing music too loudly;

2)   inserting a Schedule 2A (see Schedule 1 of this Act), which deals with the retention and disposal of musical instruments or other property seized under the power above.

CHAPTER III GREAT BRITAIN

25.– (1) After subsection (4) of section 60 (powers to stop and search in anticipation of violence) of the Criminal Justice and Public Order Act 1994 ("the 1994 Act") there shall be inserted the following subsection-

"(4A) This section also confers on any constable in uniform power-

(a) to require any person to remove any item which the constable reasonably believes that person is wearing wholly or mainly for the purpose of concealing his identity;
(b) to seize any item which the constable reasonably believes any person intends to wear wholly or mainly for that purpose."

(2) In subsection (5) of that section, for the words "those powers" there shall be substituted the words "the powers conferred by subsection (4) above".

(3) In subsection (8) of that section, for the words "to stop or (as the case may be) to stop the vehicle" there shall be substituted the following paragraphs-

"(a) to stop, or to stop a vehicle; or
(b) to remove an item worn by him,".

Section 25
This section amends the Criminal Justice and Public Order Act 1994. Where the police fear that incidents involving serious violence are imminent and have the powers to stop and search for weapons or dangerous instruments conferred by section 60 of that Act, they may also require the removal of or seize items, such as masks, that may be used to disguise or conceal a person's identity.

26. After section 60 of the 1994 Act there shall be inserted the following section-

"60A.– (1) Any things seized by a constable under section 60 may be retained in accordance with regulations made by the Secretary of State under this section.

(2) The Secretary of State may make regulations regulating the retention and safe keeping, and the disposal and destruction in prescribed circumstances, of such things.

(3) Regulations under this section may make different provisions for different classes of things or for different circumstances.

(4) The power to make regulations under this section shall be exercisable by statutory instrument which shall be subject to annulment in pursuance of a resolution of either House of Parliament."

Section 26
This section deals with the retention and disposal of items seized under section 60 of the Criminal Justice and Public Order Act 1994, such as weapons, dangerous items or masks, empowering the Secretary of State to make regulations concerning their retention and disposal.

27.– (1) In section 24(2) (arrestable offences) of the Police and Criminal Evidence Act 1984 ("the 1984 Act"), after paragraph (n) there shall be inserted-

"(o) an offence under section 60(8)(b) of the Criminal Justice and Public Order Act 1994 (failing to comply with requirement to remove mask etc.);".

(2) After section 60A of the 1994 Act there shall be inserted the following section-

"60B. In Scotland, where a constable reasonably believes that a person has committed or is committing an offence under section 60(8) he may arrest that person without warrant."

Section 27
This section amends the Police and Criminal Evidence Act 1984 making failure to remove a mask or other items worn to conceal identity when required to do so by a police officer an arrestable offence.

PART II CRIMINAL LAW

Racially-aggravated offences: England and Wales

28.– (1) An offence is racially aggravated for the purposes of sections 29 to 32 below if-

(a) at the time.of committing the offence, or immediately before or after doing so, the offender demonstrates towards the victim of the offence hostility based on the victim's membership (or presumed membership) of a racial group; or

(b) the offence is motivated (wholly or partly) by hostility towards members of a racial group based on their membership of that group.

(2) In subsection (1)(a) above-

"membership", in relation to a racial group, includes association with members of that group;

"presumed" means presumed by the offender.

(3) It is immaterial for the purposes of paragraph (a) or (b) of subsection (1) above whether or not the offender's hostility is also based, to any extent, on-

(a) the fact or presumption that any person or group of persons belongs to any religious group; or
(b) any other factor not mentioned in that paragraph.

(4) In this section "racial group" means a group of persons defined by reference to race, colour, nationality (including citizenship) or ethnic or national origins.

Section 28

1. This section defines "racially aggravated" and "racial group" for the purposes of sections 29 to 32. An offence is racially aggravated if:

1) at the time of the offence, immediately before or after it, the offender demonstrates hostility towards the victim based on his membership or presumed membership of a racial group; or

2) the offence is motivated by hostility (wholly or partly) towards members of a racial group based on their membership of that racial group.

2. "Racial group" is defined as a group defined by reference to race, colour, nationality or ethnic or national origins. "Membership" of a racial group includes association with that racial group; and "presumed" means presumed by the offender.

29.– (1) A person is guilty of an offence under this section if he commits-

(a) an offence under section 20 of the Offences Against the Person Act 1861 (malicious wounding or grievous bodily harm);
(b) an offence under section 47 of that Act (actual bodily harm); or
(c) common assault,

which is racially aggravated for the purposes of this section.

(2) A person guilty of an offence falling within subsection (1)(a) or (b) above shall be liable-

(a) on summary conviction, to imprisonment for a term not exceeding six months or to a fine not exceeding the statutory maximum, or to both;

(b) on conviction on indictment, to imprisonment for a term not exceeding seven years or to a fine, or to both.

(3) A person guilty of an offence falling within subsection (1)(c) above shall be liable-

(a) on summary conviction, to imprisonment for a term not exceeding six months or to a fine not exceeding the statutory maximum, or to both;

(b) on conviction on indictment, to imprisonment for a term not exceeding two years or to a fine, or to both.

Section 29

1.   A person is guilty of an offence under this section if he is convicted of an offence under:

1)   section 20 of the Offences Against the Person Act 1861 (malicious wounding or grievous bodily harm);

2)   section 47 of that Act (assault occasioning actual bodily harm);

3)   common assault;

which is racially aggravated.

2.   A person is liable on summary conviction under section 29(1)(a) or (b) (racially aggravated offences of malicious wounding or grievous bodily harm, or assault occasioning actual bodily harm) to 6 months imprisonment or a fine, or both; and on conviction on indictment to a term of 7 years, or a fine, or both. The maximum term on conviction on indictment for the non-racially aggravated equivalents of these offences is 5 years.

3.   A person is liable on summary conviction under section 29(1)(c) (racially aggravated common assault) to 6 months imprisonment, or a fine, or both; and on conviction on indictment to 2 years imprisonment, a fine or both. Non-racially aggravated common assault is a summary offence.

30.– (1) A person is guilty of an offence under this section if he commits an offence under section 1(1) of the Criminal Damage Act 1971 (destroying or damaging property belonging to another) which is racially aggravated for the purposes of this section.

(2) A person guilty of an offence under this section shall be liable-

(a) on summary conviction, to imprisonment for a term not exceeding six months or to a fine not exceeding the statutory maximum, or to both;

(b) on conviction on indictment, to imprisonment for a term not exceeding fourteen years or to a fine, or to both.

(3) For the purposes of this section, section 28(1)(a) above shall have effect as if the person to whom the property belongs or is treated as belonging for the purposes of that Act were the victim of the offence.

> **Section 30**
>
> *1. A person is guilty of an offence under this section if he commits criminal damage which is racially aggravated.*
>
> *2. On summary conviction a person is liable to 6 months imprisonment, a fine or both; and on conviction on indictment a person is liable to imprisonment for 14 years, or to a fine, or both.*

31.– (1) A person is guilty of an offence under this section if he commits-

   (a) an offence under section 4 of the Public Order Act 1986 (fear or provocation of violence);
   (b) an offence under section 4A of that Act (intentional harassment, alarm or distress); or
   (c) an offence under section 5 of that Act (harassment, alarm or distress),

which is racially aggravated for the purposes of this section.

(2) A constable may arrest without warrant anyone whom he reasonably suspects to be committing an offence falling within subsection (1)(a) or (b) above.

(3) A constable may arrest a person without warrant if-

   (a) he engages in conduct which a constable reasonably suspects to constitute an offence falling within subsection (1)(c) above;
   (b) he is warned by that constable to stop; and
   (c) he engages in further such conduct immediately or shortly after the warning.

The conduct mentioned in paragraph (a) above and the further conduct need not be of the same nature.

(4) A person guilty of an offence falling within subsection (1)(a) or (b) above shall be liable-

   (a) on summary conviction, to imprisonment for a term not exceeding six months or to a fine not exceeding the statutory maximum, or to both;
   (b) on conviction on indictment, to imprisonment for a term not exceeding two years or to a fine, or to both.

(5) A person guilty of an offence falling within subsection (1)(c) above shall be liable on summary conviction to a fine not exceeding level 4 on the standard scale.

(6) If, on the trial on indictment of a person charged with an offence falling within subsection (1)(a) or (b) above, the jury find him not guilty of the offence charged, they may find him guilty of the basic offence mentioned in that provision.

(7) For the purposes of subsection (1)(c) above, section 28(1)(a) above shall have effect as if the person likely to be caused harassment, alarm or distress were the victim of the offence.

Section 31

1.   A person is guilty of an offence under this section if he is convicted of an offence under:

1)   section 4 of the Public Order Act 1986 (fear or provocation of violence);

2)   section 4A of that Act (intentional harassment, alarm or distress); or

3)   section 5 of that Act (harassment, alarm or distress);

which is racially aggravated.

2.   A constable may arrest without warrant anyone he reasonably suspects to be committing an offence under section 31(1)(a) or (b) (the racially aggravated equivalents of offences under section 4 and 4A of the Public Order Act 1986).

3.   A constable may also arrest a person without warrant if he reasonably suspects that he is committing an offence under section 31(1)(c) (the racially aggravated equivalent of section 5) and, despite a warning to stop by that constable, the person continues.

4.   A person guilty of an offence under section 31(1)(a) or (b) shall be liable on summary conviction to imprisonment for 6 months, a fine or both; and on conviction on indictment to 2 years imprisonment, a fine or both. The non-racially aggravated equivalents of these offences are summary offences.

5.   A person guilty of an offence under section 31(1)(c) (the racially aggravated equivalent of section 5) is liable to a fine not exceeding level 4 on the standard scale. The fine for the non-racially aggravated equivalent is a fine not exceeding level 3.

32.– (1) A person is guilty of an offence under this section if he commits-

(a) an offence under section 2 of the Protection from Harassment Act 1997 (offence of harassment); or

(b) an offence under section 4 of that Act (putting people in fear of violence),

which is racially aggravated for the purposes of this section.

(2) In section 24(2) of the 1984 Act (arrestable offences), after paragraph (o) there shall be inserted-

"(p) an offence falling within section 32(1)(a) of the Crime and Disorder Act 1998 (racially-aggravated harassment);".

(3) A person guilty of an offence falling within subsection (1)(a) above shall be liable-

(a) on summary conviction, to imprisonment for a term not exceeding six months or to a fine not exceeding the statutory maximum, or to both;

(b) on conviction on indictment, to imprisonment for a term not exceeding two years or to a fine, or to both.

(4) A person guilty of an offence falling within subsection (1)(b) above shall be liable-

(a) on summary conviction, to imprisonment for a term not exceeding six months or to a fine not exceeding the statutory maximum, or to both;

(b) on conviction on indictment, to imprisonment for a term not exceeding seven years or to a fine, or to both.

(5) If, on the trial on indictment of a person charged with an offence falling within subsection (1)(a) above, the jury find him not guilty of the offence charged, they may find him guilty of the basic offence mentioned in that provision.

(6) If, on the trial on indictment of a person charged with an offence falling within subsection (1)(b) above, the jury find him not guilty of the offence charged, they may find him guilty of an offence falling within subsection (1)(a) above.

(7) Section 5 of the Protection from Harassment Act 1997 (restraining orders) shall have effect in relation to a person convicted of an offence under this section as if the reference in subsection (1) of that section to an offence under section 2 or 4 included a reference to an offence under this section.

Section 32

1.   A person is guilty of an offence under this section if he is convicted of an offence under:

1)   section 2 of the Protection from Harassment Act 1997 (offence of harassment);

2)   section 4 of that Act (putting people in fear of violence)

which is racially aggravated.

2.   Section 24 of the Police and Criminal Evidence Act 1984 is amended so that an offence under this section is an arrestable offence.

3.   On summary conviction of an offence under section 32(1)(a) (racially-aggravated harassment) a person is liable to 6 months imprisonment, a fine or both; and on indictment to 2 years imprisonment, a fine or both.

> *4. On summary conviction of an offence under section 32(1)(b) (the racially-aggravated putting people in fear of violence) a person is liable to 6 months imprisonment, a fine or both; and on indictment to 7 years imprisonment, a fine or both.*

Racially-aggravated offences: Scotland

33. After section 50 of the Criminal Law (Consolidation) (Scotland) Act 1995 there shall be inserted the following section-

"Racially-aggravated harassment.

50A.– (1) A person is guilty of an offence under this section if he-

- (a) pursues a racially-aggravated course of conduct which amounts to harassment of a person and-
  - (i) is intended to amount to harassment of that person; or
  - (ii) occurs in circumstances where it would appear to a reasonable person that it would amount to harassment of that person; or
- (b) acts in a manner which is racially aggravated and which causes, or is intended to cause, a person alarm or distress.

(2) For the purposes of this section a course of conduct or an action is racially aggravated if-

- (a) immediately before, during or immediately after carrying out the course of conduct or action the offender evinces towards the person affected malice and ill-will based on that person's membership (or presumed membership) of a racial group; or
- (b) the course of conduct or action is motivated (wholly or partly) by malice and ill-will towards members of a racial group based on their membership of that group.

(3) In subsection (2)(a) above-

"membership", in relation to a racial group, includes association with members of that group;

"presumed" means presumed by the offender.

(4) It is immaterial for the purposes of paragraph (a) or (b) of subsection (2) above whether or not the offender's malice and ill-will is also based, to any extent, on-

- (a) the fact or presumption that any person or group of persons belongs to any religious group; or
- (b) any other factor not mentioned in that paragraph.

(5) A person who is guilty of an offence under this section shall-

(a) on summary conviction, be liable to a fine not exceeding the statutory maximum, or imprisonment for a period not exceeding six months, or both such fine and such imprisonment; and

(b) on conviction on indictment, be liable to a fine or to imprisonment for a period not exceeding seven years, or both such fine and such imprisonment.

(6) In this section-

"conduct" includes speech;

"harassment" of a person includes causing the person alarm or distress;

"racial group" means a group of persons defined by reference to race, colour, nationality (including citizenship) or ethnic or national origins,

and a course of conduct must involve conduct on at least two occasions."

Section 33 - Scotland

1.   This section deals with racially aggravated offences in Scotland, by amending the Criminal Law (Consolidation) (Scotland) Act 1995. A section 50A is added.

2.   It is an offence to pursue a racially aggravated course of conduct that amounts to harassment of a person, and is either intended to do so or would appear to a reasonable person to do so. A course of conduct must involve conduct on at least two occasions.

3.   It is also an offence to act in a manner that is racially aggravated and which causes or is intended to cause alarm or distress.

4.   A course of conduct or an action is racially aggravated if:

1)   immediately before, during or immediately after it, the offender evinces malice and ill-will based on the victim's membership or presumed membership of a racial group; or

2)   it is motivated (wholly or partly) by malice and ill-will towards members of a racial group based on their membership, or presumed membership of that racial group.

5.   "Harassment" includes causing alarm or distress. "Conduct" includes speech.

6.   A person is liable on summary conviction to imprisonment for 6 months, a fine or both; and on conviction on indictment to imprisonment for 7 years, a fine or both.

7.   Although pursuing a racially aggravated course of conduct requires conduct on at least two occasion, whereas acting in a racially aggravated manner does not, the maximum sentence is the same.

Miscellaneous

34. The rebuttable presumption of criminal law that a child aged 10 or over is incapable of committing an offence is hereby abolished.

> **Section 34**
> *This section abolishes the presumption of* doli incapax, *the rebuttable presumption that children aged 10 to 13 inclusive do not know the difference between right and wrong. Where a child aged between 10 and 13 was charged with an offence, common law required the Crown to prove, in addition to all the other elements of the offence, that the child knew at the time of the act that it was seriously wrong, and was not just naughty or childishly mischievous. That is no longer required.*

35. In section 35 of the 1994 Act (effect of accused's silence at trial), the following provisions shall cease to have effect, namely-

(a) in subsection (1), the words "who has attained the age of fourteen years"; and
(b) subsection (6).

> **Section 35**
> *This section amends section 35 of the Criminal Justice and Public Order Act 1994, which permits a jury to draw an adverse inference from a defendant's silence at trial. Section 35 now applies where children aged between 10 and 13 are defendants, so that juries can now draw adverse inferences from the silence of children aged between 10 and 13. It is consequential upon the abolition of the presumption of doli incapax.*

36.– (1) In section I of the Treason Act (Ireland) 1537 (practising any harm etc. to, or slandering, the King, Queen or heirs apparent punishable as high treason), for the words "have and suffer such pains of death and" there shall be substituted the words "be liable to imprisonment for life and to such".

(2) In the following enactments, namely-

(a) section II of the Crown of Ireland Act 1542 (occasioning disturbance etc. to the crown of Ireland punishable as high treason);
(b) section XII of the Act of Supremacy (Ireland) 1560 (penalties for maintaining or defending foreign authority);
(c) section 3 of the Treason Act 1702 (endeavouring to hinder the succession to the Crown etc. punishable as high treason);
(d) section I of the Treason Act (Ireland) 1703 (which makes corresponding provision),

for the words "suffer pains of death" there shall be substituted the words "be liable to imprisonment for life".

(3) The following enactments shall cease to have effect, namely-

(a) the Treason Act 1790;
(b) the Treason Act 1795.

(4) In section 1 of the Treason Act 1814 (form of sentence in case of high treason), for the words "such person shall be hanged by the neck until such person be dead", there shall be substituted the words "such person shall be liable to imprisonment for life".

(5) In section 2 of the Piracy Act 1837 (punishment of piracy when murder is attempted), for the words "and being convicted thereof shall suffer death" there shall be substituted the words "and being convicted thereof shall be liable to imprisonment for life".

(6) The following enactments shall cease to have effect, namely-

(a) the Sentence of Death (Expectant Mothers) Act 1931; and
(b) sections 32 and 33 of the Criminal Justice Act Northern Ireland) 1945 (which make corresponding provision).

Section 36
This section abolishes the death penalty for treason, piracy and other offences and substitutes a liability to imprisonment for life.

PART III CRIMINAL JUSTICE SYSTEM

Youth justice

37.– (1) It shall be the principal aim of the youth justice system to prevent offending by children and young persons.

(2) In addition to any other duty to which they are subject, it shall be the duty of all persons and bodies carrying out functions in relation to the youth justice system to have regard to that aim.

Section 37
This section provides that the principal aim of the youth justice system is to prevent offending by children and young persons. All persons or bodies performing functions in relation to the youth justice system are obliged to have regard to that aim.

38. (1) It shall be the duty of each local authority, acting in co-operation with the persons and bodies mentioned in subsection (2) below, to secure that, to such extent as is appropriate for their area, all youth justice services are available there.

(2) It shall be the duty of-

(a) every chief officer of police or police authority any part of whose police area lies within the local authority's area; and

(b) every probation committee or health authority any part of whose area lies within that area,

to co-operate in the discharge by the local authority of their duty under subsection (1) above.

(3) The local authority and every person or body mentioned in subsection (2) above shall have power to make payments towards expenditure incurred in the provision of youth justice services-

(a) by making the payments directly; or

(b) by contributing to a fund, established and maintained by the local authority, out of which the payments may be made.

(4) In this section and sections 39 to 41 below "youth justice services" means any of the following, namely-

(a) the provision of persons to act as appropriate adults to safeguard the interests of children and young persons detained or questioned by police officers;

(b) the assessment of children and young persons, and the provision for them of rehabilitation programmes, for the purposes of section 66(2) below;

(c) the provision of support for children and young persons remanded or committed on bail while awaiting trial or sentence;

(d) the placement in local authority accommodation of children and young persons remanded or committed to such accommodation under section 23 of the Children and Young Persons Act 1969 ("the 1969 Act");

(e) the provision of reports or other information required by courts in criminal proceedings against children and young persons;

(f) the provision of persons to act as responsible officers in relation to parenting orders, child safety orders, reparation orders and action plan orders;

(g) the supervision of young persons sentenced to a probation order, a community service order or a combination order;

(h) the supervision of children and young persons sentenced to a detention and training order or a supervision order;

(i) the post-release supervision of children and young persons under section 37(4A) or 65 of the 1991 Act or section 31 of the Crime (Sentences) Act 1997 ("the 1997 Act");

(j) the performance of functions under subsection (1) of section 75 below by such persons as may be authorised by the Secretary of State under that subsection.

(5) The Secretary of State may by order amend subsection (4) above so as to extend, restrict or otherwise alter the definition of "youth justice services" for the time being specified in that subsection.

Section 38

1.   This section imposes a duty on each local authority to ensure that all youth justice services appropriate for its area are available in its area.

2.   A duty is also imposed on every chief officer of police or police authority and every probation committee and health authority to cooperate with the local authority in the discharge of its duty to ensure that youth justice services are available.

3.   "Youth justice services" are defined in section 38(4), and include the provision of appropriate adults to safeguard the interests of children or young persons detained by police; the provision of rehabilitation programmes; the provision of support for children and young persons on bail, and so on.

39.– (1) Subject to subsection (2) below, it shall be the duty of each local authority, acting in co-operation with the persons and bodies mentioned in subsection (3) below, to establish for their area one or more youth offending teams.

(2) Two (or more) local authorities acting together may establish one or more youth offending teams for both (or all) their areas; and where they do so-

    (a) any reference in the following provisions of this section (except subsection (4)(b)) to, or to the area of, the local authority or a particular local authority shall be construed accordingly, and

    (b) the reference in subsection (4)(b) to the local authority shall be construed as a reference to one of the authorities.

(3) It shall be the duty of-

    (a) every chief officer of police any part of whose police area lies within the local authority's area; and

    (b) every probation committee or health authority any part of whose area lies within that area,

to co-operate in the discharge by the local authority of their duty under subsection (1) above.

(4) The local authority and every person or body mentioned in subsection (3) above shall have power to make payments towards expenditure incurred by, or for purposes connected with, youth offending teams-

    (a) by making the payments directly; or

    (b) by contributing to a fund, established and maintained by the local authority, out of which the payments may be made.

(5) A youth offending team shall include at least one of each of the following, namely-

    (a) a probation officer;

    (b) a social worker of a local authority social services department;

    (c) a police officer;

    (d) a person nominated by a health authority any part of whose area lies within the local authority's area;

    (e) a person nominated by the chief education officer appointed by the local authority under section 532 of the Education Act 1996.

(6) A youth offending team may also include such other persons as the local authority thinks appropriate after consulting the persons and bodies mentioned in subsection (3) above.

(7) It shall be the duty of the youth offending team or teams established by a particular local authority-

    (a) to co-ordinate the provision of youth justice services for all those in the authority's area who need them; and

    (b) to carry out such functions as are assigned to the team or teams in the youth justice plan formulated by the authority under section 40(1) below.

Section 39

1.   This section imposes the duty on local authorities to establish youth offending teams, with the cooperation of the police, probation committees and health authorities. It also defines the duty of a youth offending team.

2.   Two or more local authorities may establish youth offending teams jointly.

3.   A duty is imposed on every chief officer of police, probation committee and health authority to cooperate in the discharge by the local authority of its duty to establish youth offending teams.

4.   A youth offending team is to include at least a probation officer, a social worker, a police officer, a person nominated by the health authority, and a person nominated by the chief education officer. It may also include such other persons as the local authority thinks fit after consultation with the police, the probation committee and the health authority.

5.   The duty of a youth offending team is to co-ordinate youth justice services and to perform the functions assigned to it under the youth justice plan formulated by the local authority under section 40.

40.– (1) It shall be the duty of each local authority, after consultation with the relevant persons and bodies, to formulate and implement for each year a plan (a "youth justice plan") setting out-

(a) how youth justice services in their area are to be provided and funded; and

(b) how the youth offending team or teams established by them (whether alone or jointly with one or more other local authorities) are to be composed and funded, how they are to operate, and what functions they are to carry out.

(2) In subsection (1) above "the relevant persons and bodies" means the persons and bodies mentioned in section 38(2) above and, where the local authority is a county council, any district councils whose districts form part of its area.

(3) The functions assigned to a youth offending team under subsection (1)(b) above may include, in particular, functions under paragraph 7(b) of Schedule 2 to the 1989 Act (local authority's duty to take reasonable steps designed to encourage children and young persons not to commit offences).

(4) A local authority shall submit their youth justice plan to the Board established under section 41 below, and shall publish it in such manner and by such date as the Secretary of State may direct.

Section 40

1.   This section imposes a duty on each local authority, after consultation with the local chief officer of police, probation committee and health authority, to formulate and implement a "youth justice plan", setting out how youth justice services are to be provided; and how youth offending teams are to be composed and funded, how they are to operate, and what functions they are to perform.

2.   The functions assigned to the youth offending team may include in particular the functions under paragraph 7(b) of Schedule 2 to the Children Act 1989 (the local authority's duty to take reasonable steps designed to encourage children and young persons not to commit offences).

3.   Local authorities are obliged to submit their youth justice plans to the Youth Justice Board, and the plan is to be published as the Secretary of State directs.

41.– (1) There shall be a body corporate to be known as the Youth Justice Board for England and Wales ("the Board").

(2) The Board shall not be regarded as the servant or agent of the Crown or as enjoying any status, immunity or privilege of the Crown; and the Board's property shall not be regarded as property of, or held on behalf of, the Crown.

(3) The Board shall consist of 10, 11 or 12 members appointed by the Secretary of State.

(4) The members of the Board shall include persons who appear to the Secretary of State to have extensive recent experience of the youth justice system.

(5) The Board shall have the following functions, namely-

(a) to monitor the operation of the youth justice system and the provision of youth justice services;

(b) to advise the Secretary of State on the following matters, namely-

    (i) the operation of that system and the provision of such services;

    (ii) how the principal aim of that system might most effectively be pursued;

    (iii) the content of any national standards he may see fit to set with respect to the provision of such services, or the accommodation in which children and young persons are kept in custody; and

    (iv) the steps that might be taken to prevent offending by children and young persons;

(c) to monitor the extent to which that aim is being achieved and any such standards met;

(d) for the purposes of paragraphs (a), (b) and (c) above, to obtain information from relevant authorities;

(e) to publish information so obtained;

(f) to identify, to make known and to promote good practice in the following matters, namely-

    (i) the operation of the youth justice system and the provision of youth justice services;

    (ii) the prevention of offending by children and young persons; and

    (iii) working with children and young persons who are or are at risk of becoming offenders;

(g) to make grants, with the approval of the Secretary of State, to local authorities or other bodies for them to develop such practice, or to commission research in connection with such practice; and

(h) themselves to commission research in connection with such practice.

(6) The Secretary of State may by order-

(a) amend subsection (5) above so as to add to, subtract from or alter any of the functions of the Board for the time being specified in that subsection; or

(b) provide that any function of his which is exercisable in relation to the youth justice system shall be exercisable concurrently with the Board.

(7) In carrying out their functions, the Board shall comply with any directions given by the Secretary of State and act in accordance with any guidance given by him.

(8) A relevant authority-

(a) shall furnish to the Board any information required for the purposes of subsection (5)(a), (b) or (c) above; and

(b) whenever so required by the Board, shall submit to the Board a report on such matters connected with the discharge of their duties under the foregoing provisions of this Part as may be specified in the requirement.

A requirement under paragraph (b) above may specify the form in which a report is to be given.

(9) The Board may arrange, or require the relevant authority to arrange, for a report under subsection (8)(b) above to be published in such manner as appears to the Board to be appropriate.

(10) In this section "relevant authority" means a local authority, a chief officer of police, a police authority, a probation committee and a health authority.

(11) Schedule 2 to this Act (which makes further provision with respect to the Board) shall have effect.

Section 41

1.   This section provides for the establishment of a Youth Justice Board.

2.   The Youth Justice Board is to consist of 10 to 12 members appointed by the Secretary of State who have extensive recent experience of the youth justice system.

3.   The Board's functions include the monitoring of the youth justice system and advising the Secretary of State on its operation, on how the principal aim might more effectively be pursued, and on the content of national standards. It can also make grants and commission research. The Board is obliged to comply with directions given by the Secretary of State.

4.   The Youth Justice Board is not to be regarded as a servant or agent of the Crown, and its property is not to be regarded as the property of, or held on behalf of the Crown. It is intended to be a public body independent of government.

5.   Local authorities, police authorities, probation committees and health authorities are obliged to provide the Board with information to enable it to perform its functions; or to prepare and publish a report on the discharge of their duties.

6.   Schedule 2 of the Act contains further provisions relating to membership of the Board, pay of Board-members and employees, the disqualification of MP's from membership of the Board, and annual reports.

42.– (1) In the foregoing provisions of this Part and this section-

"chief officer of police" has the meaning given by section 101(1) of the Police Act 1996;

"local authority" means-

(a) in relation to England, a county council, a district council whose district does not form part of an area that has a county council, a London borough council or the Common Council of the City of London;

(b) in relation to Wales, a county council or a county borough council;

"police authority" has the meaning given by section 101(1) of the Police Act 1996;

"youth justice system" means the system of criminal justice in so far as it relates to children and young persons.

(2) For the purposes of those provisions, the Isles of Scilly form part of the county of Cornwall and the Inner Temple and the Middle Temple form part of the City of London.

(3) In carrying out any of their duties under those provisions, a local authority, a police authority, a probation committee or a health authority shall act in accordance with any guidance given by the Secretary of State.

> **Section 42**
> *This section defines various terms used in sections 37 to 41.*

Time limits etc.

43.– (1) In subsection (2) of section 22 (time limits in relation to criminal proceedings) of the Prosecution of Offences Act 1985 ("the 1985 Act"), for paragraphs (a) and (b) there shall be substituted the following paragraphs-

"(a) be made so as to apply only in relation to proceedings instituted in specified areas, or proceedings of, or against persons of, specified classes or descriptions;
(b) make different provision with respect to proceedings instituted in different areas, or different provision with respect to proceedings of, or against persons of, different classes or descriptions;".

(2) For subsection (3) of that section there shall be substituted the following subsection-

"(3)The appropriate court may, at any time before the expiry of a time limit imposed by the regulations, extend, or further extend, that limit; but the court shall not do so unless it is satisfied-

(a) that the need for the extension is due to-
   (i) the illness or absence of the accused, a necessary witness, a judge or a magistrate;
   (ii) a postponement which is occasioned by the ordering by the court of separate trials in the case of two or more accused or two or more offences; or
   (iii) some other good and sufficient cause; and
(b) that the prosecution has acted with all due diligence and expedition."

(3) In subsection (4) of that section, for the words from "the accused" to the end there shall be substituted the words "the appropriate court shall stay the proceedings".

(4) In subsection (6) of that section-

(a) for the word "Where" there shall be substituted the words "Subsection (6A) below applies where"; and

(b) for the words from "the overall time limit" to the end there shall be substituted the words "and is accordingly unlawfully at large for any period."

(5) After that subsection there shall be inserted the following subsection-

"(6A) The following, namely-

(a) the period for which the person is unlawfully at large; and

(b) such additional period (if any) as the appropriate court may direct, having regard to the disruption of the prosecution occasioned by-

   (i) the person's escape or failure to surrender; and

   (ii) the length of the period mentioned in paragraph (a) above,

shall be disregarded, so far as the offence in question is concerned, for the purposes of the overall time limit which applies in his case in relation to the stage which the proceedings have reached at the time of the escape or, as the case may be, at the appointed time."

(6) In subsection (7) of that section, after the words "time limit," there shall be inserted the words "or to give a direction under subsection (6A) above,".

(7) In subsection (8) of that section, after the words "time limit" there shall be inserted the words ", or to give a direction under subsection (6A) above,".

(8) After subsection (11) of that section there shall be inserted the following subsection-

"(11ZA) For the purposes of this section, proceedings for an offence shall be taken to begin when the accused is charged with the offence or, as the case may be, an information is laid charging him with the offence."

Section 43

1.   This section amends section 22 of the Prosecution of Offences Act 1985, under which the Secretary of State may by regulation set time limits relating to the preliminary stages of criminal proceedings, and the time accused persons may be kept in custody.

2.   The effects of the main amendments are:

1)   to allow the Secretary of State to make regulations regarding time limits that would affect particular classes of accused person;

2)   to impose further limited restrictions on the court's power to extend time limits. The court has to be satisfied that either a necessary party to the trial is ill or absent, or that there is some other good and sufficient cause for extending the time limits; and that the prosecution has acted with all due diligence and expedition;

> 3) on expiry of a relevant time limit, instead of treating the accused for all purposes as acquitted, the proceedings against him are simply stayed.
>
> 3. Where proceedings have been stayed under this section, fresh proceedings may be instituted under section 22B of the Prosecution of Offences Act 1985, inserted by section 45, below.

44. After section 22 of the 1985 Act there shall be inserted the following section-

"22A.– (1) The Secretary of State may by regulations make provision-

(a) with respect to a person under the age of 18 at the time of his arrest in connection with an offence, as to the maximum period to be allowed for the completion of the stage beginning with his arrest and ending with the date fixed for his first appearance in court in connection with the offence ("the initial stage");

(b) with respect to a person convicted of an offence who was under that age at the time of his arrest for the offence or (where he was not arrested for it) the laying of the information charging him with it, as to the period within which the stage between his conviction and his being sentenced for the offence should be completed.

(2) Subsection (2) of section 22 above applies for the purposes of regulations under subsection (1) above as if-

(a) the reference in paragraph (d) to custody or overall time limits were a reference to time limits imposed by the regulations; and

(b) the reference in paragraph (e) to proceedings instituted before the commencement of any provisions of the regulations were a reference to a stage begun before that commencement.

(3) A magistrates' court may, at any time before the expiry of the time limit imposed by the regulations under subsection (1)(a) above ("the initial stage time limit"), extend, or further extend, that limit; but the court shall not do so unless it is satisfied-

(a) that the need for the extension is due to some good and sufficient cause; and

(b) that the investigation has been conducted, and (where applicable) the prosecution has acted, with all due diligence and expedition.

(4) Where the initial stage time limit (whether as originally imposed or as extended or further extended under subsection (3) above) expires before the person arrested is charged with the offence, he shall not be charged with it unless further evidence relating to it is obtained, and-

(a) if he is then under arrest, he shall be released;

(b) if he is then on bail under Part IV of the Police and Criminal Evidence Act 1984, his bail (and any duty or conditions to which it is subject) shall be discharged.

(5) Where the initial stage time limit (whether as originally imposed or as extended or further extended under subsection (3) above) expires after the person arrested is charged with the offence but before the date fixed for his first appearance in court in connection with it, the court shall stay the proceedings.

(6) Where-

(a) a person escapes from arrest; or

(b) a person who has been released on bail under Part IV of the (1984 c.60.)Police and Criminal Evidence Act 1984 fails to surrender himself at the appointed time,

and is accordingly unlawfully at large for any period, that period shall be disregarded, so far as the offence in question is concerned, for the purposes of the initial stage time limit.

(7) Subsections (7) to (9) of section 22 above apply for the purposes of this section, at any time after the person arrested has been charged with the offence in question, as if any reference (however expressed) to a custody or overall time limit were a reference to the initial stage time limit.

(8) Where a person is convicted of an offence in any proceedings, the exercise of the power conferred by subsection (3) above shall not be called into question in any appeal against that conviction.

(9) Any reference in this section (however expressed) to a person being charged with an offence includes a reference to the laying of an information charging him with it."

Section 44

1.   This section amends the Prosecution of Offences Act 1985 by adding section 22A under which the Secretary of State may by regulation set time limits relating to the length of time between the arrest of a person under the age of 18 and his initial appearance in court, and between conviction and sentence.

2.   These time limits may only be extended if the magistrates' court is satisfied that the need for an extension is due to some good and sufficient cause, and that the investigation has been conducted, and the prosecution has acted with all due diligence and expedition.

3.   If the time limits are exceeded the proceedings will be stayed, but fresh proceedings may be instituted within 3 months under section 22B of the Prosecution of Offences Act 1985, inserted by section 45, below.

45. After section 22A of the 1985 Act there shall be inserted the following section-

"**22B.**– (1) This section applies where proceedings for an offence ("the original proceedings") are stayed by a court under section 22(4) or 22A(5) of this Act.

(2) If-

    (a) in the case of proceedings conducted by the Director, the Director or a Chief Crown Prosecutor so directs;

    (b) in the case of proceedings conducted by the Director of the Serious Fraud Office, the Commissioners of Inland Revenue or the Commissioners of Customs and Excise, that Director or those Commissioners so direct; or

    (c) in the case of proceedings not conducted as mentioned in paragraph (a) or (b) above, a person designated for the purpose by the Secretary of State so directs,

fresh proceedings for the offence may be instituted within a period of three months (or such longer period as the court may allow) after the date on which the original proceedings were stayed by the court.

(3) Fresh proceedings shall be instituted as follows-

    (a) where the original proceedings were stayed by the Crown Court, by preferring a bill of indictment;

    (b) where the original proceedings were stayed by a magistrates' court, by laying an information.

(4) Fresh proceedings may be instituted in accordance with subsections (2) and (3)(b) above notwithstanding anything in section 127(1) of the Magistrates' Courts Act 1980 (limitation of time).

(5) Where fresh proceedings are instituted, anything done in relation to the original proceedings shall be treated as done in relation to the fresh proceedings if the court so directs or it was done-

    (a) by the prosecutor in compliance or purported compliance with section 3, 4, 7 or 9 of the Criminal Procedure and Investigations Act 1996; or

    (b) by the accused in compliance or purported compliance with section 5 or 6 of that Act.

(6) Where a person is convicted of an offence in fresh proceedings under this section, the institution of those proceedings shall not be called into question in any appeal against that conviction."

Section 45

1. This section amends the Prosecution of Offences Act 1985 by inserting section 22B which provides that where proceedings have been stayed as a result of the expiry of time limits under sections 22(4) or 22A(5), fresh proceedings may be instituted within 3 months.

> 2.   *Fresh proceedings may be instituted at the direction of the Director of Public Prosecutions or a Chief Crown Prosecutor; a Director of the Serious Fraud Office, the Commissioners of Inland Revenue or Customs and Excise; or by a person designated by the Secretary of State.*

46.– (1) In subsection (3) of section 47 of the 1984 Act (bail after arrest), for the words "subsection (4)" there shall be substituted the words "subsections (3A) and (4)".

(2) After that subsection there shall be inserted the following subsection-

"(3A) Where a custody officer grants bail to a person subject to a duty to appear before a magistrates' court, he shall appoint for the appearance-

(a) a date which is not later than the first sitting of the court after the person is charged with the offence; or

(b) where he is informed by the clerk to the justices for the relevant petty sessions area that the appearance cannot be accommodated until a later date, that later date."

> **Section 46**
> 1.   *This section amends section 47 of the Police and Criminal Evidence Act 1984, which deals with bail after arrest.*
>
> 2.   *Once a person is charged with an offence, a custody officer granting bail is obliged to bail him to appear at the first court sitting thereafter, unless the clerk to the justices informs him that the appearance cannot be accommodated until a later date.*

Functions of courts etc.

47.– (1) Where a person who appears or is brought before a youth court charged with an offence subsequently attains the age of 18, the youth court may, at any time-

(a) before the start of the trial; or

(b) after conviction and before sentence,

remit the person for trial or, as the case may be, for sentence to a magistrates' court (other than a youth court) acting for the same petty sessions area as the youth court.

In this subsection "the start of the trial" shall be construed in accordance with section 22(11B) of the 1985 Act.

(2) Where a person is remitted under subsection (1) above-

(a) he shall have no right of appeal against the order of remission;

(b) the remitting court shall adjourn proceedings in relation to the offence; and

(c) subsections (3) and (4) below shall apply.

(3) The following, namely-

(a) section 128 of the 1980 Act; and

(b) all other enactments (whenever passed) relating to remand or the granting of bail in criminal proceedings,

shall have effect in relation to the remitting court's power or duty to remand the person on the adjournment as if any reference to the court to or before which the person remanded is to be brought or appear after remand were a reference to the court to which he is being remitted ("the other court").

(4) The other court may deal with the case in any way in which it would have power to deal with it if all proceedings relating to the offence which took place before the remitting court had taken place before the other court.

(5) After subsection (3) of section 10 of the 1980 Act (adjournment of trial) there shall be inserted the following subsection-

"(3A) A youth court shall not be required to adjourn any proceedings for an offence at any stage by reason only of the fact-

(a) that the court commits the accused for trial for another offence; or

(b) that the accused is charged with another offence."

(6) After subsection (1) of section 24 of the 1980 Act (summary trial of information against child or young person for indictable offence) there shall be inserted the following subsection-

"(1A) Where a magistrates' court-

(a) commits a person under the age of 18 for trial for an offence of homicide; or

(b) in a case falling within subsection (1)(a) above, commits such a person for trial for an offence,

the court may also commit him for trial for any other indictable offence with which he is charged at the same time if the charges for both offences could be joined in the same indictment."

(7) In subsection (2) of section 47 (procedure in youth courts) of the Children and Young Persons Act 1933 ("the 1933 Act"), the words from the beginning to "court; and" shall cease to have effect.

> **Section 47**
> *1. This section provides that if a person brought before a youth court attains the age of 18 at any time before sentence, the youth court may remit the case to the magistrates' court.*

> 2. *The section also amends the Magistrates' Courts Act 1980 in connection with the adjournment of trials before youth courts and the committal of persons under the age of 18 for indictable offences.*
>
> 3. *The restriction imposed by section 47 of the Children and Young Persons Act 1933 on the presence in a youth court of those unconnected with the case is abolished.*

48.– (1) In paragraph 15 of Schedule 2 to the 1933 Act (constitution of youth courts)-

  (a) in paragraph (a), after the word "shall", in the first place where it occurs, there shall be inserted the words "either consist of a metropolitan stipendiary magistrate sitting alone or" and the word "shall", in the other place where it occurs, shall cease to have effect;

  (b) in paragraph (b), after the words "the chairman" there shall be inserted the words "(where applicable)"; and

  (c) in paragraph (c), after the words "the other members" there shall be inserted the words "(where applicable)".

(2) In paragraph 17 of that Schedule, the words "or, if a metropolitan stipendiary magistrate, may sit alone" shall cease to have effect.

> **Section 48**
> *This section amends the Children and Young Persons Act 1933 to allow a stipendiary magistrate to sit alone in the youth court.*

49.– (1) The following powers of a magistrates' court for any area may be exercised by a single justice of the peace for that area, namely-

  (a) to extend bail or to impose or vary conditions of bail;

  (b) to mark an information as withdrawn;

  (c) to dismiss an information, or to discharge an accused in respect of an information, where no evidence is offered by the prosecution;

  (d) to make an order for the payment of defence costs out of central funds;

  (e) to request a pre-sentence report following a plea of guilty and, for that purpose, to give an indication of the seriousness of the offence;

  (f) to request a medical report and, for that purpose, to remand the accused in custody or on bail;

  (g) to remit an offender to another court for sentence;

  (h) where a person has been granted police bail to appear at a magistrates' court, to appoint an earlier time for his appearance;

  (i) to extend, with the consent of the accused, a custody time limit or an overall time limit;

(j) where a case is to be tried on indictment, to grant representation under Part V of the Legal Aid Act 1988 for purposes of the proceedings in the Crown Court;

(k) where an accused has been convicted of an offence, to order him to produce his driving licence;

(l) to give a direction prohibiting the publication of matters disclosed or exempted from disclosure in court;

(m) to give, vary or revoke directions for the conduct of a trial, including directions as to the following matters, namely-

(i) the timetable for the proceedings;

(ii) the attendance of the parties;

(iii) the service of documents (including summaries of any legal arguments relied on by the parties);

(iv) the manner in which evidence is to be given; and

(n) to give, vary or revoke orders for separate or joint trials in the case of two or more accused or two or more informations.

(2) Without prejudice to the generality of subsection (1) of section 144 of the 1980 Act (rules of procedure)-

(a) rules under that section may, subject to subsection (3) below, provide that any of the things which, by virtue of subsection (1) above, are authorised to be done by a single justice of the peace for any area may, subject to any specified restrictions or conditions, be done by a justices' clerk for that area; and

(b) rules under that section which make such provision as is mentioned in paragraph (a) above may make different provision for different areas.

(3) Rules under that section which make such provision as is mentioned in subsection (2) above shall not authorise a justices' clerk-

(a) without the consent of the prosecutor and the accused, to extend bail on conditions other than those (if any) previously imposed, or to impose or vary conditions of bail;

(b) to give an indication of the seriousness of an offence for the purposes of a pre-sentence report;

(c) to remand the accused in custody for the purposes of a medical report or, without the consent of the prosecutor and the accused, to remand the accused on bail for those purposes on conditions other than those (if any) previously imposed;

(d) to give a direction prohibiting the publication of matters disclosed or exempted from disclosure in court; or

(e) without the consent of the parties, to give, vary or revoke orders for separate or joint trials in the case of two or more accused or two or more informations.

(4) Before making any rules under that section which make such provision as is mentioned in subsection (2) above in relation to any area, the Lord Chancellor shall consult justices of the peace and justices' clerks for that area.

(5) In this section and section 50 below "justices' clerk" has the same meaning as in section 144 of the 1980 Act.

> **Section 49**
> *This section sets out powers that may be exercised by a single justice of the peace, such as extending bail. Subject to certain restrictions, the powers may also be exercised by the clerk to the justices.*

50.– (1) Where a person ("the accused") has been charged with an offence at a police station, the magistrates' court before whom he appears or is brought for the first time in relation to the charge may, unless the accused falls to be dealt with under section 51 below, consist of a single justice.

(2) At a hearing conducted by a single justice under this section-

(a) the accused shall be asked whether he wishes to receive legal aid; and

(b) if he indicates that he does, his eligibility for it shall be determined; and

(c) if it is determined that he is eligible for it, the necessary arrangements or grant shall be made for him to obtain it.

(3) At such a hearing the single justice-

(a) may exercise, subject to subsection (2) above, such of his powers as a single justice as he thinks fit; and

(b) on adjourning the hearing, may remand the accused in custody or on bail.

(4) This section applies in relation to a justices' clerk as it applies in relation to a single justice; but nothing in subsection (3)(b) above authorises such a clerk to remand the accused in custody or, without the consent of the prosecutor and the accused, to remand the accused on bail on conditions other than those (if any) previously imposed.

(5) In this section "legal aid" means representation under Part V of the Legal Aid Act 1988.

> **Section 50**
> *A first appearance before a magistrates' court may be before a single justice, who may exercise the powers set out in section 49 above, having enquired whether the accused wishes to receive legal aid.*

51.– (1) Where an adult appears or is brought before a magistrates' court ("the court") charged with an offence triable only on indictment ("the indictable-only offence"), the court shall send him forthwith to the Crown Court for trial-

(a) for that offence, and

(b) for any either-way or summary offence with which he is charged which fulfils the requisite conditions (as set out in subsection (11) below).

(2) Where an adult who has been sent for trial under subsection (1) above subsequently appears or is brought before a magistrates' court charged with an either-way or summary offence which fulfils the requisite conditions, the court may send him forthwith to the Crown Court for trial for the either-way or summary offence.

(3) Where-

(a) the court sends an adult for trial under subsection (1) above;

(b) another adult appears or is brought before the court on the same or a subsequent occasion charged jointly with him with an either-way offence; and

(c) that offence appears to the court to be related to the indictable-only offence,

the court shall where it is the same occasion, and may where it is a subsequent occasion, send the other adult forthwith to the Crown Court for trial for the either-way offence.

(4) Where a court sends an adult for trial under subsection (3) above, it shall at the same time send him to the Crown Court for trial for any either-way or summary offence with which he is charged which fulfils the requisite conditions.

(5) Where-

(a) the court sends an adult for trial under subsection (1) or (3) above; and

(b) a child or young person appears or is brought before the court on the same or a subsequent occasion charged jointly with the adult with an indictable offence for which the adult is sent for trial,

the court shall, if it considers it necessary in the interests of justice to do so, send the child or young person forthwith to the Crown Court for trial for the indictable offence.

(6) Where a court sends a child or young person for trial under subsection (5) above, it may at the same time send him to the Crown Court for trial for any either-way or summary offence with which he is charged which fulfils the requisite conditions.

(7) The court shall specify in a notice the offence or offences for which a person is sent for trial under this section and the place at which he is to be tried; and a copy of the notice shall be served on the accused and given to the Crown Court sitting at that place.

(8) In a case where there is more than one indictable-only offence and the court includes an either-way or a summary offence in the notice under subsection (7) above, the court shall specify in that notice the indictable-only offence to which the either-way offence or, as the case may be, the summary offence appears to the court to be related.

(9) The trial of the information charging any summary offence for which a person is sent for trial under this section shall be treated as if the court had adjourned it under section 10 of the 1980 Act and had not fixed the time and place for its resumption.

(10) In selecting the place of trial for the purpose of subsection (7) above, the court shall have regard to-

    (a) the convenience of the defence, the prosecution and the witnesses;

    (b) the desirability of expediting the trial; and

    (c) any direction given by or on behalf of the Lord Chief Justice with the concurrence of the Lord Chancellor under section 75(1) of the Supreme Court Act 1981.

(11) An offence fulfils the requisite conditions if-

    (a) it appears to the court to be related to the indictable-only offence; and

    (b) in the case of a summary offence, it is punishable with imprisonment or involves obligatory or discretionary disqualification from driving.

(12) For the purposes of this section-

    (a) "adult" means a person aged 18 or over, and references to an adult include references to a corporation;

    (b) "either-way offence" means an offence which, if committed by an adult, is triable either on indictment or summarily;

    (c) an either-way offence is related to an indictable-only offence if the charge for the either-way offence could be joined in the same indictment as the charge for the indictable-only offence;

    (d) a summary offence is related to an indictable-only offence if it arises out of circumstances which are the same as or connected with those giving rise to the indictable-only offence.

Section 51

Committal proceedings are no longer necessary in connection with indictable-only offences. Where a person charged with an indictable-only offence appears before a magistrates' court, the court shall send him forthwith to be tried before the Crown Court. Related either-way or summary offences, which are punishable with imprisonment or disqualification from driving, may also be sent up to the Crown Court; as may co-defendants.

52.– (1) Subject to section 4 of the Bail Act 1976, section 41 of the 1980 Act, regulations under section 22 of the 1985 Act and section 25 of the 1994 Act, the court may send a person for trial under section 51 above-

    (a) in custody, that is to say, by committing him to custody there to be safely kept until delivered in due course of law; or

    (b) on bail in accordance with the (1976 c.63.)Bail Act 1976, that is to say, by directing him to appear before the Crown Court for trial.

(2) Where-

    (a) the person's release on bail under subsection (1)(b) above is conditional on his providing one or more sureties; and

    (b) in accordance with subsection (3) of section 8 of the (1976 c.63.)Bail Act 1976, the court fixes the amount in which a surety is to be bound with a view to his entering into his recognisance subsequently in accordance with subsections (4) and (5) or (6) of that section,

the court shall in the meantime make an order such as is mentioned in subsection (1)(a) above.

(3) The court shall treat as an indictable offence for the purposes of section 51 above an offence which is mentioned in the first column of Schedule 2 to the 1980 Act (offences for which the value involved is relevant to the mode of trial) unless it is clear to the court, having regard to any representations made by the prosecutor or the accused, that the value involved does not exceed the relevant sum.

(4) In subsection (3) above "the value involved" and "the relevant sum" have the same meanings as in section 22 of the 1980 Act (certain offences triable either way to be tried summarily if value involved is small).

(5) A magistrates' court may adjourn any proceedings under section 51 above, and if it does so shall remand the accused.

(6) Schedule 3 to this Act (which makes further provision in relation to persons sent to the Crown Court for trial under section 51 above) shall have effect.

> **Section 52**
> *This section contains provisions supplemental to section 51 (abolishing committal proceedings for indictable only offences), dealing, for example, with powers to remand in custody.*

Miscellaneous

53. For section 7A of the 1985 Act there shall be substituted the following section-

"7A.- (1) The Director may designate, for the purposes of this section, members of the staff of the Crown Prosecution Service who are not Crown Prosecutors.

(2) Subject to such exceptions (if any) as may be specified in the designation, a person so designated shall have such of the following as may be so specified, namely-

(a) the powers and rights of audience of a Crown Prosecutor in relation to-
    (i) applications for, or relating to, bail in criminal proceedings;
    (ii) the conduct of criminal proceedings in magistrates' courts other than trials;
(b) the powers of such a Prosecutor in relation to the conduct of criminal proceedings not falling within paragraph (a)(ii) above.

(3) A person so designated shall exercise any such powers subject to instructions given to him by the Director.

(4) Any such instructions may be given so as to apply generally.

(5) For the purposes of this section-

(a) "bail in criminal proceedings" has the same meaning as it would have in the Bail Act 1976 by virtue of the definition in section 1 of that Act if in that section "offence" did not include an offence to which subsection (6) below applies;
(b) "criminal proceedings" does not include proceedings for an offence to which subsection (6) below applies; and
(c) a trial begins with the opening of the prosecution case after the entry of a plea of not guilty and ends with the conviction or acquittal of the accused.

(6) This subsection applies to an offence if it is triable only on indictment, or is an offence-

(a) for which the accused has elected to be tried by a jury;
(b) which a magistrates' court has decided is more suitable to be so tried; or
(c) in respect of which a notice of transfer has been given under section 4 of the Criminal Justice Act 1987 or section 53 of the Criminal Justice Act 1991.

(7) Details of the following for any year, namely-

(a) the criteria applied by the Director in determining whether to designate persons under this section;
(b) the training undergone by persons so designated; and
(c) any general instructions given by the Director under subsection (4) above,

shall be set out in the Director's report under section 9 of this Act for that year."

Section 53
1.   This section amends section 7A of the Prosecution of Offences Act 1985 and allows the Director of the Crown Prosecution Service to designate members of the Crown Prosecution Service who are not legally qualified to have rights of audience in magistrates' courts to deal with bail applications and to conduct certain criminal proceedings other than trials. The section also gives them the powers of a Crown Prosecutor, but not the rights of audience, in relation to the conduct of other criminal proceedings.

2. *"Criminal proceedings" has a restricted meaning for the purposes of the section, with the effect that the designated members of the Crown Prosecution Service cannot deal with offences that are to be tried in the Crown Court.*

3. *Thus, certain non-legally qualified staff will have rights of audience in the magistrates' court to deal with bail applications, guilty pleas and other criminal matters, but they may not conduct trials and they may not deal with or conduct any application concerning an offence that is triable only on indictment or in respect of which the defendant has elected to be tried in the Crown Court.*

54.– (1) In subsection (5) of section 3 of the Bail Act 1976 (general provisions as to bail), the words "If it appears that he is unlikely to remain in Great Britain until the time appointed for him to surrender to custody" shall cease to have effect.

(2) In subsection (6) of that section, after paragraph (d) there shall be inserted the following paragraph-

"(e) before the time appointed for him to surrender to custody, he attends an interview with an authorised advocate or authorised litigator, as defined by section 119(1) of the Courts and Legal Services Act 1990;".

(3) In subsection (2) of section 3A of that Act (conditions of bail in the case of police bail), for the words "paragraph (d)" there shall be substituted the words paragraph (d) or (e)".

Section 54
1. *This section amends the Bail Act 1976 making it easier to require security before release on bail, by removing the requirement to show that there is reason to believe that the person is unlikely to remain in the country.*

2. *It also creates the power to make it a condition of bail that a person is to attend for interview with his legal representative.*

55. For subsections (1) and (2) of section 120 of the 1980 Act (forfeiture of recognizances) there shall be substituted the following subsections-

"(1) This section applies where-

(a) a recognizance to keep the peace or to be of good behaviour has been entered into before a magistrates' court; or
(b) any recognizance is conditioned for the appearance of a person before a magistrates' court, or for his doing any other thing connected with a proceeding before a magistrates' court.

(1A)   If, in the case of a recognizance which is conditioned for the appearance of an accused before a magistrates' court, the accused fails to appear in accordance with the condition, the court shall-

(a) declare the recognizance to be forfeited;

(b) issue a summons directed to each person bound by the recognizance as surety, requiring him to appear before the court on a date specified in the summons to show cause why he should not be adjudged to pay the sum in which he is bound;

and on that date the court may proceed in the absence of any surety if it is satisfied that he has been served with the summons.

(2) If, in any other case falling within subsection (1) above, the recognizance appears to the magistrates' court to be forfeited, the court may-

(a) declare the recognizance to be forfeited; and

(b) adjudge each person bound by it, whether as principal or surety, to pay the sum in which he is bound;

but in a case falling within subsection (1)(a) above, the court shall not declare the recognizance to be forfeited except by order made on complaint."

Section 55

This section amends section 120 of the Magistrates' Courts Act 1980. Where a surety enters into a recognizance to ensure the attendance of a person before a magistrates' court and that person fails to appear, the magistrates' court is now obliged to issue a summons requiring the attendance of the surety to consider whether he should pay the sum in which he is bound.

56. In subsection (1) of section 25 of the 1994 Act (no bail for defendants charged with or convicted of homicide or rape after previous conviction of such offences), for the words "shall not be granted bail in those proceedings" there shall be substituted the words "shall be granted bail in those proceedings only if the court or, as the case may be, the constable considering the grant of bail is satisfied that there are exceptional circumstances which justify it".

Section 56

Bail may now be granted in exceptional circumstances to those charged with or convicted of homicide, rape or attempted rape following a previous conviction for one of those offences.

57.– (1) In any proceedings for an offence, a court may, after hearing representations from the parties, direct that the accused shall be treated as being present in the court for any particular hearing before the start of the trial if, during that hearing-

(a) he is held in custody in a prison or other institution; and

(b) whether by means of a live television link or otherwise, he is able to see and hear the court and to be seen and heard by it.

(2) A court shall not give a direction under subsection (1) above unless-

(a) it has been notified by the Secretary of State that facilities are available for enabling persons held in custody in the institution in which the accused is or is to be so held to see and hear the court and to be seen and heard by it; and

(b) the notice has not been withdrawn.

(3) If in a case where it has power to do so a magistrates' court decides not to give a direction under subsection (1) above, it shall give its reasons for not doing so.

(4) In this section "the start of the trial" has the meaning given by subsection (11A) or (11B) of section 22 of the 1985 Act.

Section 57
This section empowers a court to direct that a person in custody, who is able to communicate with, hear and see the court via a live television link, or other device, be deemed to be present in court.

PART IV DEALING WITH OFFENDERS

CHAPTER I ENGLAND AND WALES

Sexual or violent offenders

58.– (1) This section applies where a court which proposes to impose a custodial sentence for a sexual or violent offence considers that the period (if any) for which the offender would, apart from this section, be subject to a licence would not be adequate for the purpose of preventing the commission by him of further offences and securing his rehabilitation.

(2) Subject to subsections (3) to (5) below, the court may pass on the offender an extended sentence, that is to say, a custodial sentence the term of which is equal to the aggregate of-

(a) the term of the custodial sentence that the court would have imposed if it had passed a custodial sentence otherwise than under this section ("the custodial term"); and

(b) a further period ("the extension period") for which the offender is to be subject to a licence and which is of such length as the court considers necessary for the purpose mentioned in subsection (1) above.

(3) Where the offence is a violent offence, the court shall not pass an extended sentence the custodial term of which is less than four years.

(4) The extension period shall not exceed-

(a) ten years in the case of a sexual offence; and
(b) five years in the case of a violent offence.

(5) The term of an extended sentence passed in respect of an offence shall not exceed the maximum term permitted for that offence.

(6) Subsection (2) of section 2 of the 1991 Act (length of custodial sentences) shall apply as if the term of an extended sentence did not include the extension period.

(7) The Secretary of State may by order amend paragraph (b) of subsection (4) above by substituting a different period, not exceeding ten years, for the period for the time being specified in that paragraph.

(8) In this section-

"licence" means a licence under Part II of the 1991 Act;

"sexual offence" and

"violent offence" have the same meanings as in Part I of that Act.

Section 58

1.   This section introduces extended sentences. An extended sentence is not simply a longer custodial sentence than would otherwise be imposed, as the name might imply. It is a sentence made up of the term of imprisonment that would have been imposed in any event, together with a further period, the "extension period", during which the offender is released on licence and subject to supervision.

2.   The extension period may be significant: up to 10 years in the case of a sexual offence, and up to 5 years in the case of a violent offence. These limits may be changed by order.

3.   Where a custodial sentence is to be imposed for a sexual or a violent offence, the period for which an offender is to be subject to a licence on release from custody may be extended where the court considers that the period of licence, but for this section, would be inadequate to prevent further offences or to rehabilitate the offender.

---

59. For section 44 of the 1991 Act there shall be substituted the following section-

"**44.**– (1) This section applies to a prisoner serving an extended sentence within the meaning of section 58 of the Crime and Disorder Act 1998.

(2) Subject to the provisions of this section and section 51(2D) below, this Part, except sections 40 and 40A, shall have effect as if the term of the extended sentence did not include the extension period.

(3) Where the prisoner is released on licence under this Part, the licence shall, subject to any revocation under section 39(1) or (2) above, remain in force until the end of the extension period.

(4) Where, apart from this subsection, the prisoner would be released unconditionally-

(a) he shall be released on licence; and
(b) the licence shall, subject to any revocation under section 39(1) or (2) above, remain in force until the end of the extension period.

(5) The extension period shall be taken to begin as follows-

(a) for the purposes of subsection (3) above, on the date given by section 37(1) above;
(b) for the purposes of subsection (4) above, on the date on which, apart from that subsection, the prisoner would have been released unconditionally.

(6) Sections 33(3) and 33A(1) above and section 46 below shall not apply in relation to the prisoner.

(7) For the purposes of sections 37(5) and 39(1) and (2) above the question whether the prisoner is a long-term or short-term prisoner shall be determined by reference to the term of the extended sentence.

(8) In this section "extension period" has the same meaning as in section 58 of the Crime and Disorder Act 1998."

Section 59
This section amends section 44 of the Criminal Justice Act 1991 providing that an offender subject to an extended sentence will be released on licence rather than unconditionally and the licence will continue until the end of the extended sentence.

60. After section 44 of the 1991 Act there shall be inserted the following section-

"**44A.**– (1) This section applies to a prisoner serving an extended sentence within the meaning of section 58 of the Crime and Disorder Act 1998 who is recalled to prison under section 39(1) or (2) above.

(2) Subject to subsection (3) below, the prisoner may require the Secretary of State to refer his case to the Board at any time.

(3) Where there has been a previous reference of the prisoner's case to the Board (whether under this section or section 39(4) above), the Secretary of State shall not be required to refer the case until after the end of the period of one year beginning with the disposal of that reference.

(4) On a reference-

   (a) under this section; or
   (b) under section 39(4) above,

the Board shall direct the prisoner's release if satisfied that it is no longer necessary for the protection of the public that he should be confined (but not otherwise).

(5) If the Board gives a direction under subsection (4) above it shall be the duty of the Secretary of State to release the prisoner on licence."

Section 60
This section inserts a new section, section 44A, into the Criminal Justice Act 1991 which deals with the re-release of prisoners serving extended sentences who have been recalled to prison.

Offenders dependent etc. on drugs

61.– (1) This section applies where a person aged 16 or over is convicted of an offence other than one for which the sentence-

   (a) is fixed by law; or
   (b) falls to be imposed under section 2(2), 3(2) or 4(2) of the 1997 Act.

(2) Subject to the provisions of this section, the court by or before which the offender is convicted may make an order (a "drug treatment and testing order") which-

   (a) has effect for a period specified in the order of not less than six months nor more than three years ("the treatment and testing period"); and
   (b) includes the requirements and provisions mentioned in section 62 below.

(3) A court shall not make a drug treatment and testing order unless it has been notified by the Secretary of State that arrangements for implementing such orders are available in the area proposed to be specified in the order and the notice has not been withdrawn.

(4) A drug treatment and testing order shall be a community order for the purposes of Part I of the 1991 Act; and the provisions of that Part, which include provisions with respect to restrictions on imposing, and procedural requirements for, community sentences (sections 6 and 7), shall apply accordingly.

(5) The court shall not make a drug treatment and testing order in respect of the offender unless it is satisfied-

   (a) that he is dependent on or has a propensity to misuse drugs; and
   (b) that his dependency or propensity is such as requires and may be susceptible to treatment.

(6) For the purpose of ascertaining for the purposes of subsection (5) above whether the offender has any drug in his body, the court may by order require him to provide samples of such description as it may specify; but the court shall not make such an order unless the offender expresses his willingness to comply with its requirements.

(7) The Secretary of State may by order amend subsection (2) above by substituting a different period for the minimum or maximum period for the time being specified in that subsection.

Section 61
Where an offender is dependent on or has a propensity to abuse drugs the court may make a "drug treatment and testing order", under which the offender is required to undergo treatment and to provide samples which may be tested for drugs. The order can only be made if the offender is willing to comply with the order, and it can last for a minimum of 6 months and a maximum of 3 years, "the treatment and testing period".

62.– (1) A drug treatment and testing order shall include a requirement ("the treatment requirement") that the offender shall submit, during the whole of the treatment and testing period, to treatment by or under the direction of a specified person having the necessary qualifications or experience ("the treatment provider") with a view to the reduction or elimination of the offender's dependency on or propensity to misuse drugs.

(2) The required treatment for any particular period shall be-

   (a) treatment as a resident in such institution or place as may be specified in the order; or
   (b) treatment as a non-resident in or at such institution or place, and at such intervals, as may be so specified;

but the nature of the treatment shall not be specified in the order except as mentioned in paragraph (a) or (b) above.

(3) A court shall not make a drug treatment and testing order unless it is satisfied that arrangements have been or can be made for the treatment intended to be specified in the order (including arrangements for the reception of the offender where he is to be required to submit to treatment as a resident).

(4) A drug treatment and testing order shall include a requirement ("the testing requirement") that, for the purpose of ascertaining whether he has any drug in his body during the treatment and testing period, the offender shall provide during that period, at such times or in such circumstances as may (subject to the provisions of the order) be determined by the treatment provider, samples of such description as may be so determined.

(5) The testing requirement shall specify for each month the minimum number of occasions on which samples are to be provided.

(6) A drug treatment and testing order shall include a provision specifying the petty sessions area in which it appears to the court making the order that the offender resides or will reside.

(7) A drug treatment and testing order shall-

    (a) provide that, for the treatment and testing period, the offender shall be under the supervision of a responsible officer, that is to say, a probation officer appointed for or assigned to the petty sessions area specified in the order;

    (b) require the offender to keep in touch with the responsible officer in accordance with such instructions as he may from time to time be given by that officer, and to notify him of any change of address; and

    (c) provide that the results of the tests carried out on the samples provided by the offender in pursuance of the testing requirement shall be communicated to the responsible officer.

(8) Supervision by the responsible officer shall be carried out to such extent only as may be necessary for the purpose of enabling him-

    (a) to report on the offender's progress to the court responsible for the order;

    (b) to report to that court any failure by the offender to comply with the requirements of the order; and

    (c) to determine whether the circumstances are such that he should apply to that court for the revocation or amendment of the order.

(9) In this section and sections 63 and 64 below, references to the court responsible for a drug treatment and testing order are references to-

    (a) the court by which the order is made; or

    (b) where another court is specified in the order in accordance with subsection (10) below, that court.

(10) Where the area specified in a drug treatment and testing order made by a magistrates' court is not the area for which the court acts, the court may, if it thinks fit, include in the order provision specifying for the purposes of subsection (9) above a magistrates' court which acts for that area.

Section 62

1.   A drug treatment and testing order requires an offender to submit to treatment for the whole of the treatment and testing period with a view to reducing or eliminating dependency on drugs.

2.   The court must specify whether the offender is to be treated as resident or non-resident in an institution; that the offender shall be under the supervision of a specified probation officer; and the minimum number of samples for drug-testing that must be provided each month by the offender.

3.   A court cannot make an order unless it is satisfied that suitable arrangements have been or can be made for the treatment.

63.– (1) A drug treatment and testing order shall-

- (a) provide for the order to be reviewed periodically at intervals of not less than one month;
- (b) provide for each review of the order to be made, subject to subsection (7) below, at a hearing held for the purpose by the court responsible for the order (a "review hearing");
- (c) require the offender to attend each review hearing;
- (d) provide for the responsible officer to make to the court, before each review, a report in writing on the offender's progress under the order; and
- (e) provide for each such report to include the test results communicated to the responsible officer under section 62(7)(c) above and the views of the treatment provider as to the treatment and testing of the offender.

(2) At a review hearing the court, after considering the responsible officer's report, may amend any requirement or provision of the order.

(3) The court-

- (a) shall not amend the treatment or testing requirement unless the offender expresses his willingness to comply with the requirement as amended;
- (b) shall not amend any provision of the order so as to reduce the treatment and testing period below the minimum specified in section 61(2) above, or to increase it above the maximum so specified; and
- (c) except with the consent of the offender, shall not amend any requirement or provision of the order while an appeal against the order is pending.

(4) If the offender fails to express his willingness to comply with the treatment or testing requirement as proposed to be amended by the court, the court may-

- (a) revoke the order; and
- (b) deal with him, for the offence in respect of which the order was made, in any manner in which it could deal with him if he had just been convicted by the court of the offence.

(5) In dealing with the offender under subsection (4)(b) above, the court-

  (a) shall take into account the extent to which the offender has complied with the requirements of the order; and

  (b) may impose a custodial sentence notwithstanding anything in section 1(2) of the 1991 Act.

(6) Where the order was made by a magistrates' court in the case of an offender under the age of 18 years in respect of an offence triable only on indictment in the case of an adult, the court's power under subsection (4)(b) above shall be a power to do either or both of the following, namely-

  (a) to impose a fine not exceeding £5,000 for the offence in respect of which the order was made;

  (b) to deal with the offender for that offence in any way in which it could deal with him if it had just convicted him of an offence punishable with imprisonment for a term not exceeding six months;

and the reference in paragraph (b) above to an offence punishable with imprisonment shall be construed without regard to any prohibition or restriction imposed by or under any enactment on the imprisonment of young offenders.

(7) If at a review hearing the court, after considering the responsible officer's report, is of the opinion that the offender's progress under the order is satisfactory, the court may so amend the order as to provide for each subsequent review to be made by the court without a hearing.

(8) If at a review without a hearing the court, after considering the responsible officer's report, is of the opinion that the offender's progress under the order is no longer satisfactory, the court may require the offender to attend a hearing of the court at a specified time and place.

(9) At that hearing the court, after considering that report, may-

  (a) exercise the powers conferred by this section as if the hearing were a review hearing; and

  (b) so amend the order as to provide for each subsequent review to be made at a review hearing.

(10) In this section any reference to the court, in relation to a review without a hearing, shall be construed-

  (a) in the case of the Crown Court, as a reference to a judge of the court;

  (b) in the case of a magistrates' court, as a reference to a justice of the peace acting for the commission area for which the court acts.

64.– (1) Before making a drug treatment and testing order, a court shall explain to the offender in ordinary language-

  (a) the effect of the order and of the requirements proposed to be included in it;

(b) the consequences which may follow (under Schedule 2 to the 1991 Act) if he fails to comply with any of those requirements;

(c) that the order may be reviewed (under that Schedule) on the application either of the offender or of the responsible officer; and

(d) that the order will be periodically reviewed at intervals as provided for in the order (by virtue of section 63 above);

and the court shall not make the order unless the offender expresses his willingness to comply with its requirements.

(2) Where, in the case of a drug treatment and testing order made by a magistrates' court, another magistrates' court is responsible for the order, the court making the order shall forthwith send copies of the order to the other court.

(3) Where a drug treatment and testing order is made or amended under section 63(2) above, the court responsible for the order shall forthwith or, in a case falling within subsection (2) above, as soon as reasonably practicable give copies of the order, or the order as amended, to a probation officer assigned to the court, and he shall give a copy-

(a) to the offender;

(b) to the treatment provider; and

(c) to the responsible officer.

(4) Where a drug treatment and testing order has been made on an appeal brought from the Crown Court, or from the criminal division of the Court of Appeal, for the purposes of sections 62 and 63 above it shall be deemed to have been made by the Crown Court.

(5) Schedule 2 to the 1991 Act (enforcement etc. of community orders) shall have effect subject to the amendments specified in Schedule 4 to this Act, being amendments for applying that Schedule to drug treatment and testing orders.

Sections 63 and 64

1.   These sections contain further provisions relating to drug treatment and testing orders.

2.   Such orders are to be reviewed periodically at intervals of not less than one month.

3.   In the event of failure to comply with the order, the court may deal with the offender in any manner in which it could have dealt with him for the original offence.

Young offenders: reprimands and warnings

65.– (1) Subsections (2) to (5) below apply where-

(a) a constable has evidence that a child or young person ("the offender") has committed an offence;

(b) the constable considers that the evidence is such that, if the offender were prosecuted for the offence, there would be a realistic prospect of his being convicted;

(c) the offender admits to the constable that he committed the offence;

(d) the offender has not previously been convicted of an offence; and

(e) the constable is satisfied that it would not be in the public interest for the offender to be prosecuted.

(2) Subject to subsection (4) below, the constable may reprimand the offender if the offender has not previously been reprimanded or warned.

(3) The constable may warn the offender if-

(a) the offender has not previously been warned; or

(b) where the offender has previously been warned, the offence was committed more than two years after the date of the previous warning and the constable considers the offence to be not so serious as to require a charge to be brought;

but no person may be warned under paragraph (b) above more than once.

(4) Where the offender has not been previously reprimanded, the constable shall warn rather than reprimand the offender if he considers the offence to be so serious as to require a warning.

(5) The constable shall-

(a) give any reprimand or warning at a police station and, where the offender is under the age of 17, in the presence of an appropriate adult; and

(b) explain to the offender and, where he is under that age, the appropriate adult in ordinary language-

(i) in the case of a reprimand, the effect of subsection (5)(a) of section 66 below;

(ii) in the case of a warning, the effect of subsections (1), (2), (4) and (5)(b) and (c) of that section, and any guidance issued under subsection (3) of that section.

(6) The Secretary of State shall publish, in such manner as he considers appropriate, guidance as to-

(a) the circumstances in which it is appropriate to give reprimands or warnings, including criteria for determining-

(i) for the purposes of subsection (3)(b) above, whether an offence is not so serious as to require a charge to be brought; and

(ii) for the purposes of subsection (4) above, whether an offence is so serious as to require a warning;

(b) the category of constable by whom reprimands and warnings may be given; and

(c) the form which reprimands and warnings are to take and the manner in which they are to be given and recorded.

(7) In this section "appropriate adult", in relation to a child or young person, means-

(a) his parent or guardian or, if he is in the care of a local authority or voluntary organisation, a person representing that authority or organisation;

(b) a social worker of a local authority social services department;

(c) if no person falling within paragraph (a) or (b) above is available, any responsible person aged 18 or over who is not a police officer or a person employed by the police.

(8) No caution shall be given to a child or young person after the commencement of this section.

(9) Any reference (however expressed) in any enactment passed before or in the same Session as this Act to a person being cautioned shall be construed, in relation to any time after that commencement, as including a reference to a child or young person being reprimanded or warned.

Section 65

1.   The system of cautioning children or young persons for offences they have committed and admitted is replaced by a system of reprimands and warnings.

2.   The system applies where a constable considers that:

1)   a child or young person has committed an offence;

2)   there is a realistic prospect of conviction;

3)   the offence is admitted;

4)   the offender has not previously been convicted of an offence; and

5)   the constable considers that prosecution would not be in the public interest.

3.   A child or young person may be reprimanded once, if he has not previously been warned.

4.   A child or young person may be warned once; or twice if the first warning was more than two years old.

5.   A warning involves referral to the youth offending team, under section 66 below. A reprimand does not.

> 6.　*Reprimands and warnings are to be given in police stations, with an appropriate adult in cases involving those not yet 17.*
>
> 7.　*The Secretary of State is obliged to publish guidance as to when reprimands or warnings would be appropriate.*

66.– (1) Where a constable warns a person under section 65 above, he shall as soon as practicable refer the person to a youth offending team.

(2) A youth offending team-

    (a) shall assess any person referred to them under subsection (1) above; and

    (b) unless they consider it inappropriate to do so, shall arrange for him to participate in a rehabilitation programme.

(3) The Secretary of State shall publish, in such manner as he considers appropriate, guidance as to-

    (a) what should be included in a rehabilitation programme arranged for a person under subsection (2) above;

    (b) the manner in which any failure by a person to participate in such a programme is to be recorded; and

    (c) the persons to whom any such failure is to be notified.

(4) Where a person who has been warned under section 65 above is convicted of an offence committed within two years of the warning, the court by or before which he is so convicted-

    (a) shall not make an order under subsection (1)(b) (conditional discharge) of section 1A of the 1973 Act in respect of the offence unless it is of the opinion that there are exceptional circumstances relating to the offence or the offender which justify its doing so; and

    (b) where it does so, shall state in open court that it is of that opinion and why it is.

(5) The following, namely-

    (a) any reprimand of a person under section 65 above;

    (b) any warning of a person under that section; and

    (c) any report on a failure by a person to participate in a rehabilitation programme arranged for him under subsection (2) above,

may be cited in criminal proceedings in the same circumstances as a conviction of the person may be cited.

(6) In this section "rehabilitation programme" means a programme the purpose of which is to rehabilitate participants and to prevent them from re-offending.

Section 66

1. A constable who warns a child or young person under section 65 is obliged to refer him to the youth offending team, which will assess and, if appropriate, arrange for him to participate in a rehabilitation programme.

2. The Secretary of State is obliged to publish guidance as to what a rehabilitation programme should involve, and the manner in which failure to participate should be recorded and to whom the failure should be notified.

3. If a child or young person is convicted of an offence within two years of a warning, a court cannot conditionally discharge him unless there are exceptional circumstances, and it must state in open court its reasons for doing so.

Young offenders: non-custodial orders

67.– (1) This section applies where a child or young person is convicted of an offence other than one for which the sentence is fixed by law.

(2) Subject to the provisions of this section and section 68 below, the court by or before which the offender is convicted may make an order (a "reparation order") which requires the offender to make reparation specified in the order-

   (a) to a person or persons so specified; or
   (b) to the community at large;

and any person so specified must be a person identified by the court as a victim of the offence or a person otherwise affected by it.

(3) The court shall not make a reparation order unless it has been notified by the Secretary of State that arrangements for implementing such orders are available in the area proposed to be named in the order and the notice has not been withdrawn.

(4) The court shall not make a reparation order in respect of the offender if it proposes-

   (a) to pass on him a custodial sentence or a sentence under section 53(1) of the 1933 Act; or
   (b) to make in respect of him a community service order, a combination order, a supervision order which includes requirements imposed in pursuance of sections 12 to 12C of the 1969 Act or an action plan order.

(5) A reparation order shall not require the offender-

   (a) to work for more than 24 hours in aggregate; or
   (b) to make reparation to any person without the consent of that person.

(6) Subject to subsection (5) above, requirements specified in a reparation order shall be such as in the opinion of the court are commensurate with seriousness of the offence, or the combination of the offence and one or more offences associated with it.

(7) Requirements so specified shall, as far as practicable, be such as to avoid-

(a) any conflict with the offender's religious beliefs or with the requirements of any community order to which he may be subject; and

(b) any interference with the times, if any, at which the offender normally works or attends school or any other educational establishment.

(8) Any reparation required by a reparation order-

(a) shall be made under the supervision of the responsible officer; and

(b) shall be made within a period of three months from the date of the making of the order.

(9) A reparation order shall name the petty sessions area in which it appears to the court making the order, or to the court varying any provision included in the order in pursuance of this subsection, that the offender resides or will reside.

(10) In this section "responsible officer", in relation to a reparation order, means one of the following who is specified in the order, namely-

(a) a probation officer;

(b) a social worker of a local authority social services department; and

(c) a member of a youth offending team.

(11) The court shall give reasons if it does not make a reparation order in a case where it has power to do so.

Section 67

1.   This section deals with reparation orders.

2.   Where a child or young person is convicted, a court may make a reparation order unless it proposes to pass a custodial sentence, detain at Her Majesty's pleasure, make a community service order, a combination order, a supervision order which includes requirements under the Children and Young Persons Act 1969, or an action plan order.

3.   A reparation order requires the offender to perform specified work, or other form of reparation, for the benefit of the victim of the offence or for the community at large, commensurate with the seriousness of the offence. The amount of work that may be imposed is limited to 24 hours work.

4.   The victim's consent is required.

5.   Reparation will be supervised by the responsible probation officer, social worker or member of the youth offending team, and is to be carried out within 3 months of the making of the order.

6.   A court cannot make a reparation order unless it has been notified by the Secretary of State that arrangements for implementing them are available.

7.   A court that does not make a reparation order is required to give its reasons for not doing so.

8.   The requirements are not to conflict with religious beliefs or with times when the offender normally works or attends school.

68.– (1) Before making a reparation order, a court shall obtain and consider a written report by a probation officer, a social worker of a local authority social services department or a member of a youth offending team, indicating-

(a) the type of work that is suitable for the offender; and
(b) the attitude of the victim or victims to the requirements proposed to be included in the order.

(2) Before making a reparation order, a court shall explain to the offender in ordinary language-

(a) the effect of the order and of the requirements proposed to be included in it;
(b) the consequences which may follow (under Schedule 5 to this Act) if he fails to comply with any of those requirements; and
(c) that the court has power (under that Schedule) to review the order on the application either of the offender or of the responsible officer.

(3) Schedule 5 to this Act shall have effect for dealing with failure to comply with the requirements of reparation orders, for varying such orders and for discharging them with or without the substitution of other sentences.

Section 68
1.   Before making a reparation order the court is obliged to obtain a report from a probation officer, social worker or member of the youth offending team which indicates the type of work that is suitable and the attitude of the victim or victims to the proposed requirements.

2.   The requirements and consequences of failure to comply with a reparation order must be explained to the offender.

3. Schedule 5 of the Act sets out the court's powers on failure to comply. They include the power to impose a fine of £1,000, and to make an attendance centre or curfew order.

69.– (1) This section applies where a child or young person is convicted of an offence other than one for which the sentence is fixed by law.

(2) Subject to the provisions of this section and section 70 below, the court by or before which the offender is convicted may, if it is of the opinion that it is desirable to do so in the interests of securing his rehabilitation, or of preventing the commission by him of further offences, make an order (an "action plan order") which-

    (a) requires the offender, for a period of three months beginning with the date of the order, to comply with an action plan, that is to say, a series of requirements with respect to his actions and whereabouts during that period;

    (b) places the offender under the supervision for that period of the responsible officer; and

    (c) requires the offender to comply with any directions given by that officer with a view to the implementation of that plan.

(3) The court shall not make an action plan order unless it has been notified by the Secretary of State that arrangements for implementing such orders are available in the area proposed to be named in the order and the notice has not been withdrawn.

(4) The court shall not make an action plan order in respect of the offender if-

    (a) he is already the subject of such an order; or

    (b) the court proposes to pass on him a custodial sentence or a sentence under section 53(1) of the 1933 Act, or to make in respect of him a probation order, a community service order, a combination order, a supervision order or an attendance centre order.

(5) Requirements included in an action plan order, or directions given by a responsible officer, may require the offender to do all or any of the following things, namely-

    (a) to participate in activities specified in the requirements or directions at a time or times so specified;

    (b) to present himself to a person or persons specified in the requirements or directions at a place or places and at a time or times so specified;

    (c) to attend at an attendance centre specified in the requirements or directions for a number of hours so specified;

    (d) to stay away from a place or places specified in the requirements or directions;

    (e) to comply with any arrangements for his education specified in the requirements or directions;

(f) to make reparation specified in the requirements or directions to a person or persons so specified or to the community at large; and

(g) to attend any hearing fixed by the court under section 70(3) below.

(6) Such requirements and directions shall, as far as practicable, be such as to avoid-

(a) any conflict with the offender's religious beliefs or with the requirements of any other community order to which he may be subject; and

(b) any interference with the times, if any, at which he normally works or attends school or any other educational establishment.

(7) Subsection (5)(c) above does not apply unless the offence committed by the offender is punishable with imprisonment in the case of a person aged 21 or over.

(8) A person shall not be specified in requirements or directions under subsection (5)(f) above unless-

(a) he is identified by the court or, as the case may be, the responsible officer as a victim of the offence or a person otherwise affected by it; and

(b) he consents to the reparation being made.

(9) An action plan order shall name the petty sessions area in which it appears to the court making the order, or to the court varying any provision included in the order in pursuance of this subsection, that the offender resides or will reside.

(10) In this section "responsible officer", in relation to an action plan order, means one of the following who is specified in the order, namely-

(a) a probation officer;

(b) a social worker of a local authority social services department; and

(c) a member of a youth offending team.

(11) An action plan order shall be a community order for the purposes of Part I of the 1991 Act; and the provisions of that Part, which include provisions with respect to restrictions on imposing, and procedural requirements for, community sentences (sections 6 and 7), shall apply accordingly.

Section 69

1.   This section deals with action plan orders.

2.   Where a child or young person is convicted, a court may make an action plan order if it considers that it is desirable to do so in the interest of securing the offender's rehabilitation. The court cannot make an order if the offender is already the subject of an action plan order or if the court proposes to pass a custodial sentence, or to make a community service order, a combination order, a supervision order or an attendance centre order.

3.   An action plan order requires the offender to comply with a series of requirements concerning his actions and whereabouts for a period of 3 months, under the supervision of the responsible probation officer, social worker or member of the youth offending team.

4.   An action plan order may require the offender:

1)   to participate in specified activities;

2)   to present himself to a specified person at specified times and places;

3)   to attend at an attendance centre for a specified number of hours (if the offence would have been punishable with imprisonment in the case of an offender aged 21 or over);

4)   to stay away from particular places;

5)   to comply with requirements concerning his education;

6)   to make reparation.

5.   The court cannot make an action plan order unless it has been notified by the Secretary of State that arrangements for implementation are available.

70.– (1) Before making an action plan order, a court shall obtain and consider-

(a) a written report by a probation officer, a social worker of a local authority social services department or a member of a youth offending team, indicating-
   (i) the requirements proposed by that person to be included in the order;
   (ii) the benefits to the offender that the proposed requirements are designed to achieve; and
   (iii) the attitude of a parent or guardian of the offender to the proposed requirements; and
(b) where the offender is under the age of 16, information about the offender's family circumstances and the likely effect of the order on those circumstances.

(2) Before making an action plan order, a court shall explain to the offender in ordinary language-

(a) the effect of the order and of the requirements proposed to be included in it;
(b) the consequences which may follow (under Schedule 5 to this Act) if he fails to comply with any of those requirements; and
(c) that the court has power (under that Schedule) to review the order on the application either of the offender or of the responsible officer.

(3) Immediately after making an action plan order, a court may-

(a) fix a further hearing for a date not more than 21 days after the making of the order; and

    (b) direct the responsible officer to make, at that hearing, a report as to the effectiveness of the order and the extent to which it has been implemented.

(4) At a hearing fixed under subsection (3) above, the court-

    (a) shall consider the responsible officer's report; and

    (b) may, on the application of the responsible officer or the offender, vary the order-

        (i) by cancelling any provision included in it; or

        (ii) by inserting in it (either in addition to or in substitution for any of its provisions) any provision that the court could originally have included in it.

(5) Schedule 5 to this Act shall have effect for dealing with failure to comply with the requirements of action plan orders, for varying such orders and for discharging them with or without the substitution of other sentences.

Section 70

1. Before making an action plan order the court is to obtain a report from a probation officer, social worker or member of the youth offending team indicating the proposed requirements, the benefits to the offender and the attitude of the parent or guardian, and, where the offender is under 16, information about his family circumstances.

2. The requirements and consequences of failure to comply with an action plan order must be explained to the offender.

3. Schedule 5 of the Act sets out the court's powers on failure to comply. They include the power to impose a fine of £1,000, and to make an attendance centre or curfew order.

4. On making an action plan order, the court may fix a date for a further hearing not more than 21 days after the making of the order to consider a report from the responsible officer on the effectiveness and the implementation of the order.

71.– (1) In subsection (3) of section 12A of the 1969 Act (young offenders), after paragraph (a) there shall be inserted the following paragraph-

    "(aa) to make reparation specified in the order to a person or persons so specified or to the community at large;".

(2) In subsection (5) of that section, for the words "subsection (3)(a) or (b)" there shall be substituted the words "subsection (3)(a), (aa) or (b)".

(3) In subsection (7) of that section, after paragraph (a) there shall be inserted the following paragraph-

    "(aa) any requirement to make reparation to any person unless that person-

(i) is identified by the court as a victim of the offence or a person otherwise affected by it; and

(ii) consents to the inclusion of the requirement; or".

(4) In subsection (6) of section 12AA of the 1969 Act (requirement for young offender to live in local authority accommodation), for paragraphs (b) to (d) there shall be substituted the following paragraphs-

"(b) that order imposed-

(i) a requirement under section 12, 12A or 12C of this Act; or

(ii) a residence requirement;

(c) he fails to comply with that requirement, or is found guilty of an offence committed while that order was in force; and

(d) the court is satisfied that-

(i) the failure to comply with the requirement, or the behaviour which constituted the offence, was due to a significant extent to the circumstances in which he was living; and

(ii) the imposition of a residence requirement will assist in his rehabilitation;".

and for the words "the condition in paragraph (d)" there shall be substituted the words "sub-paragraph (i) of paragraph (d)".

(5) In section 13 of the 1969 Act (selection of supervisor), subsection (2) shall cease to have effect.

Section 71

1. This section amends section 12A of the Children and Young Persons Act 1969 so that supervision orders may include requirements that the offender make reparation.

2. The section also amends the conditions in section 12AA of that Act before a supervision order can impose a requirement that a child or young person live in local authority accommodation.

72.– (1) In subsection (3) of section 15 of the 1969 Act (variation and discharge of supervision orders), for paragraphs (a) and (b) there shall be substituted the following paragraphs-

"(a) whether or not it also makes an order under subsection (1) above, may order him to pay a fine of an amount not exceeding œ1,000, or make in respect of him-

(i) subject to section 16A(1) of this Act, an order under section 17 of the Criminal Justice Act 1982 (attendance centre orders); or

(ii) subject to section 16B of this Act, an order under section 12 of the Criminal Justice Act 1991 (curfew orders);

(b) if the supervision order was made by a relevant court, may discharge the order and deal with him, for the offence in respect of which the order was made, in any manner in which he could have been dealt with for that offence by the court which made the order if the order had not been made; or

(c) if the order was made by the Crown Court, may commit him in custody or release him on bail until he can be brought or appear before the Crown Court."

(2) For subsections (4) to (6) of that section there shall be substituted the following subsections-

"(4) Where a court deals with a supervised person under subsection (3)(c) above, it shall send to the Crown Court a certificate signed by a justice of the peace giving-

(a) particulars of the supervised person's failure to comply with the requirement in question; and

(b) such other particulars of the case as may be desirable;

and a certificate purporting to be so signed shall be admissible as evidence of the failure before the Crown Court.

(5) Where-

(a) by virtue of subsection (3)(c) above the supervised person is brought or appears before the Crown Court; and

(b) it is proved to the satisfaction of the court that he has failed to comply with the requirement in question,

that court may deal with him, for the offence in respect of which the order was made, in any manner in which it could have dealt with him for that offence if it had not made the order.

(6) Where the Crown Court deals with a supervised person under subsection (5) above, it shall discharge the supervision order if it is still in force."

(3) In subsections (7) and (8) of that section, for the words "or (4)" there shall be substituted the words "or (5)".

> **Section 72**
> *This section amends section 15 of the Children and Young Persons Act 1969, revising the court's power to vary, discharge or impose penalties or further orders in connection with supervision orders.*

Young offenders: detention and training orders

73.– (1) Subject to section 53 of the 1933 Act, section 8 of the Criminal Justice Act 1982 ("the 1982 Act") and subsection (2) below, where-

(a) a child or young person ("the offender") is convicted of an offence which is punishable with imprisonment in the case of a person aged 21 or over; and

(b) the court is of the opinion that either or both of paragraphs (a) or (b) of subsection (2) of section 1 of the 1991 Act apply or the case falls within subsection (3) of that section,

the sentence that the court is to pass is a detention and training order.

(2) A court shall not make a detention and training order-

(a) in the case of an offender under the age of 15 at the time of the conviction, unless it is of the opinion that he is a persistent offender;

(b) in the case of an offender under the age of 12 at that time, unless-

(i) it is of the opinion that only a custodial sentence would be adequate to protect the public from further offending by him; and

(ii) the offence was committed on or after such date as the Secretary of State may by order appoint.

(3) A detention and training order is an order that the offender in respect of whom it is made shall be subject, for the term specified in the order, to a period of detention and training followed by a period of supervision.

(4) A detention and training order shall be a custodial sentence for the purposes of Part I of the 1991 Act; and the provisions of sections 1 to 4 of that Act shall apply accordingly.

(5) Subject to subsection (6) below, the term of a detention and training order shall be 4, 6, 8, 10, 12, 18 or 24 months.

(6) The term of a detention and training order may not exceed the maximum term of imprisonment that the Crown Court could (in the case of an offender aged 21 or over) impose for the offence.

(7) The following provisions, namely-

(a) section 1B of the 1982 Act (detention in young offender institutions: special provision for offenders under 18); and

(b) sections 1 to 4 of the 1994 Act (secure training orders),

which are superseded by this section and sections 74 to 78 below, shall cease to have effect.

Section 73
1.   This section introduces detention and training orders for offenders aged up to and including 17.

2.   *Where a child or young person faces a custodial sentence, apart from detention during her Majesty's pleasure or custody for life, the sentence that is to be passed is a detention and training order. Thus, apart from the exceptions already mentioned, the custodial sentence for offenders up to and including the age of 17 is a detention and training order; and the custodial sentence for offenders aged 18 up to but not including 21 is detention in a young offender institution (see section 1A of the Criminal Justice Act 1982).*

3.   *Secure training orders introduced by the Criminal Justice and Public order Act 1994 are superceded.*

4.   *An offender subject to a detention and training order is subject to detention and training for 4, 6, 8, 10, 18 or 24 months, and supervision thereafter. The term of a detention and training order cannot exceed the maximum sentence of imprisonment that a Crown Court could have imposed on an offender over 21.*

5.   *An offender under the age of 15 can only be made the subject of a detention and training order if he is a persistent offender. An offender under the age of 12 can only be made the subject of an order if it is the only way of protecting the public from further offending by him.*

74.– (1) On making a detention and training order in a case where subsection (2) of section 73 above applies, it shall be the duty of the court (in addition to the duty imposed by section 1(4) of the 1991 Act) to state in open court that it is of the opinion mentioned in paragraph (a) or, as the case may be, paragraphs (a) and (b)(i) of that subsection.

(2) Subject to subsection (3) below, where-

    (a) an offender is convicted of more than one offence for which he is liable to a detention and training order; or

    (b) an offender who is subject to a detention and training order is convicted of one or more further offences for which he is liable to such an order,

the court shall have the same power to pass consecutive detention and training orders as if they were sentences of imprisonment.

(3) A court shall not make in respect of an offender a detention and training order the effect of which would be that he would be subject to detention and training orders for a term which exceeds 24 months.

(4) Where the term of the detention and training orders to which an offender would otherwise be subject exceeds 24 months, the excess shall be treated as remitted.

(5) In determining the term of a detention and training order for an offence, the court shall take account of any period for which the offender has been remanded in custody in connection with the offence, or any other offence the charge for which was founded on the same facts or evidence.

(6) The reference in subsection (5) above to an offender being remanded in custody is a reference to his being-

(a) held in police detention;

(b) remanded in or committed to custody by an order of a court;

(c) remanded or committed to local authority accommodation under section 23 of the 1969 Act and placed and kept in secure accommodation; or

(d) remanded, admitted or removed to hospital under section 35, 36, 38 or 48 of the Mental Health Act 1983.

(7) A person is in police detention for the purposes of subsection (6) above-

(a) at any time when he is in police detention for the purposes of the 1984 Act; and

(b) at any time when he is detained under section 14 of the (1989 c.4.)Prevention of Terrorism (Temporary Provisions) Act 1989;

and in that subsection "secure accommodation" has the same meaning as in section 23 of the 1969 Act.

(8) For the purpose of any reference in this section or sections 75 to 78 below to the term of a detention and training order, consecutive terms of such orders and terms of such orders which are wholly or partly concurrent shall be treated as a single term if-

(a) the orders were made on the same occasion; or

(b) where they were made on different occasions, the offender has not been released (by virtue of subsection (2), (3), (4) or (5) of section 75 below) at any time during the period beginning with the first and ending with the last of those occasions.

> **Section 74**
>
> *1.   Where an offender under the age of 15 is made the subject of a detention and training order, the court must state that it considers the offender to be a persistent offender; and where an offender under the age 12 is made the subject of an order, the court must state that it considers that only a custodial sentence will protect the public from further offending by the offender.*
>
> *2.   A court can pass consecutive detention and training orders although the aggregate cannot exceed 24 months.*

75.– (1) An offender shall serve the period of detention and training under a detention and training order in such secure accommodation as may be determined by the Secretary of State or by such other person as may be authorised by him for that purpose.

(2) Subject to subsections (3) to (5) below, the period of detention and training under a detention and training order shall be one-half of the term of the order.

(3) The Secretary of State may at any time release the offender if he is satisfied that exceptional circumstances exist which justify the offender's release on compassionate grounds.

(4) The Secretary of State may release the offender-

(a) in the case of an order for a term of 8 months or more but less than 18 months, one month before the half-way point of the term of the order; and

(b) in the case of an order for a term of 18 months or more, one month or two months before that point.

(5) If the youth court so orders on an application made by the Secretary of State for the purpose, the Secretary of State shall release the offender-

(a) in the case of an order for a term of 8 months or more but less than 18 months, one month after the half-way point of the term of the order; and

(b) in the case of an order for a term of 18 months or more, one month or two months after that point.

(6) An offender detained in pursuance of a detention and training order shall be deemed to be in legal custody.

(7) In this section and sections 77 and 78 below "secure accommodation" means-

(a) a secure training centre;

(b) a young offender institution;

(c) accommodation provided by a local authority for the purpose of restricting the liberty of children and young persons;

(d) accommodation provided for that purpose under subsection (5) of section 82 of the 1989 Act (financial support by the Secretary of State); or

(e) such other accommodation provided for the purpose of restricting liberty as the Secretary of State may direct.

Section 75

1.   An offender will serve the period of detention and training in a secure training centre, a young offender institution, accommodation provided by the local authority, or certain other suitable accommodation determined by the Secretary of State.

2.   The period of detention and training will be half the term of the order, although the Secretary of State may release an offender early at certain specified points in the term, depending upon the length of the term. Following release the offender is subject to supervision (see section 76 below).

76.– (1) The period of supervision of an offender who is subject to a detention and training order-

(a) shall begin with the offender's release, whether at the half-way point of the term of the order or otherwise; and

(b) subject to subsection (2) below, shall end when the term of the order ends.

(2) The Secretary of State may by order provide that the period of supervision shall end at such point during the term of a detention and training order as may be specified in the order under this subsection.

(3) During the period of supervision, the offender shall be under the supervision of-

(a) a probation officer;

(b) a social worker of a local authority social services department; or

(c) a member of a youth offending team;

and the category of person to supervise the offender shall be determined from time to time by the Secretary of State.

(4) Where the supervision is to be provided by a probation officer, the probation officer shall be an officer appointed for or assigned to the petty sessions area within which the offender resides for the time being.

(5) Where the supervision is to be provided by-

(a) a social worker of a local authority social services department; or

(b) a member of a youth offending team,

the social worker or member shall be a social worker of, or a member of a youth offending team established by, the local authority within whose area the offender resides for the time being.

(6) The offender shall be given a notice from the Secretary of State specifying-

(a) the category of person for the time being responsible for his supervision; and

(b) any requirements with which he must for the time being comply.

(7) A notice under subsection (6) above shall be given to the offender-

(a) before the commencement of the period of supervision; and

(b) before any alteration in the matters specified in subsection (6)(a) or (b) above comes into effect.

Section 76

1. On release from a period of detention and training an offender will be subject to supervision for the remainder of the term, although there is provision for terminating supervision early.

2. During the period of supervision the offender will be supervised by a probation officer, a social worker or member of the youth offending team.

> *3.   At the commencement of his supervision an offender is to be given a notice identifying who is to be responsible for his supervision and specifying any requirements with which he must comply.*

77.– (1) Where a detention and training order is in force in respect of an offender and it appears on information to a justice of the peace acting for a relevant petty sessions area that the offender has failed to comply with requirements under section 76(6)(b) above, the justice-

(a) may issue a summons requiring the offender to appear at the place and time specified in the summons before a youth court acting for the area; or

(b) if the information is in writing and on oath, may issue a warrant for the offender's arrest requiring him to be brought before such a court.

(2) For the purposes of this section a petty sessions area is a relevant petty sessions area in relation to a detention and training order if-

(a) the order was made by a youth court acting for it; or

(b) the offender resides in it for the time being.

(3) If it is proved to the satisfaction of the youth court before which an offender appears or is brought under this section that he has failed to comply with requirements under section 76(6)(b) above, that court may-

(a) order the offender to be detained, in such secure accommodation as the Secretary of State may determine, for such period, not exceeding the shorter of three months or the remainder of the term of the detention and training order, as the court may specify; or

(b) impose on the offender a fine not exceeding level 3 on the standard scale.

(4) An offender detained in pursuance of an order under subsection (3) above shall be deemed to be in legal custody; and a fine imposed under that subsection shall be deemed, for the purposes of any enactment, to be a sum adjudged to be paid by a conviction.

> **Section 77**
> *On breach of requirements set out in the notice given to him under section 76 above, an offender may be detained in secure accommodation for 3 months or the remainder of the term of the detention and training order, whichever is less, or fined up to level 3.*

78.– (1) This section applies to a person subject to a detention and training order if-

(a) after his release and before the date on which the term of the order ends, he commits an offence punishable with imprisonment in the case of a person aged 21 or over; and

(b) whether before or after that date, he is convicted of that offence ("the new offence").

(2) Subject to section 7(8) of the 1969 Act, the court by or before which a person to whom this section applies is convicted of the new offence may, whether or not it passes any other sentence on him, order him to be detained in such secure accommodation as the Secretary of State may determine for the whole or any part of the period which-

(a) begins with the date of the court's order; and

(b) is equal in length to the period between the date on which the new offence was committed and the date mentioned in subsection (1) above.

(3) The period for which a person to whom this section applies is ordered under subsection (2) above to be detained in secure accommodation-

(a) shall, as the court may direct, either be served before and be followed by, or be served concurrently with, any sentence imposed for the new offence; and

(b) in either case, shall be disregarded in determining the appropriate length of that sentence.

(4) Where the new offence is found to have been committed over a period of two or more days, or at some time during a period of two or more days, it shall be taken for the purposes of this section to have been committed on the last of those days.

(5) A person detained in pursuance of an order under subsection (2) above shall be deemed to be in legal custody.

Section 78

1.   If an offender subject to a detention and training order and under supervision commits an offence, the court may detain him in secure accommodation for a period equal to that between the date of the offence and the date when his detention and training order would end.

2.   That period of detention may be concurrent or consecutive to any period of detention ordered in respect of the new offence.

79.– (1) Where a court passes a sentence of detention in a young offender institution in the case of an offender who is subject to a detention and training order, the sentence shall take effect as follows-

(a) if the offender has been released by virtue of subsection (2), (3), (4) or (5) of section 75 above, at the beginning of the day on which it is passed;

(b) if not, either as mentioned in paragraph (a) above or, if the court so orders, at the time when the offender would otherwise be released by virtue of that subsection.

(2) Where a court makes a detention and training order in the case of an offender who is subject to a sentence of detention in a young offender institution, the order shall take effect as follows-

(a) if the offender has been released under Part II of the 1991 Act, at the beginning of the day on which it is made;

(b) if not, either as mentioned in paragraph (a) above or, if the court so orders, at the time when the offender would otherwise be released under that Part.

(3) Subject to subsection (4) below, where at any time an offender is subject concurrently-

(a) to a detention and training order; and

(b) to a sentence of detention in a young offender institution,

he shall be treated for the purposes of sections 75 to 78 above, section 1C of the 1982 Act and Part II of the 1991 Act as if he were subject only to the one of them that was imposed on the later occasion.

(4) Nothing in subsection (3) above shall require the offender to be released in respect of either the order or the sentence unless and until he is required to be released in respect of each of them.

(5) Where, by virtue of any enactment giving a court power to deal with a person in a manner in which a court on a previous occasion could have dealt with him, a detention and training order for any term is made in the case of a person who has attained the age of 18, the person shall be treated as if he had been sentenced to detention in a young offender institution for the same term.

Section 79
This section deals with what happens when an offender who is subject to a detention and training order is sentenced to detention in a young offender institution, and vice versa. In effect the new sentence will take effect when the offender is released from detention under the earlier sentence.

Sentencing: general

80.– (1) This section applies where the Court-

(a) is seised of an appeal against, or a reference under section 36 of the Criminal Justice Act 1988 with respect to, the sentence passed for an offence; or

(b) receives a proposal under section 81 below in respect of a particular category of offence;

and in this section "the relevant category" means any category within which the offence falls or, as the case may be, the category to which the proposal relates.

(2) The Court shall consider-

(a) whether to frame guidelines as to the sentencing of offenders for offences of the relevant category; or

(b) where such guidelines already exist, whether it would be appropriate to review them.

(3) Where the Court decides to frame or revise such guidelines, the Court shall have regard to-

(a) the need to promote consistency in sentencing;

(b) the sentences imposed by courts in England and Wales for offences of the relevant category;

(c) the cost of different sentences and their relative effectiveness in preventing re-offending;

(d) the need to promote public confidence in the criminal justice system; and

(e) the views communicated to the Court, in accordance with section 81(4)(b) below, by the Sentencing Advisory Panel.

(4) Guidelines framed or revised under this section shall include criteria for determining the seriousness of offences, including (where appropriate) criteria for determining the weight to be given to any previous convictions of offenders or any failures of theirs to respond to previous sentences.

(5) In a case falling within subsection (1)(a) above, guidelines framed or revised under this section shall, if practicable, be included in the Court's judgment in the appeal.

(6) Subject to subsection (5) above, guidelines framed or revised under this section shall be included in a judgment of the Court at the next appropriate opportunity (having regard to the relevant category of offence).

(7) For the purposes of this section, the Court is seised of an appeal against a sentence if-

(a) the Court or a single judge has granted leave to appeal against the sentence under section 9 or 10 of the Criminal Appeal Act 1968; or

(b) in a case where the judge who passed the sentence granted a certificate of fitness for appeal under section 9 or 10 of that Act, notice of appeal has been given,

and (in either case) the appeal has not been abandoned or disposed of.

(8) For the purposes of this section, the Court is seised of a reference under section 36 of the Criminal Justice Act 1988 if it has given leave under subsection (1) of that section and the reference has not been disposed of.

(9) In this section and section 81 below-

"the Court" means the criminal division of the Court of Appeal;

"offence" means an indictable offence.

Section 80

1.   Whenever the Court of Appeal is considering an appeal against sentence for, or a reference by the Attorney General in respect of an indictable offence, or when the Sentencing Advisory Panel (established under section 81 below) proposes that sentencing guidelines be framed, the Court of Appeal shall consider whether to frame or review guidelines for the sentencing of offenders for particular categories of offence.

2.   Where the Court of Appeal frames or reviews sentencing guidelines, it is obliged to consider;

1)   the need to promote consistency in sentencing;

2)   the sentences imposed in England and Wales for offences of that category;

3)   the cost and effectiveness in preventing re-offending of different sentences;

4)   the need to promote public confidence in the criminal justice system;

5)   the views of the Sentencing Advisory Panel.

3.   Guidelines must include criteria for determining the seriousness of an offence, and they must include criteria for determining the weight to be attached to previous convictions and any failures to respond to sentences.

81.– (1) The Lord Chancellor, after consultation with the Secretary of State and the Lord Chief Justice, shall constitute a sentencing panel to be known as the Sentencing Advisory Panel ("the Panel") and appoint one of the members of the Panel to be its chairman.

(2) Where, in a case falling within subsection (1)(a) of section 80 above, the Court decides to frame or revise guidelines under that section for a particular category of offence, the Court shall notify the Panel.

(3) The Panel may at any time, and shall if directed to do so by the Secretary of State, propose to the Court that guidelines be framed or revised under section 80 above for a particular category of offence.

(4) Where the Panel receives a notification under subsection (2) above or makes a proposal under subsection (3) above, the Panel shall-

(a) obtain and consider the views on the matters in issue of such persons or bodies as may be determined, after consultation with the Secretary of State and the Lord Chief Justice, by the Lord Chancellor;

(b) formulate its own views on those matters and communicate them to the Court; and

(c) furnish information to the Court as to the matters mentioned in section 80(3)(b) and (c) above.

(5) The Lord Chancellor may pay to any member of the Panel such remuneration as he may determine.

Section 81

1.   This section obliges the Lord Chancellor, after consultation with the Secretary of State and the Lord Chief Justice, to constitute a Sentencing Advisory Panel.

2.   The Sentencing Advisory Panel may, and must if directed to do so by the Secretary of State, propose to the Court of Appeal that sentencing guidelines for specified categories of offence be framed or reviewed.

3.   Before making a proposal to the Court of Appeal the Sentencing Advisory Panel is obliged to:

1)   obtain and consider the views of the persons or bodies determined by the Lord Chancellor, after consultation with the Secretary of State and the Lord Chief Justice;

2)   formulate its own views and communicate them to the Court of Appeal;

3)   furnish information concerning the sentences that have been imposed in England and Wales for that category of offence and the cost of different sentences and their relative effectiveness at preventing re-offending.

82.– (1) This section applies where a court is considering the seriousness of an offence other than one under sections 29 to 32 above.

(2) If the offence was racially aggravated, the court-

(a) shall treat that fact as an aggravating factor (that is to say, a factor that increases the seriousness of the offence); and

(b) shall state in open court that the offence was so aggravated.

(3) Section 28 above applies for the purposes of this section as it applies for the purposes of sections 29 to 32 above.

Section 82

Where any offence is racially aggravated (see section 28 above), other than those under sections 29 to 32 of this Act which already comprise a racially aggravated element, the Court of Appeal is obliged to treat that as an aggravating factor in framing or reviewing guidelines.

Miscellaneous and supplemental

83. After subsection (9) of section 71 of the Criminal Justice Act 1988 (confiscation orders) there shall be inserted the following subsection-

"(9A) Where an offender is committed by a magistrates' court for sentence under section 38 or 38A of the Magistrates' Courts Act 1980 or section 56 of the Criminal Justice Act 1967, this section and sections 72 to 74C below shall have effect as if the offender had been convicted of the offence in the proceedings before the Crown Court and not in the proceedings before the magistrates' court."

Section 83

This section empowers the Crown Court to make a confiscation order when an offender is committed for sentence from the magistrates' court.

84.– (1) In section 16(5) of the Football Spectators Act 1989 (penalties for failure to comply with reporting duty imposed by restriction order)-

(a) for the words "one month" there shall be substituted the words "six months"; and

(b) for the words "level 3" there shall be substituted the words "level 5".

(2) In section 24(2) of the 1984 Act (arrestable offences), after paragraph (p) there shall be inserted-

"(q) an offence under section 16(4) of the Football Spectators Act 1989 (failure to comply with reporting duty imposed by restriction order)."

Section 84

This section increases penalties under the Football Spectators Act 1989.

85.– (1) In this Chapter-

"action plan order" has the meaning given by section 69(2) above;

"detention and training order" has the meaning given by section 73(3) above;

"drug treatment and testing order" has the meaning given by section 61(2) above;

"make reparation", in relation to an offender, means make reparation for the offence otherwise than by the payment of compensation;

"reparation order" has the meaning given by section 67(2) above;

"responsible officer"-

    (a) in relation to a drug treatment and testing order, has the meaning given by section 62(7) above;

    (b) in relation to a reparation order, has the meaning given by section 67(10) above;

    (c) in relation to an action plan order, has the meaning given by section 69(10) above.

(2) Where the supervision under a reparation order or action plan order is be provided by a probation officer, the probation officer shall be an officer appointed for or assigned to the petty sessions area named in the order.

(3) Where the supervision under a reparation order or action plan order is to be provided by-

    (a) a social worker of a local authority social services department; or

    (b) a member of a youth offending team,

the social worker or member shall be a social worker of, or a member of a youth offending team established by, the local authority within whose area it appears to the court that the child or young person resides or will reside.

(4) In this Chapter, in relation to a drug treatment and testing order-

"the treatment and testing period" has the meaning given by section 61(2) above;

"the treatment provider" and

"the treatment requirement" have the meanings given by subsection (1) of section 62 above;

"the testing requirement" has the meaning given by subsection (4) of that section.

(5) In this Chapter, unless the contrary intention appears, expressions which are also used in Part I of the 1991 Act have the same meanings as in that Part.

(6) For the purposes of this Chapter, a sentence falls to be imposed under section 2(2), 3(2) or 4(2) of the 1997 Act if it is required by that provision and the court is not of the opinion there mentioned.

Section 85
This is an interpretation section.

CHAPTER II SCOTLAND

Sexual or violent offenders

86.– (1) After section 210 of the 1995 Act there shall be inserted the following section-

"210A.– (1) Where a person is convicted on indictment of a sexual or violent offence, the court may, if it-

  (a) intends, in relation to-
    (i) a sexual offence, to pass a determinate sentence of imprisonment; or
    (ii) a violent offence, to pass such a sentence for a term of four years or more; and
  (b) considers that the period (if any) for which the offender would, apart from this section, be subject to a licence would not be adequate for the purpose of protecting the public from serious harm from the offender,

pass an extended sentence on the offender.

(2) An extended sentence is a sentence of imprisonment which is the aggregate of-

  (a) the term of imprisonment ("the custodial term") which the court would have passed on the offender otherwise than by virtue of this section; and
  (b) a further period ("the extension period") for which the offender is to be subject to a licence and which is, subject to the provisions of this section, of such length as the court considers necessary for the purpose mentioned in subsection (1)(b) above.

(3) The extension period shall not exceed, in the case of-

  (a) a sexual offence, ten years; and
  (b) a violent offence, five years.

(4) A court shall, before passing an extended sentence, consider a report by a relevant officer of a local authority about the offender and his circumstances and, if the court thinks it necessary, hear that officer.

(5) The term of an extended sentence passed for a statutory offence shall not exceed the maximum term of imprisonment provided for in the statute in respect of that offence.

(6) Subject to subsection (5) above, a sheriff may pass an extended sentence which is the aggregate of a custodial term not exceeding the maximum term of imprisonment which he may impose and an extension period not exceeding three years.

(7) The Secretary of State may by order-

  (a) amend paragraph (b) of subsection (3) above by substituting a different period, not exceeding ten years, for the period for the time being specified in that paragraph; and
  (b) make such transitional provision as appears to him to be necessary or expedient in connection with the amendment.

(8) The power to make an order under subsection (7) above shall be exercisable by statutory instrument; but no such order shall be made unless a draft of the order has been laid before, and approved by a resolution of, each House of Parliament.

(9) An extended sentence shall not be imposed where the sexual or violent offence was committed before the commencement of section 86 of the Crime and Disorder Act 1998.

(10) For the purposes of this section-

"licence" and"relevant officer" have the same meaning as in Part I of the Prisoners and Criminal Proceedings (Scotland) Act 1993;

"sexual offence" means-

    (i)   rape;

    (ii)   clandestine injury to women;

    (iii)   abduction of a woman or girl with intent to rape or ravish;

    (iv)   assault with intent to rape or ravish;

    (v)   indecent assault;

    (vi)   lewd, indecent or libidinous behaviour or practices;

    (vii) shameless indecency;

    (viii) sodomy;

    (ix)   an offence under section 170 of the Customs and Excise Management Act 1979 in relation to goods prohibited to be imported under section 42 of the Customs Consolidation Act 1876, but only where the prohibited goods include indecent photographs of persons;

    (x)   an offence under section 52 of the Civic Government (Scotland) Act 1982 (taking and distribution of indecent images of children);

    (xi)   an offence under section 52A of that Act (possession of indecent images of children);

    (xii) an offence under section 1 of the Criminal Law (Consolidation) (Scotland) Act 1995 (incest);

    (xiii) an offence under section 2 of that Act (intercourse with a stepchild);

    (xiv) an offence under section 3 of that Act (intercourse with child under 16 by person in position of trust);

    (xv)   an offence under section 5 of that Act (unlawful intercourse with girl under 16);

    (xvi) an offence under section 6 of that Act (indecent behaviour towards girl between 12 and 16);

    (xvii) an offence under section 8 of that Act (abduction of girl under 18 for purposes of unlawful intercourse);

    (xviii) an offence under section 10 of that Act (person having parental responsibilities causing or encouraging sexual activity in relation to a girl under 16); and

    (xix) an offence under subsection (5) of section 13 of that Act (homosexual offences);

"imprisonment" includes-

    (i) detention under section 207 of this Act; and

    (ii) detention under section 208 of this Act; and

"violent offence" means any offence (other than an offence which is a sexual offence within the meaning of this section) inferring personal violence.

(11) Any reference in subsection (10) above to a sexual offence includes-

    (a) a reference to any attempt, conspiracy or incitement to commit that offence; and

    (b) except in the case of an offence in paragraphs (i) to (viii) of the definition of "sexual offence" in that subsection, a reference to aiding and abetting, counselling or procuring the commission of that offence.".

(2) In section 209 of the 1995 Act (supervised release orders), in subsection (1)-

    (a) after the word "convicted" there shall be inserted the words "on indictment";

    (b) after the words "an offence" there shall be inserted the words ", other than a sexual offence within the meaning of section 210A of this Act,"; and

    (c) the words "not less than twelve months but" shall cease to have effect.

Section 86

1.   This section amends the Criminal Procedure (Scotland) Act 1995, adding section 210A which allows a court that is considering imposing a determinate sentence of imprisonment for a sexual offence, or a sentence of 4 years or more for a violent offence, to pass an extended sentence if it considers that it is necessary to do so to protect the public from the offender on his release.

2.   An extended sentence is the aggregate of the term of imprisonment that the court would have passed in any event together with a further period, the "extension period", during which the offender is on licence and subject to supervision.

3.   The extension period cannot exceed 10 years in the case of a sexual offence, or 5 years in the case of a violent offence.

4.   The term of an extended sentence for a statutory offence is not to exceed the maximum term of imprisonment that may be imposed for that offence. A sheriff may pass an extended sentence for a non-statutory offence the custodial term of which is equal to the maximum custodial sentence that he may impose, together with an extension period of not more than 3 years.

5.   A report about the offender and his circumstances must be obtained before an extended sentence is passed.

6.   The Secretary of State may vary the maximum extension period of 5 years in the case of violent offences up to a maximum of 10 years, by order approved by each House of Parliament.

7.   The section also defines various terms, including "sexual offence", "imprisonment" and "violent offence" for the purpose of this section; and amends section 209 of the Criminal Procedure (Scotland) Act 1995 (supervised release orders).

87. After section 26 of the Prisoners and Criminal Proceedings (Scotland) Act 1993 ("the 1993 Act") there shall be inserted the following section-

"Extended sentences

26A.– (1) This section applies to a prisoner who, on or after the date on which section 87 of the Crime and Disorder Act 1998 comes into force, has been made subject to an extended sentence within the meaning of section 210A of the 1995 Act (extended sentences).

(2) Subject to the provisions of this section, this Part of this Act, except section 1A, shall apply in relation to extended sentences as if any reference to a sentence or term of imprisonment was a reference to the custodial term of an extended sentence.

(3) Where a prisoner subject to an extended sentence is released on licence under this Part the licence shall, subject to any revocation under section 17 of this Act, remain in force until the end of the extension period.

(4) Where, apart from this subsection, a prisoner subject to an extended sentence would be released unconditionally-

(a) he shall be released on licence; and
(b) the licence shall, subject to any revocation under section 17 of this Act, remain in force until the end of the extension period.

(5) The extension period shall be taken to begin as follows-

(a) for the purposes of subsection (3) above, on the day following the date on which, had there been no extension period, the prisoner would have ceased to be on licence in respect of the custodial term;
(b) for the purposes of subsection (4) above, on the date on which, apart from that subsection, he would have been released unconditionally.

(6) Subject to section 1A(c) of this Act and section 210A(3) of the 1995 Act and to any direction by the court which imposes an extended sentence, where a prisoner is subject to two or more extended sentences, the extension period which is taken to begin in accordance with subsection (5) above shall be the aggregate of the extension period of each of those sentences.

(7) For the purposes of sections 12(3) and 17(1) of this Act, and subject to subsection (8) below, the question whether a prisoner is a long-term or short-term prisoner shall be determined by reference to the extended sentence.

(8) Where a short-term prisoner serving an extended sentence in respect of a sexual offence is released on licence under subsection (4)(a) above, the provisions of section 17 of this Act shall apply to him as if he was a long-term prisoner.

(9) In relation to a prisoner subject to an extended sentence, the reference in section 17(5) of this Act to his sentence shall be construed as a reference to the extended sentence.

(10) For the purposes of this section "custodial term", "extension period" and "imprisonment" shall have the same meaning as in section 210A of the 1995 Act.

(11) In section 1A(c) and section 16(1)(a) of this Act, the reference to the date on which a prisoner would have served his sentence in full shall mean, in relation to a prisoner subject to an extended sentence, the date on which the extended sentence, as originally imposed by the court, would expire."

> **Section 87**
>
> *1.   This section amends the Prisoners and Criminal Proceedings (Scotland) Act 1993, adding section 26A which deals with the effect of an extended sentence.*
>
> *2.   On release from the custodial term of an extended sentence, an offender will remain on licence until the end of the extension period.*

88. After section 3 of the 1993 Act there shall be inserted the following section-

"3A.– (1) This section applies to a prisoner serving an extended sentence within the meaning of section 210A of the 1995 Act (extended sentences) who has been recalled to prison under section 17(1) of this Act.

(2) Subject to subsection (3) below, a prisoner to whom this section applies may require the Secretary of State to refer his case to the Parole Board-

    (a) where his case has previously been referred to the Parole Board under this section or section 17(3) of this Act, not less than one year following the disposal of that referral;

    (b) in any other case, at any time.

(3) Where a prisoner to whom this section applies is subject to another sentence which is not treated as a single sentence with the extended sentence, the Secretary of State shall not be required to refer his case to the Parole Board before he has served one half of that other sentence.

(4) Where the case of a prisoner to whom this section applies is referred to the Parole Board under this section or section 17(3) of this Act, the Board shall, if it is satisfied that it is no longer necessary for the protection of the public from serious harm that the prisoner should be confined (but not otherwise), direct that he should be released.

(5) If the Parole Board gives a direction under subsection (4) above, the Secretary of State shall release the prisoner on licence."

Section 88

1.   This section deals with the right of a prisoner serving an extended sentence who has been recalled to prison to have his case for re-release referred to the Parole Board.

2.   If the Board is satisfied that it is not necessary to confine the prisoner to protect the public from serious harm, it is obliged to direct his re-release.

Offenders dependent etc. on drugs

89. After section 234A of the 1995 Act there shall be inserted the following section-

"**234B.**– (1) This section applies where a person of 16 years of age or more is convicted of an offence, other than one for which the sentence is fixed by law, committed on or after the date on which section 89 of the Crime and Disorder Act 1998 comes into force.

(2) Subject to the provisions of this section, the court by or before which the offender is convicted may, if it is of the opinion that it is expedient to do so instead of sentencing him, make an order (a "drug treatment and testing order") which shall-

(a) have effect for a period specified in the order of not less than six months nor more than three years ("the treatment and testing period"); and

(b) include the requirements and provisions mentioned in section 234C of this Act.

(3) A court shall not make a drug treatment and testing order unless it-

(a) has been notified by the Secretary of State that arrangements for implementing such orders are available in the area of the local authority proposed to be specified in the order under section 234C(6) of this Act and the notice has not been withdrawn;

(b) has obtained a report by, and if necessary heard evidence from, an officer of the local authority in whose area the offender is resident about the offender and his circumstances; and

(c) is satisfied that-

(i) the offender is dependent on, or has a propensity to misuse, drugs;

(ii) his dependency or propensity is such as requires and is susceptible to treatment; and

(iii) he is a suitable person to be subject to such an order.

(4) For the purpose of determining for the purposes of subsection (3)(c) above whether the offender has any drug in his body, the court may by order require him to provide samples of such description as it may specify.

(5) A drug treatment and testing order or an order under subsection (4) above shall not be made unless the offender expresses his willingness to comply with its requirements.

(6) The Secretary of State may by order-

   (a) amend paragraph (a) of subsection (2) above by substituting a different period for the minimum or the maximum period for the time being specified in that paragraph; and

   (b) make such transitional provisions as appear to him necessary or expedient in connection with any such amendment.

(7) The power to make an order under subsection (6) above shall be exercisable by statutory instrument; but no such order shall be made unless a draft of the order has been laid before and approved by resolution of each House of Parliament.

(8) A drug treatment and testing order shall be as nearly as may be in the form prescribed by Act of Adjournal."

Section 89

1. This section adds section 234B to the Criminal Procedure (Scotland) Act 1995. It deals with drug treatment and testing orders.

2. Where a person over 16 is convicted of an offence other than one for which the sentence is fixed by law, and the court considers it expedient to do so rather than sentencing him, the court may make a drug treatment and testing order for a specified period between 6 months and 3 years.

3. A court can only make a drug treatment and testing order if:

1) it has been notified by the Secretary of State that arrangements for implementing the order have been made; and

2) it has obtained a report from an officer of the local authority dealing with the offender's circumstances; and

3) the offender is dependent on or has a propensity to misuse drugs which can be treated, and he is suitable; and

4) the offender is willing to comply.

90. After section 234B of the 1995 Act there shall be inserted the following section-

"234C.– (1) A drug treatment and testing order shall include a requirement ("the treatment requirement") that the offender shall submit, during the whole of the treatment and testing period, to treatment by or under the direction of a specified person having the necessary qualifications or experience ("the treatment provider") with a view to the reduction or elimination of the offender's dependency on or propensity to misuse drugs.

(2) The required treatment for any particular period shall be-

(a) treatment as a resident in such institution or place as may be specified in the order; or

(b) treatment as a non-resident in or at such institution or place, and at such intervals, as may be so specified;

but the nature of the treatment shall not be specified in the order except as mentioned in paragraph (a) or (b) above.

(3) A court shall not make a drug treatment and testing order unless it is satisfied that arrangements have been made for the treatment intended to be specified in the order (including arrangements for the reception of the offender where he is required to submit to treatment as a resident).

(4) A drug treatment and testing order shall include a requirement ("the testing requirement") that, for the purpose of ascertaining whether he has any drug in his body during the treatment and testing period, the offender shall provide during that period, at such times and in such circumstances as may (subject to the provisions of the order) be determined by the treatment provider, samples of such description as may be so determined.

(5) The testing requirement shall specify for each month the minimum number of occasions on which samples are to be provided.

(6) A drug treatment and testing order shall specify the local authority in whose area the offender will reside when the order is in force and require that authority to appoint or assign an officer (a "supervising officer") for the purposes of subsections (7) and (8) below.

(7) A drug treatment and testing order shall-

(a) provide that, for the treatment and testing period, the offender shall be under the supervision of a supervising officer;

(b) require the offender to keep in touch with the supervising officer in accordance with such instructions as he may from time to time be given by that officer, and to notify him of any change of address; and

(c) provide that the results of the tests carried out on the samples provided by the offender in pursuance of the testing requirement shall be communicated to the supervising officer.

(8) Supervision by the supervising officer shall be carried out to such extent only as may be necessary for the purpose of enabling him-

(a) to report on the offender's progress to the appropriate court;

(b) to report to that court any failure by the offender to comply with the requirements of the order; and

(c) to determine whether the circumstances are such that he should apply to that court for the variation or revocation of the order."

Section 90

1.   This section adds section 234C to the Criminal Procedure (Scotland) Act 1995. It deals with the effect of a drug treatment and testing order.

2.   A drug treatment and testing order requires the offender:

1)   to submit to treatment by or under the direction of a specified person with the necessary qualifications or experience, for the whole of the treatment and testing period, with a view to reducing or eliminating his dependency on or propensity to misuse drugs;

2)   to provide such samples for drug testing as are necessary on a specified number of occasions per month during the currency of the order;

3)   to submit to supervision by the supervising officer.

3.   The order may specify that treatment should be as resident of a specified institution, or as a non-resident and at such intervals as the nature of the treatment requires.

4.   A court cannot make a drug treatment and testing order unless arrangements have been made for the treatment intended.

5.   A drug treatment and testing order must specify the local authority in whose area the offender is to reside and require that authority to appoint a supervising officer.

6.   The supervision must only be what is necessary to enable the supervising officer to report on the offender's progress and any failures to comply with requirements, and to decide whether or not to apply to the court to vary the terms of the order.

91. After section 234C of the 1995 Act there shall be inserted the following section-

"234D.– (1) Before making a drug treatment and testing order, a court shall explain to the offender in ordinary language-

(a) the effect of the order and of the requirements proposed to be included in it;
(b) the consequences which may follow under section 234G of this Act if he fails to comply with any of those requirements;
(c) that the court has power under section 234E of this Act to vary or revoke the order on the application of either the offender or the supervising officer; and
(d) that the order will be periodically reviewed at intervals provided for in the order.

(2) Upon making a drug treatment and testing order the court shall-

(a) give, or send by registered post or the recorded delivery service, a copy of the order to the offender;

(b) send a copy of the order to the treatment provider;

(c) send a copy of the order to the chief social work officer of the local authority specified in the order in accordance with section 234C(6) of this Act; and

(d) where it is not the appropriate court, send a copy of the order (together with such documents and information relating to the case as are considered useful) to the clerk of the appropriate court.

(3) Where a copy of a drug treatment and testing order has under subsection (2)(a) been sent by registered post or by the recorded delivery service, an acknowledgment or certificate of delivery of a letter containing a copy order issued by the Post Office shall be sufficient evidence of the delivery of the letter on the day specified in such acknowledgement or certificate."

Section 91

This section adds section 234D to the Criminal Procedure (Scotland) Act 1995, and provides that the court is obliged to explain the effect of a drug treatment and testing order and the consequences of failure to comply with it to the offender. The offender is also to be given an appropriate notice in writing.

92. After section 234D of the 1995 Act there shall be inserted the following sections-

"234E.– (1) Where a drug treatment and testing order is in force either the offender or the supervising officer may apply to the appropriate court for variation or revocation of the order.

(2) Where an application is made under subsection (1) above by the supervising officer, the court shall issue a citation requiring the offender to appear before the court.

(3) On an application made under subsection (1) above and after hearing both the offender and the supervising officer, the court may by order, if it appears to it in the interests of justice to do so-

(a) vary the order by-
(i) amending or deleting any of its requirements or provisions;
(ii) inserting further requirements or provisions; or
(iii) subject to subsection (4) below, increasing or decreasing the treatment and testing period; or
(b) revoke the order.

(4) The power conferred by subsection (3)(a)(iii) above shall not be exercised so as to increase the treatment and testing period above the maximum for the time being specified in section 234B(2)(a) of this Act, or to decrease it below the minimum so specified.

(5) Where the court, on the application of the supervising officer, proposes to vary (otherwise than by deleting a requirement or provision) a drug treatment and testing order, sections 234B(5) and 234D(1) of this Act shall apply to the variation of such an order as they apply to the making of such an order.

(6) If an offender fails to appear before the court after having been cited in accordance with subsection (2) above, the court may issue a warrant for his arrest.

"234F.– (1) A drug treatment and testing order shall-

   (a) provide for the order to be reviewed periodically at intervals of not less than one month;

   (b) provide for each review of the order to be made, subject to subsection (5) below, at a hearing held for the purpose by the appropriate court (a "review hearing");

   (c) require the offender to attend each review hearing;

   (d) provide for the supervising officer to make to the court, before each review, a report in writing on the offender's progress under the order; and

   (e) provide for each such report to include the test results communicated to the supervising officer under section 234C(7)(c) of this Act and the views of the treatment provider as to the treatment and testing of the offender.

(2) At a review hearing the court, after considering the supervising officer's report, may amend any requirement or provision of the order.

(3) The court-

   (a) shall not amend the treatment or testing requirement unless the offender expresses his willingness to comply with the requirement as amended;

   (b) shall not amend any provision of the order so as reduce the treatment and testing period below the minimum specified in section 234B(2)(a) of this Act or to increase it above the maximum so specified; and

   (c) except with the consent of the offender, shall not amend any requirement or provision of the order while an appeal against the order is pending.

(4) If the offender fails to express his willingness to comply with the treatment or testing requirement as proposed to be amended by the court, the court may revoke the order.

(5) If at a review hearing the court, after considering the supervising officer's report, is of the opinion that the offender's progress under the order is satisfactory, the court may so amend the order as to provide for each subsequent review to be made without a hearing.

(6) A review without a hearing shall take place in chambers without the parties being present.

(7) If at a review without a hearing the court, after considering the supervising officer's report, is of the opinion that the offender's progress is no longer satisfactory, the court may issue a warrant for the arrest of the offender or may, if it thinks fit, instead of issuing a warrant in the first instance, issue a citation

requiring the offender to appear before that court as such time as may be specified in the citation.

(8) Where an offender fails to attend-

(a) a review hearing in accordance with a requirement contained in a drug treatment and testing order; or

(b) a court at the time specified in a citation under subsection (7) above,

the court may issue a warrant for his arrest.

(9) Where an offender attends the court at a time specified by a citation issued under subsection (7) above-

(a) the court may exercise the powers conferred by this section as if the court were conducting a review hearing; and

(b) so amend the order as to provide for each subsequent review to be made at a review hearing."

Section 92

1.   This section inserts sections 234E and 234F into the Criminal Procedure (Scotland) Act 1995.

2.   Section 234E gives the court wide powers to vary or revoke a drug treatment and testing order, to include deleting or inserting requirements, and increasing or decreasing the drug treatment and testing period within the maximum and minimum limits.

3.   Section 234F provides for periodic review of a drug treatment and testing order at intervals of not less than one month, with a report from the supervising officer which contains details of recent drug tests on the offender and the views of the treatment provider.

4.   At a review hearing the court may amend any requirement in the order but only if the offender expresses his willingness to comply. If the offender does not wish to comply the court may revoke the order.

5.   If an offender's progress is satisfactory, further reviews may take place without a hearing. If progress declines the court may issue a citation requiring the offender to appear before the court, or the court may issue a warrant for the offender's arrest.

93. After section 234F of the 1995 Act there shall be inserted the following sections-

"234G.– (1) If at any time when a drug treatment and testing order is in force it appears to the appropriate court that the offender has failed to comply with any requirement of the order, the court may issue a citation requiring the offender to appear before the court at such time as may be specified in the citation or, if it appears to the court to be appropriate, it may issue a warrant for the arrest of the offender.

(2) If it is proved to the satisfaction of the appropriate court that the offender has failed without reasonable excuse to comply with any requirement of the order, the court may by order-

(a) without prejudice to the continuation in force of the order, impose a fine not exceeding level 3 on the standard scale;
(b) vary the order; or
(c) revoke the order.

(3) For the purposes of subsection (2) above, the evidence of one witness shall be sufficient evidence.

(4) A fine imposed under this section in respect of a failure to comply with the requirements of a drug treatment and testing order shall be deemed for the purposes of any enactment to be a sum adjudged to be paid by or in respect of a conviction or a penalty imposed on a person summarily convicted.

234H.– (1) Where the court revokes a drugs treatment and testing order under section 234E(3)(b), 234F(4) or 234G(2)(c) of this Act, it may dispose of the offender in any way which would have been competent at the time when the order was made.

(2) In disposing of an offender under subsection (1) above, the court shall have regard to the time for which the order has been in operation.

(3) Where the court revokes a drug treatment and testing order as mentioned in subsection (1) above and the offender is subject to-

(a) a probation order, by virtue of section 234J of this Act; or
(b) a restriction of liberty order, by virtue of section 245D of this Act; or
(c) a restriction of liberty order and a probation order, by virtue of the said section 245D,

the court shall, before disposing of the offender under subsection (1) above-

(i) where he is subject to a probation order, discharge that order;
(ii) where he is subject to a restriction of liberty order, revoke that order; and
(iii) where he is subject to both such orders, discharge the probation order and revoke the restriction of liberty order."

Section 93

1.   *This section inserts sections 234G and 234H into the Criminal Procedure (Scotland) Act 1995.*

2.   *Section 234G deals with the consequences of breach of a drug treatment and testing order.*

3.   *Where a court is satisfied that a drug treatment and testing order has been breached it may issue a citation or a warrant for the arrest of the offender, and may impose a fine not exceeding level 3 and vary or revoke the order.*

4.   *The evidence of one witness shall be sufficient proof of breach.*

5.   *It is a defence for the offender to prove reasonable excuse.*

6.   *A fine imposed under this section is deemed to be a fine imposed on conviction.*

7.   *Section 234H provides that when the court revokes a drug treatment and testing order, it may deal with the offender in any way in which it could have dealt with him when the order was made.*

8.   *If the offender is subject to a probation order by virtue of section 234J, a restriction of liberty order by virtue of section 245D, or both a restriction of liberty order and a probation order by virtue of section 245D of the Criminal Procedure (Scotland) Act 1995, the court is to revoke those orders before dealing with the offender under section 234H.*

94.– (1) After section 234H of the 1995 Act there shall be inserted the following

"234J.– (1) Notwithstanding sections 228(1) and 234B(2) of this Act, where the court considers it expedient that the offender should be subject to a drug treatment and testing order and to a probation order, it may make both such orders in respect of the offender.

(2) In deciding whether it is expedient for it to exercise the power conferred by subsection (1) above, the court shall have regard to the circumstances, including the nature of the offence and the character of the offender and to the report submitted to it under section 234B(3)(b) of this Act.

(3) Where the court makes both a drug treatment and testing order and a probation order by virtue of subsection (1) above, the clerk of the court shall send a copy of each of the orders to the following-

(a) the treatment provider within the meaning of section 234C(1);
(b) the officer of the local authority who is appointed or assigned to be the supervising officer under section 234C(6) of this Act; and
(c) if he would not otherwise receive a copy of the order, the officer of the local authority who is to supervise the probationer.

(4) Where the offender by an act or omission fails to comply with a requirement of an order made by virtue of subsection (1) above-

(a) if the failure relates to a requirement contained in a probation order and is dealt with under section 232(2)(c) of this Act, the court may, in addition, exercise the power conferred by section 234G(2)(b) of this Act in relation to the drug treatment and testing order; and

(b) if the failure relates to a requirement contained in a drug treatment and testing order and is dealt with under section 234G(2)(b) of this Act, the court may, in addition, exercise the power conferred by section 232(2)(c) of this Act in relation to the probation order.

(5) Where an offender by an act or omission fails to comply with both a requirement contained in a drug treatment and testing order and in a probation order to which he is subject by virtue of subsection (1) above, he may, without prejudice to subsection (4) above, be dealt with as respects that act or omission either under section 232(2) of this Act or under section 234G(2) of this Act but he shall not be liable to be otherwise dealt with in respect of that act or omission."

(2) Schedule 6 to this Act (Part I of which makes further provision in relation to the combination of drug treatment and testing orders with other orders and Part II of which makes provision in relation to appeals) shall have effect.

Section 94

1.   This section inserts section 234J into the Criminal Procedure (Scotland) Act 1995.

2.   The court may make a drug treatment and testing order and a probation order at the same time where it considers it expedient to do so, in the light of all the circumstances including the offence, the character of the offender, and the report from the local authority officer about the offender and his circumstances.

3.   Where a drugs treatment and testing order and a probation order have been made at the same time, pursuant to section 234J(1), if the offender acts in breach of either one, the court may also vary the other.

4.   Schedule 6 is given effect by this section. Please see below.

95.– (1) After section 234J of the 1995 Act there shall be inserted the following section-

"234K.In sections 234B to 234J of this Act-

"the appropriate court" means-

(a) where the drug treatment and testing order has been made by the High Court, that court;

(b) in any other case, the court having jurisdiction in the area of the local authority for the time being specified in the order under section 234C(6) of this Act, being a sheriff or district court according to whether the order has been made by a sheriff or district court, but in a case where an order has been made by a district court and there is no district court in that area, the sheriff court; and

"local authority" means a council constituted under section 2 of the Local Government etc. (Scotland) Act 1994 and any reference to the area of such an authority is a reference to the local government area within the meaning of that Act for which it is so constituted."

(2) In section 307(1) of the 1995 Act (interpretation), after the definition of "diet" there shall be inserted the following definition-

""drug treatment and testing order" has the meaning assigned to it in section 234B(2) of this Act;".

Section 95
This is an interpretation section.

Racial aggravation

96.– (1) The provisions of this section shall apply where it is-

(a) libelled in an indictment; or
(b) specified in a complaint,

and, in either case, proved that an offence has been racially aggravated.

(2) An offence is racially aggravated for the purposes of this section if-

(a) at the time of committing the offence, or immediately before or after doing so, the offender evinces towards the victim (if any) of the offence malice and ill-will based on the victim's membership (or presumed membership) of a racial group; or
(b) the offence is motivated (wholly or partly) by malice and ill-will towards members of a racial group based on their membership of that group,

and evidence from a single source shall be sufficient evidence to establish, for the purposes of this subsection, that an offence is racially aggravated.

(3) In subsection (2)(a) above-

"membership", in relation to a racial group, includes association with members of that group;

"presumed" means presumed by the offender.

(4) It is immaterial for the purposes of paragraph (a) or (b) of subsection (2) above whether or not the offender's malice and ill-will is also based, to any extent, on-

(a) the fact or presumption that any person or group of persons belongs to any religious group; or

(b) any other factor not mentioned in that paragraph.

(5) Where this section applies, the court shall, on convicting a person, take the aggravation into account in determining the appropriate sentence.

(6) In this section

"racial group" means a group of persons defined by reference to race, colour, nationality (including citizenship) or ethnic or national origins.

Section 96

1.   Wherever an offence is racially aggravated, the court is to take that into account on sentence, provided that it is libelled in an indictment or specified in a complaint.

2.   An offence is racially aggravated if at the time or immediately before or after it the offender evinces towards the victim malice and ill-will based upon the victim's membership or presumed membership of a racial group; or the offence is wholly or partly motivated by malice or ill-will towards members of a racial group based on their membership of that group.

3.   A "racial group" is defined as a group of persons defined by reference to race, colour, nationality or ethnic or national origins. "Membership" of a racial group includes association with it; "presumed" means presumed by the offender.

4.   Evidence from a single source is sufficient to establish that an offence is racially aggravated.

PART V MISCELLANEOUS AND SUPPLEMENTAL

Remands and committals

97.– (1) In subsection (4) of section 23 of the 1969 Act (remands and committals to local authority accommodation), for the words "Subject to subsection (5) below," there shall be substituted the words "Subject to subsections (5) and (5A) below,".

(2) In subsection (5) of that section, for the words "a young person who has attained the age of fifteen" there shall be substituted the words "a child who has attained the age of twelve, or a young person, who (in either case) is of a prescribed description".

(3) After that subsection there shall be inserted the following subsection-

"(5A) A court shall not impose a security requirement in respect of a child or young person who is not legally represented in the court unless-

(a) he applied for legal aid and the application was refused on the ground that it did not appear his means were such that he required assistance; or

(b) having been informed of his right to apply for legal aid and had the opportunity to do so, he refused or failed to apply."

(4) In subsection (12) of that section, after the definition of "imprisonable offence" there shall be inserted the following definition-

""prescribed description" means a description prescribed by reference to age or sex or both by an order of the Secretary of State;".

(5) Section 20 of the 1994 Act (which has not been brought into force and is superseded by this section) is hereby repealed.

Section 97
1.   This section amends section 23 of the Children and Young Persons Act 1969. The effect of the amendment is that a court can only impose a security requirement relating to a child of 12 or more, or a young person, if the child or young person:

1)   is of the age and sex to be prescribed by the Secretary of State; and

2)   is either legally represented, or legal aid has been refused or not applied for.

2.   A security requirement is a requirement on a local authority to keep a person in secure accommodation.

98.– (1) Section 23 of the 1969 Act shall have effect with the modifications specified in subsections (2) to (6) below in relation to any male person who-

(a) is of the age of 15 or 16; and

(b) is not of a description prescribed for the purposes of subsection (5) of that section.

(2) In subsection (1), immediately before the words "the remand" there shall be inserted the words "then, unless he is remanded to a remand centre or a prison in pursuance of subsection (4)(b) or (c) below,".

(3) For subsections (4) to (5A) there shall be substituted the following subsections-

"(4) Where a court, after consultation with a probation officer, a social worker of a local authority social services department or a member of a youth offending team, declares a person to be one to whom subsection (5) below applies-

(a) it shall remand him to local authority accommodation and require him to be placed and kept in secure accommodation, if-

   (i) it also, after such consultation, declares him to be a person to whom
      subsection (5A) below applies; and

   (ii) it has been notified that secure accommodation is available for him;

(b) it shall remand him to a remand centre, if paragraph (a) above does not apply
   and it has been notified that such a centre is available for the reception from
   the court of persons to whom subsection (5) below applies; and

(c) it shall remand him to a prison, if neither paragraph (a) nor paragraph (b)
   above applies.

(4A) A court shall not declare a person who is not legally represented in the court to be
   a person to whom subsection (5) below applies unless-

   (a) he applied for legal aid and the application was refused on the ground that it
      did not appear his means were such that he required assistance; or

   (b) having been informed of his right to apply for legal aid and had the
      opportunity to do so, he refused or failed to apply.

(5) This subsection applies to a person who-

   (a) is charged with or has been convicted of a violent or sexual offence, or an
      offence punishable in the case of an adult with imprisonment for a term of
      fourteen years or more; or

   (b) has a recent history of absconding while remanded to local authority
      accommodation, and is charged with or has been convicted of an imprisonable
      offence alleged or found to have been committed while he was so remanded,

if (in either case) the court is of opinion that only remanding him to a remand centre
or prison, or to local authority accommodation with a requirement that he be placed
and kept in secure accommodation, would be adequate to protect the public from
serious harm from him.

(5A) This subsection applies to a person if the court is of opinion that, by reason of his
   physical or emotional immaturity or a propensity of his to harm himself, it would
   be undesirable for him to be remanded to a remand centre or a prison."

(4) In subsection (6)-

   (a) for the words "imposes a security requirement in respect of a young person"
      there shall be substituted the words "declares a person to be one to whom
      subsection (5) above applies"; and

   (b) for the words "subsection (5) above" there shall be substituted the words "that
      subsection".

(5) In subsection (7), after the words "a security requirement" there shall be inserted
   the words "(that is to say, a requirement imposed under subsection (4)(a) above
   that the person be placed and kept in secure accommodation)".

(6) After subsection (9) there shall be inserted the following subsection-

"(9A) Where a person is remanded to local authority accommodation without the imposition of a security requirement, a relevant court may, on the application of the designated authority, declare him to be a person to whom subsection (5) above applies; and on its doing so, subsection (4) above shall apply."

(7) Section 62 of the 1991 Act (which is superseded by this section) shall cease to have effect.

Section 98

1.   This section provides that section 23 of the Children and Young Persons Act 1969 is to have effect with the modifications set out in this section in the cases of males aged 15 or 16 who are not of the prescribed description.

2.   There are therefore two alternative versions of section 23 of the Children and Young Persons Act 1969, depending upon whether the case involves a male of 15 or 16, or not.

3.   The effect of this alternative wording of section 23 is to allow the court to remand males of 15 or 16 to secure local authority accommodation, a remand centre or to prison, depending upon whether the person is charged with or convicted of a violent or sexual offence, or has a history of absconding, and it is necessary to protect the public, and whether the person may harm himself if remanded to prison.

Release and recall of prisoners

99. Immediately before section 35 of the 1991 Act there shall be inserted the following section-

"34A.– (1) Subject to subsection (2) below, subsection (3) below applies where a short-term prisoner aged 18 or over is serving a sentence of imprisonment for a term of three months or more.

(2) Subsection (3) below does not apply where-

    (a) the sentence is an extended sentence within the meaning of section 58 of the Crime and Disorder Act 1998;

    (b) the sentence is for an offence under section 1 of the Prisoners (Return to Custody) Act 1995;

    (c) the sentence was imposed under paragraph 3(1)(d) or 4(1)(d) of Schedule 2 to this Act in a case where the prisoner had failed to comply with a requirement of a curfew order;

    (d) the prisoner is subject to a hospital order, hospital direction or transfer direction under section 37, 45A or 47 of the Mental Health Act 1983;

    (e) the prisoner is liable to removal from the United Kingdom for the purposes of section 46 below;

(f) the prisoner has been released on licence under this section at any time and has been recalled to prison under section 38A(1)(a) below;

(g) the prisoner has been released on licence under this section or section 36 below during the currency of the sentence, and has been recalled to prison under section 39(1) or (2) below;

(h) the prisoner has been returned to prison under section 40 below at any time; or

(j) the interval between-

(i) the date on which the prisoner will have served the requisite period for the term of the sentence; and

(ii) the date on which he will have served one-half of the sentence,

is less than 14 days.

(3) After the prisoner has served the requisite period for the term of his sentence, the Secretary of State may, subject to section 37A below, release him on licence.

(4) In this section "the requisite period" means-

(a) for a term of three months or more but less than four months, a period of 30 days;

(b) for a term of four months or more but less than eight months, a period equal to one-quarter of the term;

(c) for a term of eight months or more, a period that is 60 days less than one-half of the term.

(5) The Secretary of State may by order made by statutory instrument-

(a) repeal the words "aged 18 or over" in subsection (1) above;

(b) amend the definition of "the requisite period" in subsection (4) above; and

(c) make such transitional provision as appears to him necessary or expedient in connection with the repeal or amendment.

(6) No order shall be made under subsection (5) above unless a draft of the order has been laid before and approved by a resolution of each House of Parliament."

Section 99

1.   This section inserts section 34A into the Criminal Justice Act 1991, which gives the Secretary of State power to release short-term prisoners aged 18 or more early on licence and subject to a curfew condition (see section 37A, inserted by section 100 below).

2.   A prisoner serving a sentence of:

1)   between 3 and 4 months, must serve 30 days;

2)   4 and 8 months, must serve one quarter of the term;

3)   8 months or more, must serve one half the term less 60 days.

> 3. *The section does not apply to extended sentences, or when prisoners on licence have been recalled to prison. There are also other circumstances when the section does not apply.*

100.– (1) After section 37 of the 1991 Act there shall be inserted the following section-

"**37A.**– (1) A person shall not be released under section 34A(3) above unless the licence includes a condition ("the curfew condition") which-

   (a) requires the released person to remain, for periods for the time being specified in the condition, at a place for the time being so specified (which may be an approved probation hostel); and
   (b) includes requirements for securing the electronic monitoring of his whereabouts during the periods for the time being so specified.

(2) The curfew condition may specify different places or different periods for different days, but shall not specify periods which amount to less than 9 hours in any one day (excluding for this purpose the first and last days of the period for which the condition is in force).

(3) The curfew condition shall remain in force until the date when the released person would (but for his release) have served one-half of his sentence.

(4) The curfew condition shall include provision for making a person responsible for monitoring the released person's whereabouts during the periods for the time being specified in the condition; and a person who is made so responsible shall be of a description specified in an order made by the Secretary of State.

(5) The power conferred by subsection (4) above-

   (a) shall be exercisable by statutory instrument; and
   (b) shall include power to make different provision for different cases or classes of case or for different areas.

(6) Nothing in this section shall be taken to require the Secretary of State to ensure that arrangements are made for the electronic monitoring of released persons' whereabouts in any particular part of England and Wales;

(7) In this section "approved probation hostel" has the same meaning as in the Probation Service Act 1993."

(2) Immediately before section 39 of the 1991 Act there shall be inserted the following section-

"**38A.**– (1) If it appears to the Secretary of State, as regards a person released on licence under section 34A(3) above-

   (a) that he has failed to comply with the curfew condition;

(b) that his whereabouts can no longer be electronically monitored at the place for the time being specified in that condition; or

(c) that it is necessary to do so in order to protect the public from serious harm from him,

the Secretary of State may, if the curfew condition is still in force, revoke the licence and recall the person to prison.

(2) A person whose licence under section 34A(3) above is revoked under this section-

(a) may make representations in writing with respect to the revocation;

(b) on his return to prison, shall be informed of the reasons for the revocation and of his right to make representations.

(3) The Secretary of State, after considering any representations made under subsection (2)(b) above or any other matters, may cancel a revocation under this section.

(4) Where the revocation of a person's licence is cancelled under subsection (3) above, the person shall be treated for the purposes of sections 34A(2)(f) and 37(1B) above as if he had not been recalled to prison under this section.

(5) On the revocation under this section of a person's licence under section 34A(3) above, he shall be liable to be detained in pursuance of his sentence and, if at large, shall be deemed to be unlawfully at large.

(6) In this section "the curfew condition" has the same meaning as in section 37A above."

Section 100

1.   This section inserts sections 37A and 38A into the Criminal Justice Act 1991. Prisoners released early on licence under section 34A (see above) will be subject to a curfew condition.

2.   A curfew condition requires the released person to remain in a specified place monitored by an electronic monitoring system for at least 9 hours per day, although the place and the period specified may vary from day to day.

3.   The curfew condition would remain in force until half the sentence would, but for the release, have been served.

4.   Section 38A provides that on failure to comply with a curfew condition offenders may be recalled to prison.

101.– (1) For subsection (2) of section 51 of the 1991 Act (interpretation of Part II) there shall be substituted the following subsections-

"(2) For the purposes of any reference in this Part, however expressed, to the term of imprisonment to which a person has been sentenced or which, or part of which, he has served, consecutive terms and terms which are wholly or partly concurrent shall be treated as a single term if-

(a) the sentences were passed on the same occasion; or
(b) where they were passed on different occasions, the person has not been released under this Part at any time during the period beginning with the first and ending with the last of those occasions.

(2A) Where a suspended sentence of imprisonment is ordered to take effect, with or without any variation of the original term, the occasion on which that order is made shall be treated for the purposes of subsection (2) above as the occasion on which the sentence is passed.

(2B) Where a person has been sentenced to two or more terms of imprisonment which are wholly or partly concurrent and do not fall to be treated as a single term-

(a) nothing in this Part shall require the Secretary of State to release him in respect of any of the terms unless and until the Secretary of State is required to release him in respect of each of the others;
(b) nothing in this Part shall require the Secretary of State or the Board to consider his release in respect of any of the terms unless and until the Secretary of State or the Board is required to consider his release, or the Secretary of State is required to release him, in respect of each of the others;
(c) on and after his release under this Part he shall be on licence for so long, and subject to such conditions, as is required by this Part in respect of any of the sentences; and
(d) the date mentioned in section 40(1) above shall be taken to be that on which he would (but for his release) have served each of the sentences in full.

(2C) Where a person has been sentenced to one or more terms of imprisonment and to one or more life sentences (within the meaning of section 34 of the Crime (Sentences) Act 1997), nothing in this Part shall-

(a) require the Secretary of State to release the person in respect of any of the terms unless and until the Secretary of State is required to release him in respect of each of the life sentences; or
(b) require the Secretary of State or the Board to consider the person's release in respect of any of the terms unless and until the Secretary of State or the Board is required to consider his release in respect of each of the life sentences.

(2D) Subsections (2B) and (2C) above shall have effect as if the term of an extended sentence (within the meaning of section 58 of the Crime and Disorder Act 1998) included the extension period (within the meaning of that section)."

(2) After subsection (3) of section 34 of the 1997 Act (interpretation of Chapter II) there shall be inserted the following subsection-

"(4) Where a person has been sentenced to one or more life sentences and to one or more terms of imprisonment, nothing in this Chapter shall require the Secretary of State to release the person in respect of any of the life sentences unless and until the Secretary of State is required to release him in respect of each of the terms."

Section 101

This section amends section 51 of the Criminal Justice Act 1991 and provides that, for the purposes of determining early release, consecutive and concurrent sentences are to be treated as single terms if they are passed on the same occasion, or if one is passed before another has been fully served.

102.– (1) A court sentencing a person to a term of imprisonment shall not order or direct that the term shall commence on the expiration of any other sentence of imprisonment from which he has been released under Part II of the 1991 Act.

(2) Expressions used in this section shall be construed as if they were contained in that Part.

Section 102

This section provides that a court cannot impose a sentence of imprisonment to commence on the expiration of any other sentence of imprisonment from which the offender has been released.

103.– (1) This section has effect for the purpose of securing that, subject to section 100(2) above, the circumstances in which prisoners released on licence under Part II of the 1991 Act may be recalled to prison are the same for short-term prisoners as for long-term prisoners.

(2) Section 38 of the 1991 Act (breach of licence conditions by short-term prisoners) shall cease to have effect.

(3) In subsection (1) of section 39 of the 1991 Act (recall of long-term prisoners while on licence), after the words "in the case of a" there shall be inserted the words "short-term or".

> **Section 103**
> *This section amends section 39 of the Criminal Justice Act 1991 with the effect that the Parole Board is responsible for considering whether short-term prisoners as well as long-term prisoners released on licence should be recalled to prison for failure to comply with the licence. Prior to this amendment, section 38, which now ceases to have effect, imposed responsibility for short-term prisoners on the courts.*

104.– (1) In subsection (3) of section 33 of the 1991 Act (duty to release short-term and long-term prisoners), for the word "unconditionally" there shall be substituted the words "on licence".

(2) After subsection (1) of section 37 of that Act (duration and conditions of licences) there shall be inserted the following subsection-

"(1A) Where a prisoner is released on licence under section 33(3) or (3A) above, subsection (1) above shall have effect as if for the reference to three-quarters of his sentence there were substituted a reference to the whole of that sentence."

> **Section 104**
> *This section amends section 33 of the Criminal Justice Act 1991 so that prisoners are released on licence rather than unconditionally; and prisoners who are re-released having been recalled to prison are re-released on licence for the whole of the sentence rather than for three quarters.*

105. After section 40 of the 1991 Act there shall be inserted the following section-

"**40A.**– (1) This section applies (in place of sections 33, 33A, 37(1) and 39 above) where a court passes on a person a sentence of imprisonment which-

(a) includes, or consists of, an order under section 40 above; and
(b) is for a term of twelve months or less.

(2) As soon as the person has served one-half of the sentence, it shall be the duty of the Secretary of State to release him on licence.

(3) Where the person is so released, the licence shall remain in force for a period of three months.

(4) If the person fails to comply with such conditions as may for the time being be specified in the licence, he shall be liable on summary conviction-

(a) to a fine not exceeding level 3 on the standard scale; or
(b) to a sentence of imprisonment for a term not exceeding the relevant period,

but not liable to be dealt with in any other way.

(5) In subsection (4) above

"the relevant period" means a period which is equal in length to the period between the date on which the failure occurred or began and the date of the expiry of the licence.

(6) As soon as a person has served one-half of a sentence passed under subsection (4) above, it shall be the duty of the Secretary of State to release him, subject to the licence if it is still subsisting."

Section 105

This section inserts section 40A into the Criminal Justice Act 1991. When a court makes an order that an offender is to be returned to prison under section 40 for breach of his licence, and imposes a sentence of 12 months or less for the new offence, the Secretary of State is obliged to re-release him on licence once he has served half his sentence.

Miscellaneous

106.The enactments mentioned in Schedule 7 to this Act shall have effect subject to the amendments there specified, being amendments designed to facilitate, or otherwise desirable in connection with, the consolidation of certain enactments relating to the powers of courts to deal with offenders or defaulters.

Section 106

This section gives effect to Schedule 7 which sets out consequential amendments.

107.– (1) Chapter I of Part II of the 1997 Act (which relates to the effect of determinate custodial sentences) shall be amended as follows.

(2) Sections 8 and 10 to 27 are hereby repealed.

(3) After subsection (7) of section 9 (crediting of periods of remand in custody) there shall be inserted the following subsection-

"(7A) Such rules may make such incidental, supplemental and consequential provisions as may appear to the Secretary of State to be necessary or expedient."

(4) After subsection (10) of that section there shall be inserted the following subsections-

"(11) In this section "sentence of imprisonment" does not include a committal-

(a) in default of payment of any sum of money other than one adjudged to be paid by a conviction;
(b) for want of sufficient distress to satisfy any sum of money; or
(c) for failure to do or abstain from doing anything required to be done or left undone;

and cognate expressions shall be construed accordingly.

(12) For the purposes of any reference in this section, however expressed, to the term of imprisonment to which a person has been sentenced, consecutive terms and terms which are wholly or partly concurrent shall be treated as a single term if-

(a) the sentences were passed on the same occasion; or
(b) where they were passed on different occasions, the person has not been released under Part II of the 1991 Act at any time during the period beginning with the first and ending with the last of those occasions."

(5) After that section there shall be inserted the following section-

"9A.– (1) Section 9 above applies to-

(a) a sentence of detention in a young offender institution; and
(b) a determinate sentence of detention under section 53 of the Children and Young Persons Act 1933 ("the 1933 Act"),

as it applies to an equivalent sentence of imprisonment.

(2) Section 9 above applies to-

(a) persons remanded or committed to local authority accommodation under section 23 of the Children and Young Persons Act 1969 ("the 1969 Act") and placed and kept in secure accommodation; and
(b) persons remanded, admitted or removed to hospital under section 35, 36, 38 or 48 of the Mental Health Act 1983 ("the 1983 Act"),as it applies to persons remanded in or committed to custody by an order of a court.

(3) In this section "secure accommodation" has the same meaning as in section 23 of the 1969 Act."

Section 107

1.   This section repeals most of Chapter I of Part II of the Crime (Sentences) Act 1977, which dealt with time to be served, early release and supervision after release.

2.   The section also amends section 9 of that Act, which remains in force and which deals with the crediting of periods of remand in custody. As a result of the amendments:

> 1)   *the Secretary of State may make incidental regulations;*
>
> 2)   *concurrent and consecutive sentences are generally treated for the purposes of the section as a single sentence; and*
>
> 3)   *a section 9A is inserted with the effect that section 9 applies to the detention of children or young persons.*

108. Chapter I of Part III of the Crime and Punishment (Scotland) Act 1997 (early release of prisoners) shall cease to have effect.

109.– (1) Section 16 of the (1997 c.48.)Crime and Punishment (Scotland) Act 1997 (designated life prisoners) shall have effect and shall be deemed always to have had effect with the amendments made by subsections (2) and (3) below.

(2) In subsection (2), at the beginning there shall be inserted the words "Except in a case to which subsection (3A) or (3B) below applies,".

(3) After subsection (3) there shall be inserted the following subsections-

"(3A) This subsection applies in a case where a person-

(a) was sentenced, prior to 20 October 1997, in respect of a murder committed by him before he attained the age of 18 years; and
(b) has been released on licence, other than under section 3 of the 1993 Act, whether before or on that date.

(3B) This subsection applies in a case where a person-

(a) was sentenced, prior to 20 October 1997, in respect of a murder committed by him before he attained the age of 18 years; and
(b) has been released on licence, other than under section 3 of the 1993 Act, after that date without his case having been considered under subsection (2) above.

(3C) In a case to which subsection (3A) or (3B) applies, Part I of the 1993 Act shall apply as if the person were a designated life prisoner, within the meaning of section 2 of that Act, whose licence had been granted under subsection (4) of that section on his having served the designated part of his sentence."

(4) Where, prior to the commencement of this section, a certificate has been issued under subsection (2) of section 16 of the Crime and Punishment (Scotland) Act 1997 in respect of a case to which subsection (3A) of that section applies, the certificate shall be disregarded.

110. In section 24 of the Criminal Law (Consolidation) (Scotland) Act 1995 (detention and questioning by customs officers), in subsection (4)-

    (a) for the words from "he" to "be" there shall be substituted the words "and is"; and

    (b) after the word "detention" there shall be inserted the words ", the period of six hours mentioned in subsection (2) above shall be reduced by the length of that earlier detention".

111.– (1) After section 1 of the 1993 Act there shall be inserted the following section-

"1A.   Where a prisoner has been sentenced to two or more terms of imprisonment which are wholly or partly concurrent and do not fall to be treated as a single term by virtue of section 27(5) of this Act-

    (a) nothing in this Part of this Act shall require the Secretary of State to release him in respect of any of the terms unless and until the Secretary of State is required to release him in respect of each of the other terms;

    (b) nothing in this Part of this Act shall require the Secretary of State or the Parole Board to consider his release in respect of any of the terms unless and until the Secretary of State or the Parole Board is required to consider his release, or the Secretary of State is required to release him, in respect of each of the other terms; and

    (c) where he is released on licence under this Part of this Act, he shall be on a single licence which-

        (i) shall (unless revoked) remain in force until the date on which he would (but for his release) have served in full all the sentences in respect of which he has been so released; and

        (ii) shall be subject to such conditions as may be specified or required by this Part of this Act in respect of any of the sentences."

(2) After subsection (7) of section 16 of the 1993 Act (orders for return to prison on commission of further offence) there shall be inserted the following subsection-

"(8) Where a prisoner has been sentenced to two or more terms of imprisonment which are wholly or partly concurrent and do not fall to be treated as a single term by virtue of section 27(5) of this Act, the date mentioned in subsection (1)(a) above shall be taken to be that on which he would (but for his release) have served all of the sentences in full."

(3) For subsection (5) of section 27 of the 1993 Act (interpretation of Part I) there shall be substituted the following subsection-

"(5) For the purposes of any reference, however expressed, in this Part of this Act to the term of imprisonment or other detention to which a person has been sentenced or which, or any part of which, he has served, consecutive terms and terms which are wholly or partly concurrent shall be treated as a single term if-

(a) the sentences were passed at the same time; or
(b) where the sentences were passed at different times, the person has not been released under this Part of this Act at any time during the period beginning with the passing of the first sentence and ending with the passing of the last."

(4) In sub-paragraph (1) of paragraph 6B of Schedule 6 to the 1993 Act (aggregation of old and new sentences)-

(a) for the words "a prisoner" there shall be substituted the words "an existing prisoner";
(b) the word "and" after head (a) shall cease to have effect;
(c) in head (b), for the words "that date" there shall be inserted the words "the date on which section 111 of the Crime and Disorder Act 1998 comes into force"; and
(d) after head (b) there shall be inserted the following-

"; and

(c) he has not at any time prior to the passing of the sentence or sentences mentioned in head (b) above been released from the sentence or sentences mentioned in head (a) above under the existing provisions."

(5) After that paragraph there shall be inserted the following paragraph-

"6C.– (1) This paragraph applies where-

(a) an existing prisoner was, at the relevant date, serving a sentence or sentences of imprisonment, on conviction of an offence, passed before that date;
(b) on or after the date on which section 111 of the Crime and Disorder Act 1998 comes into force he is, or has been, sentenced to a further term or terms of imprisonment on conviction of an offence, to be served wholly or partly concurrently with the sentence or sentences mentioned in head (a); and
(c) the sentences do not fall to be treated as a single term by virtue of paragraph 6B(2)(a) above.

(2) In a case to which this paragraph applies the Secretary of State shall not release, or be required to consider the release of, the prisoner unless and until the requirements for release, or for consideration of his release, of the new and the existing provisions are satisfied in relation to each sentence to which they respectively apply.

(3) In a case to which this paragraph applies the Parole Board shall not be required to consider the release of the prisoner unless and until the requirements for release, or for consideration for release, of the new and the existing provisions are satisfied in relation to each sentence to which they respectively apply.

(4) In a case to which this paragraph applies, where the prisoner is released on licence, he shall be on a single licence which-

   (a) shall (unless revoked) remain in force until the later of-
      (i) the date on which he would have been discharged from prison on remission of part of his sentence or sentences under the existing provisions if, after his release, he had not forfeited remission of any part of that sentence under those provisions; or
      (ii) the date on which he would (but for his release) have served in full all the sentences in respect of which he was released on licence and which were imposed after the relevant date; and
   (b) shall be deemed to be granted under the new provisions and, subject to sub-paragraph (5) below, those provisions so far as relating to conditions of licences, and recall or return to prison, shall apply as they apply in respect of a prisoner on licence in respect of a sentence passed after the relevant date.

(5) In the application of section 16 to a person whose licence is deemed to be granted under the new provisions by virtue of sub-paragraph (4)(b) above, the reference to the original sentence (within the meaning of that section) shall be construed as a reference to the further term or terms mentioned in head (b) of sub-paragraph (1) above."

(6) Subject to subsection (7) below, the amendments made by subsections (1) to (5) above apply where one or more of the sentences concerned was passed after the commencement of this section.

(7) Where the terms of two or more sentences passed before the commencement of this section have been treated, by virtue of section 27(5) of, or paragraph 6B of Schedule 6 to, the 1993 Act, as a single term for the purposes of Part I of that Act, they shall continue to be so treated after that commencement.

(8) In relation to a prisoner released on licence at any time under section 16(7)(b) of the 1993 Act, section 17(1)(a) of that Act shall have effect as if after the word "Act" there were inserted the words "or a short term prisoner has been released on licence by virtue of section 16(7)(b) of this Act".

112. After section 204 of the 1995 Act there shall be inserted the following section-

"204A. A court sentencing a person to imprisonment or other detention shall not order or direct that the term of imprisonment or detention shall commence on the expiration of any other such sentence from which he has been released at any time under the existing or new provisions within the meaning of Schedule 6 to the Prisoners and Criminal Proceedings (Scotland) Act 1993."

113.– (1) In subsection (1) of section 94 of the Police Act 1997 (authorisations given in absence of authorising officer), for the words "(f) or (g)" there shall be substituted the words "(f), (g) or (h)".

(2) In subsection (3) of that section, for paragraphs (a) and (b) there shall be substituted the words "he holds the rank of assistant chief constable in that Service or Squad".

(3) In subsection (4) of that section, the word "and" immediately preceding paragraph (c) shall cease to have effect and after that paragraph there shall be inserted the words "and

(d) in the case of an authorising officer within paragraph (h) of section 93(5), means the customs officer designated by the Commissioners of Customs and Excise to act in his absence for the purposes of this paragraph."

Supplemental

114.– (1) Any power of a Minister of the Crown to make an order or regulations under this Act-

(a) is exercisable by statutory instrument; and
(b) includes power to make such transitional provision as appears to him necessary or expedient in connection with any provision made by the order or regulations.

(2) A statutory instrument containing an order under section 5(2) or (3) or 10(6) above, or regulations under paragraph 1 of Schedule 3 to this Act, shall be subject to annulment in pursuance of a resolution of either House of Parliament.

(3) No order under section 38(5), 41(6), 58(7), 61(7), 73(2)(b)(ii) or 76(2) above shall be made unless a draft of the order has been laid before and approved by a resolution of each House of Parliament.

> **Section 114**
> *This section deals with the power to make regulations under this Act.*

115.– (1) Any person who, apart from this subsection, would not have power to disclose information-

(a) to a relevant authority; or
(b) to a person acting on behalf of such an authority,

shall have power to do so in any case where the disclosure is necessary or expedient for the purposes of any provision of this Act.

(2) In subsection (1) above "relevant authority" means-

(a) the chief officer of police for a police area in England and Wales;
(b) the chief constable of a police force maintained under the Police (Scotland) Act 1967;
(c) a police authority within the meaning given by section 101(1) of the Police Act 1996;
(d) a local authority, that is to say-
    (i) in relation to England, a county council, a district council, a London borough council or the Common Council of the City of London;
    (ii) in relation to Wales, a county council or a county borough council;
    (iii) in relation to Scotland, a council constituted under section 2 of the Local Government etc. (Scotland) Act 1994;
(e) a probation committee in England and Wales;
(f) a health authority.

> **Section 115**
> *This section authorises the police, a local authority, a probation committee and a health authority to disclose information which, but for this section, it would not have power to disclose, where the disclosure is necessary or expedient for the purposes of any provision of this Act.*

116.– (1) The Secretary of State may by order provide that, in relation to any time before the commencement of section 73 above, a court shall not make an order under-

  (a) section 1 of the 1994 Act (secure training orders); or

  (b) subsection (3)(a) of section 4 of that Act (breaches of supervision requirements),

unless it has been notified by the Secretary of State that accommodation at a secure training centre, or accommodation provided by a local authority for the purpose of restricting the liberty of children and young persons, is immediately available for the offender, and the notice has not been withdrawn.

(2) An order under this section may provide that sections 2 and 4 of the 1994 Act shall have effect, in relation to any such time, as if-

  (a) for subsections (2) and (3) of section 2 there were substituted the following subsection-

"(2) Where accommodation for the offender at a secure training centre is not immediately available-

    (a) the court shall commit the offender to accommodation provided by a local authority for the purpose of restricting the liberty of children and young persons until such time as accommodation for him at such a centre is available; and

    (b) the period of detention in the centre under the order shall be reduced by the period spent by the offender in the accommodation so provided.";

  (b) in subsection (5) of that section, for the words "subsections (2)(a)(ii) and (4)(b) apply" there were substituted the words "subsection (4)(b) applies";

  (c) for subsection (8) of that section there were substituted the following subsection-

"(8) In this section "local authority" has the same meaning as in the Children Act 1989."; and

  (d) in subsection (4) of section 4, for the words "paragraphs (a), (b) and (c) of subsection (2) and subsections (5), (7) and (8) of section 2" there were substituted the words "paragraphs (a) and (b) of subsection (2) and subsections (7) and (8) of section 2".

(3) In relation to any time before the commencement of section 73 above, section 4 of the 1994 Act shall have effect as if after subsection (4) there were inserted the following subsection-

"(4A) A fine imposed under subsection (3)(b) above shall be deemed, for the purposes of any enactment, to be a sum adjudged to be paid by a conviction."

(4) In relation to any time before the commencement of section 73 above, section 1B of the 1982 Act (special provision for offenders under 18) shall have effect as if-

(a) in subsection (4), immediately before the words "a total term" there were inserted the words "a term or (in the case of an offender to whom subsection (6) below applies)";

(b) in subsection (5)-
  (i) immediately before the words "total term" there were inserted the words "term or (as the case may be)"; and
  (ii) for the words "the term" there were substituted the word "it"; and

(c) for subsection (6) there were substituted the following subsection-

"(6) This subsection applies to an offender sentenced to two or more terms of detention in a young offender institution which are consecutive or wholly or partly concurrent if-

(a) the sentences were passed on the same occasion; or

(b) where they were passed on different occasions, the offender has not been released under Part II of the Criminal Justice Act 1991 at any time during the period beginning with the first and ending with the last of those occasions;

and in subsections (4) and (5) above "the total term", in relation to such an offender, means the aggregate of those terms."

(5) In this section "local authority" has the same meaning as in the 1989 Act.

117.– (1) In this Act-

"the 1933 Act" means the Children and Young Persons Act 1933;

"the 1969 Act" means the Children and Young Persons Act 1969;

"the 1973 Act" means the Powers of Criminal Courts Act 1973;

"the 1980 Act" means the Magistrates' Courts Act 1980;

"the 1982 Act" means the Criminal Justice Act 1982;

"the 1984 Act" means the Police and Criminal Evidence Act 1984;

"the 1985 Act" means the Prosecution of Offences Act 1985;

"the 1989 Act" means the Children Act 1989;

"the 1991 Act" means the Criminal Justice Act 1991;

"the 1994 Act" means the Criminal Justice and Public Order Act 1994;

"the 1997 Act" means the Crime (Sentences) Act 1997;

"caution" has the same meaning as in Part V of the Police Act 1997;

"child" means a person under the age of 14;

"commission area" has the same meaning as in the Justices of the Peace Act 1997;

"custodial sentence" has the same meaning as in Part I of the 1991 Act;

"guardian" has the same meaning as in the 1933 Act;

"prescribed" means prescribed by an order made by the Secretary of State;

"young person" means a person who has attained the age of 14 and is under the age of 18;

"youth offending team" means a team established under section 39 above.

(2) In this Act-

"the 1993 Act" means the Prisoners and Criminal Proceedings (Scotland) Act 1993; and

"the 1995 Act" means the Criminal Procedure (Scotland) Act 1995.

(3) For the purposes of this Act, the age of a person shall be deemed to be that which it appears to the court to be after considering any available evidence.

118. An Order in Council under paragraph 1(1)(b) of Schedule 1 to the Northern Ireland Act 1974 (legislation for Northern Ireland in the interim period) which contains a statement that it is made only for purposes corresponding to those of sections 2 to 4, 34, 47(5), 57, 61 to 64 and 85 above-

(a) shall not be subject to paragraph 1(4) and (5) of that Schedule (affirmative resolution of both Houses of Parliament); but
(b) shall be subject to annulment in pursuance of a resolution of either House of Parliament.

119. The enactments mentioned in Schedule 8 to this Act shall have effect subject to the amendments there specified, being minor amendments and amendments consequential on the provisions of this Act.

120.– (1) The transitional provisions and savings contained in Schedule 9 to this Act shall have effect; but nothing in this subsection shall be taken as prejudicing the operation of sections 16 and 17 of the Interpretation Act 1978 (which relate to the effect of repeals).

(2) The enactments specified in Schedule 10 to this Act, which include some that are spent, are hereby repealed to the extent specified in the third column of that Schedule.

121.– (1) This Act may be cited as the Crime and Disorder Act 1998.

(2) This Act, except this section, sections 109 and 111(8) above and paragraphs 55, 99 and 117 of Schedule 8 to this Act, shall come into force on such day as the Secretary of State may by order appoint; and different days may be appointed for different purposes or different areas.

(3) Without prejudice to the provisions of Schedule 9 to this Act, an order under subsection (2) above may make such transitional provisions and savings as appear to the Secretary of State necessary or expedient in connection with any provision brought into force by the order.

(4) Subject to subsections (5) to (12) below, this Act extends to England and Wales only.

(5) The following provisions extend to Scotland only, namely-

(a) Chapter II of Part I;
(b) section 33;
(c) Chapter II of Part IV;
(d) sections 108 to 112 and 117(2); and
(e) paragraphs 55, 70, 71, 98 to 108, 115 to 124 and 140 to 143 of Schedule 8 and section 119 above so far as relating to those paragraphs.

(6) The following provisions also extend to Scotland, namely-

(a) Chapter III of Part I;
(b) section 36(3) to (5);
(c) section 65(9);
(d) section 115;
(e) paragraph 3 of Schedule 3 to this Act and section 52(6) above so far as relating to that paragraph;
(f) paragraph 15 of Schedule 7 to this Act and section 106 above so far as relating to that paragraph;
(g) paragraphs 1, 7(1) and (3), 14(1) and (2), 35, 36, 45, 135, 136 and 138 of Schedule 8 to this Act and section 119 above so far as relating to those paragraphs; and
(h) this section.

(7) Sections 36(1), (2)(a), (b) and (d) and (6)(b) and section 118 above extend to Northern Ireland only.

(8) Section 36(3)(b), (4) and (5) above, paragraphs 7(1) and (3), 45, 135 and 138 of Schedule 8 to this Act, section 119 above so far as relating to those paragraphs and this section also extend to Northern Ireland.

(9) Section 36(5) above, paragraphs 7(1) and (3), 45 and 134 of Schedule 8 to this Act, section 119 above so far as relating to those paragraphs and this section also extend to the Isle of Man.

(10) Section 36(5) above, paragraphs 7(1) and (3), 45 and 135 of Schedule 8 to this Act, section 119 above so far as relating to those paragraphs and this section also extend to the Channel Islands.

(11) The repeals in Schedule 10 to this Act, and section 120(2) above so far as relating to those repeals, have the same extent as the enactments on which the repeals operate.

(12) Section 9(4) of the Repatriation of Prisoners Act 1984 (power to extend Act to Channel Islands and Isle of Man) applies to the amendments of that Act made by paragraphs 56 to 60 of Schedule 8 to this Act; and in Schedule 1 to the 1997 Act-

    (a) paragraph 14 (restricted transfers between the United Kingdom and the Channel Islands) as applied in relation to the Isle of Man; and
    (b) paragraph 19 (application of Schedule in relation to the Isle of Man),

apply to the amendments of that Schedule made by paragraph 135 of Schedule 8 to this Act.

Sections 116 to 121
These sections deal with transitional provisions, consequential amendments, short title and commencement.

SCHEDULES

SCHEDULE 1

Application

1. This schedule applies to property seized under section 54(2A) of this Act.

Retention

2.– (1) Subject to sub-paragraph (2) below, property to which this Schedule applies may be retained for a period of twenty-eight days beginning with the day on which it was seized.

(2) Where proceedings for an offence are instituted within the period specified in sub-paragraph (1) above against any person, the property may be retained for a period beginning on the day on which it was seized and ending on the day when-

  (a) the prosecutor certifies that the property is not, or is no longer, required as a production in criminal proceedings or for any purpose relating to such proceedings;

  (b) the accused in such proceedings-

    (i) is sentenced or otherwise dealt with for the offence; or

    (ii) is acquitted of the offence; or

  (c) the proceedings are expressly abandoned by the prosecutor or are deserted *simpliciter*.

Arrangements for custody of property

3.– (1) Subject to the proviso to section 17(3)(b) of the Police (Scotland) Act 1967 (duty to comply with instructions received from prosecutor), the chief constable shall, in accordance with the provisions of this Schedule, make such arrangements as he considers appropriate for the care, custody, return or disposal of property to which this Schedule applies.

(2) Any reference in this Schedule to property being in the possession of, delivered by or disposed of by, the chief constable includes a reference to its being in the possession of, delivered by or disposed of by, another person under arrangements made under sub-paragraph (1) above.

Disposal

4. Where the period of retention permitted by paragraph 2 above expires and the chief constable has reason to believe that the person from whom the property was seized is not the owner or the person having right to possession of it, he shall take reasonable steps to ascertain the identity of the owner or of the person with that right and to notify him of the procedures determined under paragraph 5(1) below.

5.– (1) Subject to sub-paragraphs (5) and (6) below, the owner or any person having right to possession of any property to which this Schedule applies and which, at the expiry of the period of retention permitted by paragraph 2 above, is in the possession of the chief constable may at any time prior to its disposal under paragraph 6 below claim that property in accordance with such procedure as the chief constable may determine.

(2) Subject to sub-paragraphs (3), (5) and (6) below, where the chief constable considers that the person making a claim in accordance with the procedure determined under sub-paragraph (1) above is the owner of the property or has a right to possession of it, he shall deliver the property to the claimant.

(3) Subject to sub-paragraph (4) below, the chief constable may impose such conditions connected with the delivery to the claimant of property under sub-paragraph (2) above as he thinks fit and, without prejudice to that generality, such conditions may relate to the payment of such reasonable charges (including any reasonable expenses incurred in relation to the property by or on behalf of him) as he may determine.

(4) No condition relating to the payment of any charge shall be imposed by the chief constable on the owner or person having right of possession of the property where he is satisfied that that person did not know, and had no reason to suspect, that the property to which this Schedule applies was likely to be used in a manner which gave rise to its seizure.

(5) This paragraph does not apply where the period of retention expires in such manner as is mentioned in paragraph 2(2)(b)(i) above and the court by which he was convicted has made a suspended forfeiture order or a restraint order in respect of the property to which this Schedule applies.

(6) This paragraph shall cease to apply where at any time-

    (a) the property to which this Schedule applies-
        (i) is seized under any other power available to a constable; or
        (ii) passes into the possession of the prosecutor; or
    (b) proceedings for an offence are instituted, where the property to which this Schedule applies is required as a production.

6.– (1) Where this sub-paragraph applies, the chief constable may-

    (a) sell property to which this Schedule applies; or
    (b) if in his opinion it would be impracticable to sell such property, dispose of it.

(2) Sub-paragraph (1) above applies-

    (a) at any time after the expiry of the relevant period where, within that period-
        (i) no claim has been made under paragraph 5 above; or
        (ii) any such a claim which has been made has been rejected by the chief constable; and

(b) where a claim has been made under paragraph 5 above and not determined within the relevant period, at any time after the rejection of that claim by the chief constable.

(3) In sub-paragraph (2) above, the "relevant period" means a period of six months beginning with the day on which the period of retention permitted by paragraph 2 above expired.

(4) Sections 71, 72 and 77(1) of this Act shall apply to a disposal under this paragraph as they apply to a disposal under section 68 of this Act.

Appeals

7.– (1) A claimant under sub-paragraph (2) of paragraph 5 above may appeal to the sheriff against any decision of the chief constable made under that paragraph as respects the claim.

(2) The previous owner of any property disposed of for value under paragraph 6 above may appeal to the sheriff against any decision of the chief constable made under section 72 of this Act as applied by sub-paragraph (4) of that paragraph.

(3) Subsections (3) to (5) of section 76 of this Act shall apply to an appeal under this paragraph as they apply to an appeal under that section.

Interpretation

8. In this Schedule-

"chief constable" means the chief constable for the police area in which the property to which this Schedule applies was seized, and includes a constable acting under the direction of the chief constable for the purposes of this Schedule;

"restraint order" shall be construed in accordance with section 28(1) of the Proceeds of Crime (Scotland) Act 1995;

"suspended forfeiture order" shall be construed in accordance with section 21(2) of that Act."

Schedule 1
This schedule is inserted as Schedule 2A to the Civic Government (Scotland) Act 1982, and deals with the retention and disposal of musical instruments and other devices played too loudly and seized under section 54(2A) (inserted by section 24 above).

SCHEDULE 2

Membership

1. The Secretary of State shall appoint one of the members of the Board to be their chairman.

2.- (1) Subject to the following provisions of this paragraph, a person shall hold and vacate office as a member of the Board, or as chairman of the Board, in accordance with the terms of his appointment.

(2) An appointment as a member of the Board may be full-time or part-time.

(3) The appointment of a person as a member of the Board, or as chairman of the Board, shall be for a fixed period of not longer than five years.

(4) Subject to sub-paragraph (5) below, a person whose term of appointment as a member of the Board, or as chairman of the Board, expires shall be eligible for re-appointment.

(5) No person may hold office as a member of the Board for a continuous period which is longer than ten years.

(6) A person may at any time resign his office as a member of the Board, or as chairman of the Board, by notice in writing addressed to the Secretary of State.

(7) The terms of appointment of a member of the Board, or the chairman of the Board, may provide for his removal from office (without cause being assigned) on notice from the Secretary of State of such length as may be specified in those terms, subject (if those terms so provide) to compensation from the Secretary of State; and in any such case the Secretary of State may remove that member from office in accordance with those terms.

(8) Where-

    (a) the terms of appointment of a member of the Board, or the chairman of the Board, provide for compensation on his removal from office in pursuance of sub-paragraph (7) above; and

    (b) the member or chairman is removed from office in pursuance of that sub-paragraph,

the Board shall pay to him compensation of such amount, and on such terms, as the Secretary of State may with the approval of the Treasury determine.

(9) The Secretary of State may also at any time remove a person from office as a member of the Board if satisfied-

    (a) that he has without reasonable excuse failed to discharge his functions as a member for a continuous period of three months beginning not earlier than six months before that time;

    (b) that he has been convicted of a criminal offence;

(c) that a bankruptcy order has been made against him, or his estate has been sequestrated, or he has made a composition or arrangement with, or granted a trust deed for, his creditors; or

(d) that he is unable or unfit to discharge his functions as a member.

(10) The Secretary of State shall remove a member of the Board, or the chairman of the Board, from office in pursuance of this paragraph by declaring his office as a member of the Board to be vacant and notifying that fact in such manner as the Secretary of State thinks fit; and the office shall then become vacant.

(11) If the chairman of the Board ceases to be a member of the Board he shall also cease to be chairman.

Members and employees

3.– (1) The Board shall-

(a) pay to members of the Board such remuneration;

(b) pay to or in respect of members of the Board any such allowances, fees, expenses and gratuities; and

(c) pay towards the provision of pensions to or in respect of members of the Board any such sums,

as the Board are required to pay by or in accordance with directions given by the Secretary of State.

(2) Where a member of the Board was, immediately before becoming a member, a participant in a scheme under section 1 of the Superannuation Act 1972, the Minister for the Civil Service may determine that his term of office as a member shall be treated for the purposes of the scheme as if it were service in the employment or office by reference to which he was a participant in the scheme; and his rights under the scheme shall not be affected by sub-paragraph (1)(c) above.

(3) Where-

(a) a person ceases to hold office as a member of the Board otherwise than on the expiry of his term of appointment; and

(b) it appears to the Secretary of State that there are special circumstances which make it right for him to receive compensation,

the Secretary of State may direct the Board to make to the person a payment of such amount as the Secretary of State may determine.

4.– (1) The Board may appoint a chief executive and such other employees as the Board think fit, subject to the consent of the Secretary of State as to their number and terms and conditions of service.

(2) The Board shall-

(a) pay to employees of the Board such remuneration; and

(b) pay to or in respect of employees of the Board any such allowances, fees, expenses and gratuities, as the Board may, with the consent of the Secretary of State, determine.

(3) Employment by the Board shall be included among the kinds of employment to which a scheme under section 1 of the Superannuation Act 1972 may apply.

5. The Board shall pay to the Minister for the Civil Service, at such times as he may direct, such sums as he may determine in respect of any increase attributable to paragraph 3(2) or 4(3) above in the sums payable out of money provided by Parliament under the Superannuation Act 1972.

House of Commons disqualification

6. In Part II of Schedule 1 to the House of Commons Disqualification Act 1975 (bodies of which all members are disqualified), there shall be inserted at the appropriate place the following entry-

"The Youth Justice Board for England and Wales".

Procedure

7.– (1) The arrangements for the procedure of the Board (including the quorum for meetings) shall be such as the Board may determine.

(2) The validity of any proceedings of the Board (or of any committee of the Board) shall not be affected by-

(a) any vacancy among the members of the Board or in the office of chairman of the Board; or
(b) any defect in the appointment of any person as a member of the Board or as chairman of the Board.

Annual reports and accounts

8.– (1) As soon as possible after the end of each financial year of the Board, the Board shall send to the Secretary of State a report on the discharge of their functions during that year.

(2) The Secretary of State shall lay before each House of Parliament, and cause to be published, a copy of every report sent to him under this paragraph.

9.– (1) The Board shall-

(a) keep proper accounts and proper records in relation to the accounts; and
(b) prepare a statement of accounts in respect of each financial year of the Board.

(2) The statement of accounts shall contain such information and shall be in such form as the Secretary of State may, with the consent of the Treasury, direct.

(3) The Board shall send a copy of the statement of accounts to the Secretary of State and to the Comptroller and Auditor General within such period after the end of the financial year to which the statement relates as the Secretary of State may direct.

(4) The Comptroller and Auditor General shall-

(a) examine, certify and report on the statement of accounts; and
(b) lay a copy of the statement of accounts and of his report before each House of Parliament.

10. For the purposes of this Schedule the Board's financial year shall be the period of twelve months ending with 31st March; but the first financial year of the Board shall be the period beginning with the date of establishment of the Board and ending with the first 31st March which falls at least six months after that date.

Expenses

11. The Secretary of State shall out of money provided by Parliament pay to the Board such sums towards their expenses as he may determine.

Schedule 2
This schedule, given effect by section 41(11), deals with membership of the Youth Justice Board, containing provisions concerning, amongst other matters, the appointment, membership, tenure of office, removal from the Board, and pay of members of the Board.

SCHEDULE 3

PROCEDURE WHERE PERSONS ARE SENT FOR TRIAL UNDER SECTION 51

Regulations

1. The Attorney General shall by regulations provide that, where a person is sent for trial under section 51 of this Act on any charge or charges, copies of the documents containing the evidence on which the charge or charges are based shall, on or before the relevant date-

(a) be served on that person; and
(b) be given to the Crown Court sitting at the place specified in the notice under subsection (7) of that section.

(2) In sub-paragraph (1) above "the relevant date" means the date prescribed by the regulations.

Applications for dismissal

2.– (1) A person who is sent for trial under section 51 of this Act on any charge or charges may, at any time-

(a) after he is served with copies of the documents containing the evidence on which the charge or charges are based; and

(b) before he is arraigned (and whether or not an indictment has been preferred against him),

apply orally or in writing to the Crown Court sitting at the place specified in the notice under subsection (7) of that section for the charge, or any of the charges, in the case to be dismissed.

(2) The judge shall dismiss a charge (and accordingly quash any count relating to it in any indictment preferred against the applicant) which is the subject of any such application if it appears to him that the evidence against the applicant would not be sufficient for a jury properly to convict him.

(3) No oral application may be made under sub-paragraph (1) above unless the applicant has given to the Crown Court sitting at the place in question written notice of his intention to make the application.

(4) Oral evidence may be given on such an application only with the leave of the judge or by his order; and the judge shall give leave or make an order only if it appears to him, having regard to any matters stated in the application for leave, that the interests of justice require him to do so.

(5) If the judge gives leave permitting, or makes an order requiring, a person to give oral evidence, but that person does not do so, the judge may disregard any document indicating the evidence that he might have given.

(6) If the charge, or any of the charges, against the applicant is dismissed-

(a) no further proceedings may be brought on the dismissed charge or charges except by means of the preferment of a voluntary bill of indictment; and

(b) unless the applicant is in custody otherwise than on the dismissed charge or charges, he shall be discharged.

(7) Crown Court Rules may make provision for the purposes of this paragraph and, without prejudice to the generality of this sub-paragraph, may make provision-

(a) as to the time or stage in the proceedings at which anything required to be done is to be done (unless the court grants leave to do it at some other time or stage);

(b) as to the contents and form of notices or other documents;

(c) as to the manner in which evidence is to be submitted; and

(d) as to persons to be served with notices or other material.

Reporting restrictions

3.– (1) Except as provided by this paragraph, it shall not be lawful-

- (a) to publish in Great Britain a written report of an application under paragraph 2(1) above; or
- (b) to include in a relevant programme for reception in Great Britain a report of such an application,

if (in either case) the report contains any matter other than that permitted by this paragraph.

(2) An order that sub-paragraph (1) above shall not apply to reports of an application under paragraph 2(1) above may be made by the judge dealing with the application.

(3) Where in the case of two or more accused one of them objects to the making of an order under sub-paragraph (2) above, the judge shall make the order if, and only if, he is satisfied, after hearing the representations of the accused, that it is in the interests of justice to do so.

(4) An order under sub-paragraph (2) above shall not apply to reports of proceedings under sub-paragraph (3) above, but any decision of the court to make or not to make such an order may be contained in reports published or included in a relevant programme before the time authorised by sub-paragraph (5) below.

(5) It shall not be unlawful under this paragraph to publish or include in a relevant programme a report of an application under paragraph 2(1) above containing any matter other than that permitted by sub-paragraph (8) below where the application is successful.

(6) Where-

- (a) two or more persons were jointly charged; and
- (b) applications under paragraph 2(1) above are made by more than one of them,

sub-paragraph (5) above shall have effect as if for the words "the application is" there were substituted the words "all the applications are".

(7) It shall not be unlawful under this paragraph to publish or include in a relevant programme a report of an unsuccessful application at the conclusion of the trial of the person charged, or of the last of the persons charged to be tried.

(8) The following matters may be contained in a report published or included in a relevant programme without an order under sub-paragraph (2) above before the time authorised by sub-paragraphs (5) and (6) above, that is to say-

- (a) the identity of the court and the name of the judge;
- (b) the names, ages, home addresses and occupations of the accused and witnesses;
- (c) the offence or offences, or a summary of them, with which the accused is or are charged;
- (d) the names of counsel and solicitors engaged in the proceedings;

(e) where the proceedings are adjourned, the date and place to which they are adjourned;

(f) the arrangements as to bail;

(g) whether legal aid was granted to the accused or any of the accused.

(9) The addresses that may be published or included in a relevant programme under sub-paragraph (8) above are addresses-

(a) at any relevant time; and

(b) at the time of their publication or inclusion in a relevant programme.

(10) If a report is published or included in a relevant programme in contravention of this paragraph, the following persons, that is to say-

(a) in the case of a publication of a written report as part of a newspaper or periodical, any proprietor, editor or publisher of the newspaper or periodical;

(b) in the case of a publication of a written report otherwise than as part of a newspaper or periodical, the person who publishes it;

(c) in the case of the inclusion of a report in a relevant programme, any body corporate which is engaged in providing the service in which the programme is included and any person having functions in relation to the programme corresponding to those of the editor of a newspaper;

shall be liable on summary conviction to a fine not exceeding level 5 on the standard scale.

(11) Proceedings for an offence under this paragraph shall not, in England and Wales, be instituted otherwise than by or with the consent of the Attorney General.

(12) Sub-paragraph (1) above shall be in addition to, and not in derogation from, the provisions of any other enactment with respect to the publication of reports of court proceedings.

(13) In this paragraph-

"publish", in relation to a report, means publish the report, either by itself or as part of a newspaper or periodical, for distribution to the public;
"relevant programme" means a programme included in a programme service (within the meaning of the Broadcasting Act 1990);
"relevant time" means a time when events giving rise to the charges to which the proceedings relate occurred.

Power of justice to take depositions etc.

4.– (1) Sub-paragraph (2) below applies where a justice of the peace for any commission area is satisfied that-

(a) any person in England and Wales ("the witness") is likely to be able to make on behalf of the prosecutor a written statement containing material evidence, or produce on behalf of the prosecutor a document or other exhibit likely to be material evidence, for the purposes of proceedings for an offence for which a person has been sent for trial under section 51 of this Act by a magistrates' court for that area; and

(b) the witness will not voluntarily make the statement or produce the document or other exhibit.

(2) In such a case the justice shall issue a summons directed to the witness requiring him to attend before a justice at the time and place appointed in the summons, and to have his evidence taken as a deposition or to produce the document or other exhibit.

(3) If a justice of the peace is satisfied by evidence on oath of the matters mentioned in sub-paragraph (1) above, and also that it is probable that a summons under sub-paragraph (2) above would not procure the result required by it, the justice may instead of issuing a summons issue a warrant to arrest the witness and to bring him before a justice at the time and place specified in the warrant.

(4) A summons may also be issued under sub-paragraph (2) above if the justice is satisfied that the witness is outside the British Islands, but no warrant may be issued under sub-paragraph (3) above unless the justice is satisfied by evidence on oath that the witness is in England and Wales.

(5) If-

(a) the witness fails to attend before a justice in answer to a summons under this paragraph;

(b) the justice is satisfied by evidence on oath that the witness is likely to be able to make a statement or produce a document or other exhibit as mentioned in sub-paragraph (1)(a) above;

(c) it is proved on oath, or in such other manner as may be prescribed, that he has been duly served with the summons and that a reasonable sum has been paid or tendered to him for costs and expenses; and

(d) it appears to the justice that there is no just excuse for the failure,

the justice may issue a warrant to arrest the witness and to bring him before a justice at the time and place specified in the warrant.

(6) Where-

(a) a summons is issued under sub-paragraph (2) above or a warrant is issued under sub-paragraph (3) or (5) above; and

(b) the summons or warrant is issued with a view to securing that the witness has his evidence taken as a deposition,

the time appointed in the summons or specified in the warrant shall be such as to enable the evidence to be taken as a deposition before the relevant date.

(7) If any person attending or brought before a justice in pursuance of this paragraph refuses without just excuse to have his evidence taken as a deposition, or to produce the document or other exhibit, the justice may do one or both of the following-

    (a) commit him to custody until the expiration of such period not exceeding one month as may be specified in the summons or warrant or until he sooner has his evidence taken as a deposition or produces the document or other exhibit;

    (b) impose on him a fine not exceeding £2,500.

(8) A fine imposed under sub-paragraph (7) above shall be deemed, for the purposes of any enactment, to be a sum adjudged to be paid by a conviction.

(9) If in pursuance of this paragraph a person has his evidence taken as a deposition, the clerk of the justice concerned shall as soon as is reasonably practicable send a copy of the deposition to the prosecutor and the Crown Court.

(10) If in pursuance of this paragraph a person produces an exhibit which is a document, the clerk of the justice concerned shall as soon as is reasonably practicable send a copy of the document to the prosecutor and the Crown Court.

(11) If in pursuance of this paragraph a person produces an exhibit which is not a document, the clerk of the justice concerned shall as soon as is reasonably practicable inform the prosecutor and the Crown Court of that fact and of the nature of the exhibit.

(12) In this paragraph-

"prescribed" means prescribed by rules made under section 144 of the 1980 Act;

"the relevant date" has the meaning given by paragraph 1(2) above.

Use of depositions as evidence

5.– (1) Subject to sub-paragraph (3) below, sub-paragraph (2) below applies where in pursuance of paragraph 4 above a person has his evidence taken as a deposition.

(2) Where this sub-paragraph applies the deposition may without further proof be read as evidence on the trial of the accused, whether for an offence for which he was sent for trial under section 51 of this Act or for any other offence arising out of the same transaction or set of circumstances.

(3) Sub-paragraph (2) above does not apply if-

    (a) it is proved that the deposition was not signed by the justice by whom it purports to have been signed;

    (b) the court of trial at its discretion orders that sub-paragraph (2) above shall not apply; or

    (c) a party to the proceedings objects to sub-paragraph (2) above applying.

(4) If a party to the proceedings objects to sub-paragraph (2) applying the court of trial may order that the objection shall have no effect if the court considers it to be in the interests of justice so to order.

Power of Crown Court to deal with summary offence

6.– (1) This paragraph applies where a magistrates' court has sent a person for trial under section 51 of this Act for offences which include a summary offence.

(2) If the person is convicted on the indictment, the Crown Court shall consider whether the summary offence is related to the offence that is triable only on indictment or, as the case may be, any of the offences that are so triable.

(3) If it considers that the summary offence is so related, the court shall state to the person the substance of the offence and ask him whether he pleads guilty or not guilty.

(4) If the person pleads guilty, the Crown Court shall convict him, but may deal with him in respect of the summary offence only in a manner in which a magistrates' court could have dealt with him.

(5) If he does not plead guilty, the powers of the Crown Court shall cease in respect of the summary offence except as provided by sub-paragraph (6) below.

(6) If the prosecution inform the court that they would not desire to submit evidence on the charge relating to the summary offence, the court shall dismiss it.

(7) The Crown Court shall inform the clerk of the magistrates' court of the outcome of any proceedings under this paragraph.

(8) If the summary offence is one to which section 40 of the Criminal Justice Act 1988 applies, the Crown Court may exercise in relation to the offence the power conferred by that section; but where the person is tried on indictment for such an offence, the functions of the Crown Court under this paragraph in relation to the offence shall cease.

(9) Where the Court of Appeal allows an appeal against conviction of an indictable-only offence which is related to a summary offence of which the appellant was convicted under this paragraph-

   (a) it shall set aside his conviction of the summary offence and give the clerk of the magistrates' court notice that it has done so; and
   (b) it may direct that no further proceedings in relation to the offence are to be undertaken;

and the proceedings before the Crown Court in relation to the offence shall thereafter be disregarded for all purposes.

(10) A notice under sub-paragraph (9) above shall include particulars of any direction given under paragraph (b) of that sub-paragraph in relation to the offence.

(11) The references to the clerk of the magistrates' court in this paragraph shall be construed in accordance with section 141 of the 1980 Act.

(12) An offence is related to another offence for the purposes of this paragraph if it arises out of circumstances which are the same as or connected with those giving rise to the other offence.

Procedure where no indictable-only offence remains

7.– (1) Subject to paragraph 13 below, this paragraph applies where-

    (a) a person has been sent for trial under section 51 of this Act but has not been arraigned; and

    (b) the person is charged on an indictment which (following amendment of the indictment, or as a result of an application under paragraph 2 above, or for any other reason) includes no offence that is triable only on indictment.

(2) Everything that the Crown Court is required to do under the following provisions of this paragraph must be done with the accused present in court.

(3) The court shall cause to be read to the accused each count of the indictment that charges an offence triable either way.

(4) The court shall then explain to the accused in ordinary language that, in relation to each of those offences, he may indicate whether (if it were to proceed to trial) he would plead guilty or not guilty, and that if he indicates that he would plead guilty the court must proceed as mentioned in sub-paragraph (6) below.

(5) The court shall then ask the accused whether (if the offence in question were to proceed to trial) he would plead guilty or not guilty.

(6) If the accused indicates that he would plead guilty the court shall proceed as if he had been arraigned on the count in question and had pleaded guilty.

(7) If the accused indicates that he would plead not guilty, or fails to indicate how he would plead, the court shall consider whether the offence is more suitable for summary trial or for trial on indictment.

(8) Subject to sub-paragraph (6) above, the following shall not for any purpose be taken to constitute the taking of a plea-

    (a) asking the accused under this paragraph whether (if the offence were to proceed to trial) he would plead guilty or not guilty;

    (b) an indication by the accused under this paragraph of how he would plead.

8.– (1) Subject to paragraph 13 below, this paragraph applies in a case where-

    (a) a person has been sent for trial under section 51 of this Act but has not been arraigned;

    (b) he is charged on an indictment which (following amendment of the indictment, or as a result of an application under paragraph 2 above, or for any other reason) includes no offence that is triable only on indictment;

    (c) he is represented by a legal representative;

    (d) the Crown Court considers that by reason of his disorderly conduct before the court it is not practicable for proceedings under paragraph 7 above to be conducted in his presence; and

    (e) the court considers that it should proceed in his absence.

(2) In such a case-

    (a) the court shall cause to be read to the representative each count of the indictment that charges an offence triable either way;

    (b) the court shall ask the representative whether (if the offence in question were to proceed to trial) the accused would plead guilty or not guilty;

    (c) if the representative indicates that the accused would plead guilty the court shall proceed as if the accused had been arraigned on the count in question and had pleaded guilty;

    (d) if the representative indicates that the accused would plead not guilty, or fails to indicate how the accused would plead, the court shall consider whether the offence is more suitable for summary trial or for trial on indictment.

(3) Subject to sub-paragraph (2)(c) above, the following shall not for any purpose be taken to constitute the taking of a plea-

    (a) asking the representative under this section whether (if the offence were to proceed to trial) the accused would plead guilty or not guilty;

    (b) an indication by the representative under this paragraph of how the accused would plead.

9.– (1) This paragraph applies where the Crown Court is required by paragraph 7(7) or 8(2)(d) above to consider the question whether an offence is more suitable for summary trial or for trial on indictment.

(2) Before considering the question, the court shall afford first the prosecutor and then the accused an opportunity to make representations as to which mode of trial would be more suitable.

(3) In considering the question, the court shall have regard to-

    (a) any representations made by the prosecutor or the accused;

    (b) the nature of the case;

    (c) whether the circumstances make the offence one of a serious character;

    (d) whether the punishment which a magistrates' court would have power to impose for it would be adequate; and

    (e) any other circumstances which appear to the court to make it more suitable for the offence to be dealt tried in one way rather than the other.

10.– (1) This paragraph applies (unless excluded by paragraph 15 below) where the Crown Court considers that an offence is more suitable for summary trial.

(2) The court shall explain to the accused in ordinary language-

    (a) that it appears to the court more suitable for him to be tried summarily for the offence, and that he can either consent to be so tried or, of he wishes, be tried by a jury; and

(b) that if he is tried summarily and is convicted by the magistrates' court, he may be committed for sentence to the Crown Court under section 38 of the 1980 Act if the convicting court is of such opinion as is mentioned in subsection (2) of that section.

(3) After explaining to the accused as provided by sub-paragraph (2) above the court shall ask him whether he wishes to be tried summarily or by a jury, and-

(a) if he indicates that he wishes to be tried summarily, shall remit him for trial to a magistrates' court acting for the place where he was sent to the Crown Court for trial;

(b) if he does not give such an indication, shall retain its functions in relation to the offence and proceed accordingly.

11. If the Crown Court considers that an offence is more suitable for trial on indictment, the court-

(a) shall tell the accused that it has decided that it is more suitable for him to be tried for the offence by a jury; and

(b) shall retain its functions in relation to the offence and proceed accordingly.

12.– (1) Where the prosecution is being carried on by the Attorney General, the Solicitor General or the Director of Public Prosecutions and he applies for an offence which may be tried on indictment to be so tried-

(a) sub-paragraphs (4) to (8) of paragraph 7, sub-paragraphs (2)(b) to (d) and (3) of paragraph 8 and paragraphs 9 to 11 above shall not apply; and

(b) the Crown Court shall retain its functions in relation to the offence and proceed accordingly.

(2) The power of the Director of Public Prosecutions under this paragraph to apply for an offence to be tried on indictment shall not be exercised except with the consent of the Attorney General.

13.– (1) This paragraph applies, in place of paragraphs 7 to 12 above, in the case of a child or young person who-

(a) has been sent for trial under section 51 of this Act but has not been arraigned; and

(b) is charged on an indictment which (following amendment of the indictment, or as a result of an application under paragraph 2 above, or for any other reason) includes no offence that is triable only on indictment.

(2) The Crown Court shall remit the child or young person for trial to a magistrates' court acting for the place where he was sent to the Crown Court for trial unless-

(a) he is charged with such an offence as is mentioned in subsection (2) of section 53 of the 1933 Act (punishment of certain grave crimes) and the Crown Court considers that if he is found guilty of the offence it ought to be possible to sentence him in pursuance of subsection (3) of that section; or

(b) he is charged jointly with an adult with an offence triable either way and the Crown Court considers it necessary in the interests of justice that they both be tried for the offence in the Crown Court.

(3) In sub-paragraph (2) above "adult" has the same meaning as in section 51 of this Act.

Procedure for determining whether offences of criminal damage etc. are summary offences

14.– (1) This paragraph applies where the Crown Court has to determine, for the purposes of this Schedule, whether an offence which is listed in the first column of Schedule 2 to the 1980 Act (offences for which the value involved is relevant to the mode of trial) is a summary offence.

(2) The court shall have regard to any representations made by the prosecutor or the accused.

(3) If it appears clear to the court that the value involved does not exceed the relevant sum, it shall treat the offence as a summary offence.

(4) If it appears clear to the court that the value involved exceeds the relevant sum, it shall treat the offence as an indictable offence.

(5) If it appears to the court for any reason not clear whether the value involved does or does not exceed the relevant sum, the court shall ask the accused whether he wishes the offence to be treated as a summary offence.

(6) Where sub-paragraph (5) above applies-

(a) if the accused indicates that he wishes the offence to be treated as a summary offence, the court shall so treat it;

(b) if the accused does not give such an indication, the court shall treat the offence as an indictable offence.

(7) In this paragraph "the value involved" and "the relevant sum" have the same meanings as in section 22 of the 1980 Act (certain offences triable either way to be tried summarily if value involved is small).

Power of Crown Court, with consent of legally-represented accused, to proceed in his absence

15.– (1) The Crown Court may proceed in the absence of the accused in accordance with such of the provisions of paragraphs 9 to 14 above as are applicable in the circumstances if-

(a) the accused is represented by a legal representative who signifies to the court the accused's consent to the proceedings in question being conducted in his absence; and

(b) the court is satisfied that there is good reason for proceeding in the absence of the accused.

(2) Sub-paragraph (1) above is subject to the following provisions of this paragraph which apply where the court exercises the power conferred by that sub-paragraph.

(3) If, where the court has considered as required by paragraph 7(7) or 8(2)(d) above, it appears to the court that an offence is more suitable for summary trial, paragraph 10 above shall not apply and-

(a) if the legal representative indicates that the accused wishes to be tried summarily, the court shall remit the accused for trial to a magistrates' court acting for the place where he was sent to the Crown Court for trial;

(b) if the legal representative does not give such an indication, the court shall retain its functions and proceed accordingly.

(4) If, where the court has considered as required by paragraph 7(7) or 8(2)(d) above, it appears to the court that an offence is more suitable for trial on indictment, paragraph 11 above shall apply with the omission of paragraph (a).

(5) Where paragraph 14 above applies and it appears to the court for any reason not clear whether the value involved does or does not exceed the relevant sum, sub-paragraphs (5) and (6) of that paragraph shall not apply and-

(a) the court shall ask the legal representative whether the accused wishes the offence to be treated as a summary offence;

(b) if the legal representative indicates that the accused wishes the offence to be treated as a summary offence, the court shall so treat it;

(c) if the legal representative does not give such an indication, the court shall treat the offence as an indictable offence.

Schedule 3

1.   This schedule:

1)   empowers the Attorney General to make regulations to deal with the procedure to be adopted when a case is sent for trial under section 51, which obviates the need for committal proceedings for indictable only offences;

2)   it creates a procedure similar to committal proceedings allowing applications before arraignment to a judge sitting in the Crown Court to dismiss charges, provided that written notice has been given to the Crown Court; (see paragraph 2)

3)   it contains restrictions on the reporting of applications before arraignment to the Crown Court for the dismissal of charges;

4) *it contains a procedure whereby an unwilling witness can be compelled to make a deposition before a justice of the peace on behalf of the prosecution which can be used at trial in the Crown Court without further proof; (see paragraphs 4 and 5)*

5) *it deals with the powers of the Crown Court to deal with summary offences sent with indictable only offences under section 51, and the procedure to be adopted; and the procedure to be adopted in determining mode of trial of such offences where no indictable only offence remains on the indictment;*

6) *it sets out the procedure for determining value, where value is relevant to the mode of trial such as in cases of criminal damage;*

7) *provides that when determining mode of trial, the Crown Court may, subject to legal representation and consent, proceed in the absence of the accused.*

2. *When a person is sent for trial under section 51 (without committal) he may apply before he is arraigned for any charge against him to be dismissed, provided he has given notice of the application. The judge is obliged to dismiss any charge and quash any count relating to it in an indictment, if it appears to him that the evidence would not be sufficient for a jury properly to convict him.*

3. *The judge has a discretion to hear oral evidence.*

4. *If a charge is dismissed, it may only then be brought by a voluntary bill of indictment.*

SCHEDULE 4

ENFORCEMENT ETC. OF DRUG TREATMENT AND TESTING ORDERS

Preliminary

1. Schedule 2 to the 1991 Act (enforcement etc. of community orders) shall be amended as follows.

Meaning of "relevant order" etc.

2.– (1) In sub-paragraph (1) of paragraph 1 (preliminary)-

   (a) after the words "a probation order," there shall be inserted the words "a drug treatment and testing order,"; and
   (b) in paragraph (a), for the words "probation or community service order" there shall be substituted the words "probation, community service or drug treatment and testing order".

(2) After sub-paragraph (3) of that paragraph there shall be inserted the following sub-paragraph-

"(4) In this Schedule, references to the court responsible for a drug treatment and testing order shall be construed in accordance with section 62(9) of the Crime and Disorder Act 1998."

Breach of requirements of order

3. In sub-paragraph (2) of paragraph 2 (issue of summons or warrant), for the words "before a magistrates' court acting for the petty sessions area concerned" there shall be substituted the following paragraphs-

"(a) except where the relevant order is a drug treatment and testing order, before a magistrates' court acting for the petty sessions area concerned;
(b) in the excepted case, before the court responsible for the order."

4. In sub-paragraph (1) of paragraph 4 (powers of Crown Court), after the word "Where" there shall be inserted the words "under paragraph 2 or".

5. In sub-paragraph (2) of paragraph 5 (exclusions), for the words "is required by a probation order to submit to treatment for his mental condition, or his dependency on drugs or alcohol," there shall be substituted the following paragraphs-

"(a) is required by a probation order to submit to treatment for his mental condition, or his dependency on or propensity to misuse drugs or alcohol; or
(b) is required by a drug treatment and testing order to submit to treatment for his dependency on or propensity to misuse drugs,".

Revocation of order

6.– (1) In sub-paragraph (1) of paragraph 7 (revocation of order by magistrates' court), after the words "the petty sessions area concerned" there shall be inserted the words "or, where the relevant order is a drug treatment and testing order for which a magistrates' court is responsible, to that court".

(2) In sub-paragraph (3) of that paragraph-

(a) after the words "a probation order" there shall be inserted the words "or drug treatment and testing order"; and
(b) after the word "supervision" there shall be inserted the words "or, as the case may be, treatment".

7.– (1) After sub-paragraph (1) of paragraph 8 (revocation of order by Crown Court) there shall be inserted the following sub-paragraph-

"(1A) This paragraph also applies where-

(a) a drug treatment and testing order made by the Crown Court is in force in respect of an offender; and

(b) the offender or the responsible officer applies to the Crown Court for the order to be revoked or for the offender to be dealt with in some other manner for the offence in respect of which the order was made."

(2) In sub-paragraph (3) of that paragraph-

(a) after the words "a probation order" there shall be inserted the words "or drug treatment and testing order"; and

(b) after the word "supervision" there shall be inserted the words "or, as the case may be, treatment".

8. In sub-paragraph (1) of paragraph 9 (revocation of order following custodial sentence), for paragraph (a) there shall be substituted the following paragraph-

"(a) an offender in respect of whom a relevant order is in force is convicted of an offence–
   (i) by a magistrates' court other than a magistrates' court acting for the petty sessions area concerned; or
   (ii) where the relevant order is a drug treatment and testing order, by a magistrates' court which is not responsible for the order; and".

"Amendment of order

9. In sub-paragraph (1) of paragraph 12 (amendment by reason of change of residence), after the words "a relevant order" there shall be inserted the words "(other than a drug treatment and testing order)".

10. After paragraph 14 there shall be inserted the following paragraph-

Amendment of drug treatment and testing order

14A.– (1) Without prejudice to the provisions of section 63(2), (7) and (9) of the Crime and Disorder Act 1998, the court responsible for a drug treatment and testing order may by order-

(a) vary or cancel any of the requirements or provisions of the order on an application by the responsible officer under sub-paragraph (2) or (3)(a) or (b) below; or

(b) amend the order on an application by that officer under sub-paragraph (3)(c) below.

(2) Where the treatment provider is of the opinion that the treatment or testing requirement of the order should be varied or cancelled-

(a) he shall make a report in writing to that effect to the responsible officer; and

(b) that officer shall apply to the court for the variation or cancellation of the requirement.

(3) Where the responsible officer is of the opinion-

    (a) that the treatment or testing requirement of the order should be so varied as to specify a different treatment provider;

    (b) that any other requirement of the order, or a provision of the order, should be varied or cancelled; or

    (c) that the order should be so amended as to provide for each subsequent review under section 63 of the Crime and Disorder Act 1998 to be made without a hearing instead of at a review hearing, or vice versa,

he shall apply to the court for the variation or cancellation of the requirement or provision or the amendment of the order.

(4) The court-

    (a) shall not amend the treatment or testing requirement unless the offender expresses his willingness to comply with the requirement as amended; and

    (b) shall not amend any provision of the order so as to reduce the treatment and testing period below the minimum specified in section 61(2) of the Crime and Disorder Act 1998 or to increase it above the maximum so specified.

(5) If the offender fails to express his willingness to comply with the treatment or testing requirement as proposed to be amended by the court, the court may-

    (a) revoke the order; and

    (b) deal with him, for the offence in respect of which the order was made, in any manner in which it could deal with him if he had just been convicted by the court of the offence.

(6) In dealing with the offender under sub-paragraph (5)(b) above, the court-

    (a) shall take into account the extent to which the offender has complied with the requirements of the order; and

    (b) may impose a custodial sentence notwithstanding anything in section 1(2) of this Act.

(7) Paragraph 6A above shall apply for the purposes of this paragraph as it applies for the purposes of paragraph 3 above, but as if for the words "paragraph 3(1)(d) above" there were substituted the words "paragraph 14A(5)(b) below".

(8) In this paragraph-

"review hearing" has the same meaning as in section 63 of the Crime and Disorder Act 1998;

"the treatment requirement" and

"the testing requirement" have the same meanings as in Chapter I of Part IV of that Act."

11. In paragraph 16 (order not to be amended pending appeal), after the words "paragraph 13 or 15 above" there shall be inserted the words "or, except with the consent of the offender, under paragraph 14A above".

12.– (1) In sub-paragraph (1) of paragraph 18 (notification of amended order), after the words "a relevant order" there shall be inserted the words "(other than a drug treatment and testing order)".

(2) After that sub-paragraph there shall be inserted the following sub-paragraph-

"(1A) On the making under this Part of this Schedule of an order amending a drug treatment and testing order, the clerk to the court shall forthwith give copies of the amending order to the responsible officer."

(3) In sub-paragraph (2) of that paragraph, after the words "sub-paragraph (1)" there shall be inserted the words "or (1A)".

> **Schedule 4**
> *This schedule amends schedule 2 to the Criminal Justice Act 1991 to cater for the enforcement, revocation and amendment of drug treatment and testing orders.*

SCHEDULE 5

ENFORCEMENT ETC. OF REPARATION AND ACTION PLAN ORDERS

Preliminary

1. In this Schedule-

"the appropriate court", in relation to a reparation order or action plan order, means the youth court acting for the petty sessions area for the time being named in the order in pursuance of section 67(9) or, as the case may be, section 69(9) of this Act;

"local authority accommodation" means accommodation provided by or on behalf of a local authority (within the meaning of the 1989 Act).

General power to discharge or vary order

2.– (1) If while a reparation order or action plan order is in force in respect of an offender it appears to the appropriate court, on the application of the responsible officer or the offender, that it is appropriate to make an order under this sub-paragraph, the court may make an order discharging the reparation order or action plan order or varying it-

(a) by cancelling any provision included in it; or

(b) by inserting in it (either in addition to or in substitution for any of its provisions) any provision that could have been included in the order if the court had then had power to make it and were exercising the power.

(2) Where an application under this paragraph for the discharge of a reparation order or action plan order is dismissed, no further application for its discharge shall be made under this paragraph by any person except with the consent of the appropriate court.

Failure to comply with order

3.– (1) This paragraph applies where a reparation order or action plan order is in force and it is proved to the satisfaction of the appropriate court, on the application of the responsible officer, that the offender has failed to comply with any requirement included in the order.

(2) The court-

(a) whether or not it also makes an order under paragraph 2 above, may order the offender to pay a fine of an amount not exceeding £1,000, or make an attendance centre order or curfew order in respect of him; or

(b) if the reparation order or action plan order was made by a youth court, may discharge the order and deal with him, for the offence in respect of which the order was made, in any manner in which he could have been dealt with for that offence by the court which made the order if the order had not been made; or

(c) if the reparation order or action plan order was made by the Crown Court, may commit him in custody or release him on bail until he can be brought or appear before the Crown Court.

(3) For the purposes of sub-paragraph (2)(b) and (c) above, a reparation order or action plan order made on appeal from a decision of a magistrates' court or the Crown Court shall be treated as if it had been made by a magistrates' court or the Crown Court, as the case may be.

(4) Where a court deals with an offender under sub-paragraph (2)(c) above, it shall send to the Crown Court a certificate signed by a justice of the peace giving-

(a) particulars of the offender's failure to comply with the requirement in question; and

(b) such other particulars of the case as may be desirable;

and a certificate purporting to be so signed shall be admissible as evidence of the failure before the Crown Court.

(5) Where-

(a) by virtue of sub-paragraph (2)(c) above the offender is brought or appears before the Crown Court; and

(b) it is proved to the satisfaction of the court that he has failed to comply with the requirement in question, that court may deal with him, for the offence in respect of which the order was made, in any manner in which it could have dealt with him for that offence if it had not made the order.

(6) Where the Crown Court deals with an offender under sub-paragraph (5) above, it shall revoke the reparation order or action plan order if it is still in force.

(7) A fine imposed under this paragraph shall be deemed, for the purposes of any enactment, to be a sum adjudged to be paid by a conviction.

(8) In dealing with an offender under this paragraph, a court shall take into account the extent to which he has complied with the requirements of the reparation order or action plan order.

Presence of offender in court, remands etc.

4.– (1) Where the responsible officer makes an application under paragraph 2 or 3 above to the appropriate court, he may bring the offender before the court and, subject to sub-paragraph (9) below, the court shall not make an order under that paragraph unless the offender is present before it.

(2) Without prejudice to any power to issue a summons or warrant apart from this sub-paragraph, the court to which an application under paragraph 2 or 3 above is made may issue a summons or warrant for the purpose of securing the attendance of the offender before it.

(3) Subsections (3) and (4) of section 55 of the 1980 Act (which among other things restrict the circumstances in which a warrant may be issued) shall apply with the necessary modifications to a warrant under sub-paragraph (2) above as they apply to a warrant under that section and as if in subsection (3) after the word "summons" there were inserted the words "cannot be served or".

(4) Where the offender is arrested in pursuance of a warrant under sub-paragraph (2) above and cannot be brought immediately before the appropriate court, the person in whose custody he is-

(a) may make arrangements for his detention in a place of safety for a period of not more than 72 hours from the time of the arrest (and it shall be lawful for him to be detained in pursuance of the arrangements); and

(b) shall within that period bring him before a youth court.

(5) Where an offender is, under sub-paragraph (4) above, brought before a youth court other than the appropriate court, that court may-

(a) direct that he be released forthwith; or

(b) subject to sub-paragraph (6) below, remand him to local authority accommodation.

(6) Where the offender is aged 18 or over at the time when he is brought before the court, he shall not be remanded to local authority accommodation but may instead be remanded-

(a) to a remand centre, if the court has been notified that such a centre is available for the reception of persons under this sub-paragraph; or

(b) to a prison, if it has not been so notified.

(7) Where an application is made to a court under paragraph 2(1) above, the court may remand (or further remand) the offender to local authority accommodation if-

(a) a warrant has been issued under sub-paragraph (2) of this paragraph for the purpose of securing the attendance of the offender before the court; or

(b) the court considers that remanding (or further remanding) him will enable information to be obtained which is likely to assist the court in deciding whether and, if so, how to exercise its powers under paragraph 2(1) above.

(8) A court remanding an offender to local authority accommodation under this paragraph shall designate, as the authority who are to receive him, the local authority for the area in which the offender resides or, where it appears to the court that he does not reside in the area of a local authority, the local authority-

(a) specified by the court; and

(b) in whose area the offence or an offence associated with it was committed.

(9) A court may make an order under paragraph 2 above in the absence of the offender if the effect of the order is one or more of the following, that is to say-

(a) discharging the reparation order or action plan order;

(b) cancelling a requirement included in the reparation order or action plan order;

(c) altering in the reparation order or action plan order the name of any area;

(d) changing the responsible officer.

Supplemental

5.– (1) The provisions of section 17 of the 1982 Act (attendance centre orders) shall apply for the purposes of paragraph 3(2)(a) above but as if-

(a) in subsection (1), for the words from "has power" to "probation order" there were substituted the words "considers it appropriate to make an attendance centre order in respect of any person in pursuance of paragraph 3(2) of Schedule 5 to the Crime and Disorder Act 1998"; and

(b) subsection (13) were omitted.

(2) Sections 18 and 19 of the 1982 Act (discharge and variation of attendance centre order and breach of attendance centre orders or attendance centre rules) shall also apply for the purposes of that paragraph but as if there were omitted-

(a) from subsection (4A) of section 18 and subsections (3) and (5) of section 19, the words ", for the offence in respect of which the order was made," and "for that offence"; and

(b) from subsection (4B) of section 18 and subsection (6) of section 19, the words "for an offence".

(3) The provisions of section 12 of the 1991 Act (curfew orders) shall apply for the purposes of paragraph 3(2)(a) above but as if-

  (a) in subsection (1), for the words from the beginning to "before which he is convicted" there were substituted the words "Where a court considers it appropriate to make a curfew order in respect of any person in pursuance of paragraph 3(2)(a) of Schedule 5 to the Crime and Disorder Act 1998, the court"; and

  (b) in subsection (8), for the words "on conviction" there were substituted the words "on the date on which his failure to comply with a requirement included in the reparation order or action plan order was proved to the court".

(4) Schedule 2 to the 1991 Act (enforcement etc. of community orders), so far as relating to curfew orders, shall also apply for the purposes of that paragraph but as if-

  (a) the power conferred on the magistrates' court by each of paragraphs 3(1)(d) and 7(2)(a)(ii) to deal with the offender for the offence in respect of which the order was made were a power to deal with the offender, for his failure to comply with a requirement included in the reparation order or action plan order, in any manner in which the appropriate court could deal with him for that failure to comply if it had just been proved to the satisfaction of that court;

  (b) the power conferred on the Crown Court by paragraph 4(1)(d) to deal with the offender for the offence in respect of which the order was made were a power to deal with the offender, for his failure to comply with such a requirement, in any manner in which that court could deal with him for that failure to comply if it had just been proved to its satisfaction;

  (c) the reference in paragraph 7(1)(b) to the offence in respect of which the order was made were a reference to the failure to comply in respect of which the curfew order was made; and

  (d) the power conferred on the Crown Court by paragraph 8(2)(b) to deal with the offender for the offence in respect of which the order was made were a power to deal with the offender, for his failure to comply with a requirement included in the reparation order or action plan order, in any manner in which the appropriate court (if that order was made by a magistrates' court) or the Crown Court (if that order was made by the Crown Court) could deal with him for that failure to comply if it had just been proved to the satisfaction of that court.

(5) For the purposes of the provisions mentioned in sub-paragraph (4)(a) and (d) above, as applied by that sub-paragraph, if the reparation order or action plan order is no longer in force the appropriate court's powers shall be determined on the assumption that it is still in force.

(6) If while an application to the appropriate court in pursuance of paragraph 2 or 3 above is pending the offender attains the age of 18 years, the court shall, subject to paragraph 4(6) above, deal with the application as if he had not attained that age.

(7) The offender may appeal to the Crown Court against-

(a) any order made under paragraphs 2 or 3 above, except an order made or which could have been made in his absence (by virtue of paragraph 4(9) above);

(b) the dismissal of an application under paragraph 2 above to discharge a reparation order or action plan order.

Schedule 5

This schedule:

1) empowers the youth court to discharge or vary reparation and action plan orders;

2) empowers the youth court to deal with a breach of an action plan order or a reparation order by:

–   imposing a fine up to £1,000;

–   dealing with the offender in any manner in which he could have been dealt with for the original offence; or by

–   sending the offender to the Crown Court to be dealt with if the reparation or action plan order was made by the Crown Court;

3) contains provisions dealing with the issue of summonses or warrants for the purpose of securing the attendance of offenders before the court.

SCHEDULE 6

DRUG TREATMENT AND TESTING ORDERS: AMENDMENT OF THE 1995 ACT

Amendments relating to combination of orders

1. In section 228(1) (probation orders), for the words "section 245D" there shall be substituted the words "sections 234J and 245D".

2.– (1) Section 232 (failure to comply with requirements of probation orders) shall be amended as follows.

(2) In subsection (3A)-

(a) for the words "a restriction of liberty order" there shall be substituted-
"(a) a restriction of liberty order; or
(b) a restriction of liberty order and a drug treatment and testing order,"; and

(b) at the end there shall be added the words "or, as the case may be, the restriction of liberty order and the drug treatment and testing order."

(3) After that subsection there shall be inserted the following subsection-

"(3B) Where the court intends to sentence an offender under subsection (2)(b) above and the offender is by virtue of section 234J of this Act subject to a drug treatment and testing order, it shall, before sentencing the offender under that paragraph, revoke the drug treatment and testing order."

3. For section 245D there shall be substituted the following section-

"**245D.**– (1) Subsection (3) applies where the court-

    (a) intends to make a restriction of liberty order under section 245A(1) of this Act; and

    (b) considers it expedient that the offender should also be subject to a probation order made under section 228(1) of this Act or to a drug treatment and testing order made under section 234B(2) of this Act or to both such orders.

(2) In deciding whether it is expedient to make a probation order or a drug treatment and testing order by virtue of paragraph (b) of subsection (1) above, the court shall-

    (a) have regard to the circumstances, including the nature of the offence and the character of the offender; and

    (b) obtain a report as to the circumstances and character of the offender.

(3) Where this subsection applies, the court, notwithstanding sections 228(1), 234B(2) and 245A(1) of this Act, may make a restriction of liberty order and either or both of a probation order and a drug treatment and testing order.

(4) Where the court makes a restriction of liberty order and a probation order by virtue of subsection (3) above, the clerk of the court shall send a copy of each order to-

    (a) any person responsible for monitoring the offender's compliance with the restriction of liberty order; and

    (b) the officer of the local authority who is to supervise the probationer.

(5) Where the court makes a restriction of liberty order and a drug treatment and testing order by virtue of subsection (3) above, the clerk of the court shall send a copy of each order to-

    (a) any person responsible for monitoring the offender's compliance with the restriction of liberty order;

    (b) the treatment provider, within the meaning of section 234C(1) of this Act; and

    (c) the officer of the local authority who is appointed or assigned to be the supervising officer under section 234C(6) of this Act.

(6) Where the court makes a restriction of liberty order, a probation order and a drug treatment and testing order the clerk of the court shall send copies of each of the orders to the persons mentioned-

    (a) in subsection (4) above;

    (b) in paragraph (b) of subsection (5) above; and

(c) in paragraph (c) of that subsection, if that person would not otherwise receive such copies.

(7) Where the offender by an act or omission fails to comply with a requirement of an order made by virtue of subsection (3) above-

(a) if the failure relates to a requirement contained in a probation order and is dealt with under section 232(2)(c) of this Act, the court may, in addition, exercise the powers conferred by section 234G(2)(b) of this Act in relation to a drug treatment and testing order to which the offender is subject by virtue of subsection (3) above and by section 245F(2) of this Act in relation to the restriction of liberty order;

(b) if the failure relates to a requirement contained in a drug treatment and testing order and is dealt with under section 234G(2)(b) of this Act, the court may, in addition, exercise the powers conferred by section 232(2)(c) of this Act in relation to a probation order to which the offender is subject by virtue of subsection (3) above and by section 245F(2)(b) of this Act in relation to the restriction of liberty order; and

(c) if the failure relates to a requirement contained in a restriction of liberty order and is dealt with under section 245F(2)(b) of this Act, the court may, in addition, exercise the powers conferred by section 232(2)(c) of this Act in relation to a probation order and by section 234G(2)(b) of this Act in relation to a drug treatment and testing order to which, in either case, the offender is subject by virtue of subsection (3) above.

(8) In any case to which this subsection applies, the offender may, without prejudice to subsection (7) above, be dealt with as respects that case under section 232(2) or, as the case may be, section 234G or section 245F(2) of this Act but he shall not be liable to be otherwise dealt with as respects that case.

(9) Subsection (8) applies in a case where-

(a) the offender by an act or omission fails to comply with both a requirement contained in a restriction of liberty order and in a probation order to which he is subject by virtue of subsection (3) above;

(b) the offender by an act or omission fails to comply with both a requirement contained in a restriction of liberty order and in a drug treatment and testing order to which he is subject by virtue of subsection (3) above;

(c) the offender by an act or omission fails to comply with a requirement contained in each of a restriction of liberty order, a probation order and a drug treatment and testing order to which he is subject by virtue of subsection (3) above."

4.– (1) Section 245G (disposal on revocation of restriction of liberty order) shall be amended as follows.

(2) In subsection (2), for the words from "by" to the end there shall be substituted the words "by virtue of section 245D(3) of this Act, subject to a probation order or a drug treatment and testing order or to both such orders, it shall, before disposing the offender under subsection (1) above-

(a) where he is subject to a probation order, discharge that order;
(b) where he is subject to a drug treatment and testing order, revoke that order; and
(c) where he is subject to both such orders, discharge the probation order and revoke the drug treatment and testing order."

(3) After subsection (2) there shall be added-

"(3) Where the court orders a probation order discharged or a drug treatment and testing order revoked the clerk of the court shall forthwith give copies of that order to the persons mentioned in subsection (4) or, as the case may be, (5) of section 245D of this Act.

(4) Where the court orders a probation order discharged and a drug treatment and testing order revoked, the clerk of the court shall forthwith give copies of that order to the persons mentioned in section 245D(6) of this Act."

Amendments relating to appeals

5. In section 106 (solemn appeals), in paragraph (d), after the words "probation order" there shall be inserted the words ", drug treatment and testing order".

6.– (1) Section 108 (right of appeal of prosecutor) shall be amended as follows.

(2) In subsection (1), after paragraph (d) there shall be inserted the following paragraph-

"(dd) a drug treatment and testing order;".

(3) In subsection (2)(b)(iii), for the word "or", where it first occurs, there shall be substituted the word "to".

7.– (1) Section 175 (appeals in summary cases) shall be amended as follows.

(2) In subsection (2)(c), after the words "probation order" there shall be inserted the words ", drug treatment and testing order".

(3) In subsection (4), after paragraph (d) there shall be inserted the following paragraph-

"(dd) a drug treatment and testing order;".

(4) In subsection (4A)(b)(iii), for the word "or", where it first occurs, there shall be substituted the word "to".

> **Schedule 6**
> *This schedule contains consequential amendments to the Criminal Procedure (Scotland) Act 1995 to deal with drug treatment and testing orders.*

SCHEDULE 7

PRE-CONSOLIDATION AMENDMENTS: POWERS OF CRIMINAL COURTS

Children and Young Persons Act 1933 (c.12)

1.– (1) In subsection (1A) of section 55 of the 1933 Act (power to order parent or guardian to pay fine etc.), in paragraph (a), for the words "section 15(2A)" there shall be substituted the words "section 15(3)(a)".

(2) For paragraph (b) of that subsection there shall be substituted the following paragraphs-

"(b) a court would impose a fine on a child or young person under section 19(3) of the Criminal Justice Act 1982 (breach of attendance centre order or attendance centre rules); or

(bb) a court would impose a fine on a child or young person under paragraph 3(1)(a) or 4(1)(a) of Schedule 2 to the Criminal Justice Act 1991 (breach of requirement of a relevant order (within the meaning given by that Schedule) or of a combination order);".

(3) After subsection (5) of that section there shall be added the following subsection-

"(6) In relation to any other child or young person, references in this section to his parent shall be construed in accordance with section 1 of the Family Law Reform Act 1987."

Criminal Justice Act 1967 (c.80)

2.– (1) In subsection (1)(b)(i) of section 56 of the Criminal Justice Act 1967 (committal for sentence for offences tried summarily), for the words from "section 93" to "34 to 36" there shall be substituted the words "section 34, 35 or 36".

(2) In subsection (2) of that section, for the words from "section 8(6)" to the end there shall be substituted the words "section 1B(5) of the Powers of Criminal Courts Act 1973 (conditionally discharged person convicted of further offence) and section 24(2) of that Act (offender convicted during operational period of suspended sentence)."

(3) Subsection (3) of that section shall cease to have effect.

(4) For subsection (5) of that section there shall be substituted the following subsections-

"(5) Where under subsection (1) above a magistrates' court commits a person to be dealt with by the Crown Court in respect of an offence, the Crown Court may after inquiring into the circumstances of the case deal with him in any way in which the magistrates' court could deal with him if it had just convicted him of the offence.

(5A) Subsection (5) above does not apply where under subsection (1) above a magistrates' court commits a person to be dealt with by the Crown Court in respect of a suspended sentence, but in such a case the powers under section 23 of the Powers of Criminal Courts Act 1973 (power of court to deal with suspended sentence) shall be exercisable by the Crown Court.

(5B) Without prejudice to subsections (5) and (5A) above, where under subsection (1) above or any enactment to which this section applies a magistrates' court commits a person to be dealt with by the Crown Court, any duty or power which, apart from this subsection, would fall to be discharged or exercised by the magistrates' court shall not be discharged or exercised by that court but shall instead be discharged or may instead be exercised by the Crown Court.

(5C) Where under subsection (1) above a magistrates' court commits a person to be dealt with by the Crown Court in respect of an offence triable only on indictment in the case of an adult (being an offence which was tried summarily because of the offender's being under 18 years of age), the Crown Court's powers under subsection (5) above in respect of the offender after he attains the age of 18 years shall be powers to do either or both of the following-

(a) to impose a fine not exceeding £5,000;
(b) to deal with the offender in respect of the offence in any way in which the magistrates' court could deal with him if it had just convicted him of an offence punishable with imprisonment for a term not exceeding six months.

(5D) For the purposes of this section the age of an offender shall be deemed to be that which it appears to the court to be after considering any available evidence."

(5) Subsection (13) of that section shall cease to have effect.

Children and Young Persons Act 1969 (c.54)

3. After subsection (8) of section 7 of the 1969 Act (alterations in treatment of young offenders etc.) there shall be added the following subsection-

"(9) The reference in subsection (8) above to a person's parent shall be construed in accordance with section 1 of the Family Law Reform Act 1987 (and not in accordance with section 70(1A) of this Act)."

4. In section 12 of the 1969 Act (power to include requirements in supervision orders), after subsection (3) there shall be added the following subsection-

"(4) Directions given by the supervisor by virtue of subsection (2)(b) or (c) above shall, as far as practicable, be such as to avoid-

(a) any conflict with the offender's religious beliefs or with the requirements of any other community order (within the meaning of Part I of the Criminal Justice Act 1991) to which he may be subject; and

(b) any interference with the times, if any, at which he normally works or attends school or any other educational establishment."

5.– (1) In subsection (1) of section 12B of the 1969 Act (power to include in supervision order requirements as to mental treatment)-

(a) for the words "medical practitioner", in the first place where they occur, there shall be substituted the words "registered medical practitioner";

(b) for the words "his detention in pursuance of a hospital order under Part III" there shall be substituted the words "the making of a hospital order or guardianship order within the meaning";

(c) in paragraph (a), for the words "fully registered medical practitioner" there shall be substituted the words "registered medical practitioner";

(d) after that paragraph there shall be inserted the following paragraph-
   "(aa) treatment by or under the direction of a chartered psychologist specified in the order;";

(e) in paragraph (b), for the words "a place" there shall be substituted the words "an institution or place"; and

(f) in paragraph (c), for the words "the said Act of 1983" there shall be substituted the words "the Mental Health Act 1983".

(2) After that subsection there shall be inserted the following subsection-

"(1A) In subsection (1) of this section "registered medical practitioner" means a fully registered person within the meaning of the Medical Act 1983 and "chartered psychologist" means a person for the time being listed in the British Psychological Society's Register of Chartered Psychologists."

(3) After subsection (2) of that section there shall be added the following subsection-

"(3) Subsections (2) and (3) of section 54 of the (1983 c.20.)Mental Health Act 1983 shall have effect with respect to proof for the purposes of subsection (1) above of a supervised person's mental condition as they have effect with respect to proof of an offender's mental condition for the purposes of section 37(2)(a) of that Act."

6. In section 16(11) of the 1969 Act (provisions supplementary to section 15), the words "seventeen or" shall cease to have effect.

7.– (1) In subsection (1)(a) of section 16A of the 1969 Act (application of sections 17 to 19 of Criminal Justice Act 1982), for the words "section 15(2A) or (4)" there shall be substituted the words "section 15(3)(a)".

(2) In subsection (2)(b) of that section-

  (a) in sub-paragraph (i), after the word "from" there shall be inserted the words "subsection (4A) of section 18 and"; and
  (b) in sub-paragraph (ii), for the words "subsection (6)" there shall be substituted the words "subsection (4B) of section 18 and subsection (6) of section 19".

8. In section 34(1)(c) of the 1969 Act (power of Secretary of State to amend references to young person), the words "7(7), 7(8)," shall cease to have effect.

9. Section 69(5) of the 1969 Act (power to include in commencement order certain consequential provisions) shall cease to have effect.

10. In section 70 of the 1969 Act (interpretation), for subsections (1A) and (1B) there shall be substituted the following subsections-

"(1A) In the case of a child or young person-

  (a) whose father and mother were not married to each other at the time of his birth, and
  (b) with respect to whom a residence order is in force in favour of the father,

any reference in this Act to the parent of the child or young person includes (unless the contrary intention appears) a reference to the father.

(1B) In subsection (1A) of this section, the reference to a child or young person whose father and mother were not married to each other at the time of his birth shall be construed in accordance with section 1 of the Family Law Reform Act 1987 and "residence order" has the meaning given by section 8(1) of the Children Act 1989."

11. In Schedule 6 to the 1969 Act (repeals), the entries relating to sections 55, 56(1) and 59(1) of the 1933 Act (which entries have never come into force or are spent) are hereby repealed.

Criminal Justice Act 1972 (c.71)

12. Section 49 of the Criminal Justice Act 1972 (community service order in lieu of warrant of commitment for failure to pay fine etc.) shall cease to have effect.

Powers of Criminal Courts Act 1973 (c.62)

13.– (1) In subsection (6) of section 1 of the 1973 Act (deferment of sentence), for the words "13(1), (2) and (5)" there shall be substituted the words "13(1) to (3) and (5)".

(2) In subsection (8) of that section, for paragraph (a) there shall be substituted the following paragraph-

"(a) is power to deal with him, in respect of the offence for which passing of sentence has been deferred, in any way in which the court which deferred passing sentence could have dealt with him; and".

14.– (1) In subsection (9) of section 1B of the 1973 Act (commission of further offence by person conditionally discharged), for the words from "those which" to the end there shall be substituted the words "powers to do either or both of the following-

(a) to impose a fine not exceeding £5,000 for the offence in respect of which the order was made;

(b) to deal with the offender for that offence in any way in which a magistrates' court could deal with him if it had just convicted him of an offence punishable with imprisonment for a term not exceeding six months."

(2) Subsection (10) of that section (which is superseded by provision inserted by this Schedule in section 57 of the 1973 Act) shall cease to have effect.

15. In section 1C(1) of the 1973 Act (effect of absolute or conditional discharge)-

(a) in paragraph (a), for the words "the following provisions" there shall be substituted the words "section 1B"; and

(b) paragraph (b) and the word "and" immediately preceding it shall cease to have effect.

16. In section 2(1) of the 1973 Act (probation orders), the words from "For the purposes" to "available evidence" (which are superseded by provision inserted by this Schedule in section 57 of the 1973 Act) shall cease to have effect.

17. Section 11 of the 1973 Act (which is superseded by the paragraph 8A inserted by this Schedule in Schedule 2 to the 1991 Act) shall cease to have effect.

18.– (1) For subsection (2) of section 12 of the 1973 Act (supplementary provision as to probation and discharge) there shall be substituted the following subsection-

"(2) Where an order for conditional discharge has been made on appeal, for the purposes of this Act it shall be deemed-

(a) if it was made on an appeal brought from a magistrates' court, to have been made by that magistrates' court;

(b) if it was made on an appeal brought from the Crown Court or from the criminal division of the Court of Appeal, to have been made by the Crown Court."

(2) In subsection (3) of that section, for the words from "any question whether a probationer" to "period of conditional discharge," there shall be substituted the words "any question whether any person in whose case an order for conditional discharge has been made has been convicted of an offence committed during the period of conditional discharge".

(3) For subsection (4) of that section there shall be substituted the following subsection-

"(4) Nothing in section 1A of this Act shall be construed as preventing a court, on discharging an offender absolutely or conditionally in respect of any offence, from making an order for costs against the offender or imposing any disqualification on him or from making in respect of the offence an order under section 35 or 43 of this Act or section 28 of the Theft Act 1968."

19.– (1) In subsection (1) of section 14 of the 1973 Act (community service orders in respect of convicted persons), after the word "imprisonment", in the first place where it occurs, there shall be inserted the words "(not being an offence the sentence for which is fixed by law or falls to be imposed under section 2(2), 3(2) or 4(2) of the Crime (Sentences) Act 1997)".

(2) In that subsection, after the words "young offenders" there shall be inserted the words "; and for the purposes of this subsection a sentence falls to be imposed under section 2(2), 3(2) or 4(2) of the (1997 c.43.)Crime (Sentences) Act 1997 if it is required by that provision and the court is not of the opinion there mentioned".

(3) In subsection (7) of that section, for the words "paragraph (b)(i) or (ii)" there shall be substituted the words "paragraph (b)".

(4) Subsection (8) of that section shall cease to have effect.

20. For subsection (3) of section 15 of the 1973 Act (obligations of person subject to community service order) there shall be substituted the following subsection-

"(3) The instructions given by the relevant officer under this section shall, as far as practicable, be such as to avoid-

(a) any conflict with the offender's religious beliefs or with the requirements of any other community order (within the meaning of Part I of the Criminal Justice Act 1991) to which he may be subject; and

(b) any interference with the times, if any, at which he normally works or attends school or any other educational establishment."

21. In section 21(3)(b) of the 1973 Act (meaning of "sentence of imprisonment" for purposes of restriction on imposing sentences of imprisonment on persons not legally represented), after the words "contempt of court" there shall be inserted the words "or any kindred offence".

22. In subsection (3) of section 22 of the 1973 Act (suspended sentences of imprisonment)-

(a) for the words "make a probation order in his case in respect of another offence" there shall be substituted the words "impose a community sentence in his case in respect of that offence or any other offence"; and

(b) at the end there shall be inserted the words "; and in this subsection "community sentence" has the same meaning as in Part I of the Criminal Justice Act 1991."

23.– (1) In section 31 of the 1973 Act (powers etc. of Crown Court in relation to fines and forfeited recognizances), the following provisions shall cease to have effect-

(a) in subsection (3A), the words "Subject to subsections (3B) and (3C) below,";
(b) subsections (3B) and (3C); and
(c) in subsection (4), the words "4 or".

(2) In subsection (6) of that section-

(a) the words "about committal by a magistrates' court to the Crown Court" shall cease to have effect; and
(b) after the words "dealt with him" there shall be inserted the words "or could deal with him".

(3) In subsection (8) of that section, for the words "(2) to (3C)" there shall be substituted the words "(2) to (3A)".

24.– (1) In subsection (2) of section 32 of the 1973 Act (enforcement etc. of fines imposed and recognizances forfeited by Crown Court), for the words "section 85(1)" there shall be substituted the words "section 85(2)".

(2) In subsection (3) of that section, after the words "to the Crown Court" there shall be inserted the words "(except the reference in subsection (1)(b) above)".

(3) For subsection (4) of that section there shall be substituted the following subsection-

"(4) A magistrates' court shall not, under section 85(1) or 120 of the Magistrates' Courts Act 1980 as applied by subsection (1) above, remit the whole or any part of a fine imposed by, or sum due under a recognizance forfeited by-

(a) the Crown Court,
(b) the criminal division of the Court of Appeal, or
(c) the House of Lords on appeal from that division,

without the consent of the Crown Court."

(4) Subsection (5) of that section shall cease to have effect.

25. In section 46 of the 1973 Act (reports of probation officers), after subsection (2) there shall be added the following subsection-

"(3) For the purposes of this section-

(a) references to an offender's parent shall be construed in accordance with section 1 of the Family Law Reform Act 1987; and
(b) "guardian" has the same meaning as in the Children and Young Persons Act 1933."

26.– (1) For subsection (5) of section 57 of the 1973 Act (interpretation) there shall be substituted the following subsection-

"(5) Where a compensation order or supervision order has been made on appeal, for the purposes of this Act (except section 26(5)) it shall be deemed-

(a) if it was made on an appeal brought from a magistrates' court, to have been made by that magistrates' court;

(b) if it was made on an appeal brought from the Crown Court or from the criminal division of the Court of Appeal, to have been made by the Crown Court."

(2) After subsection (6) of that section there shall be added the following subsection-

"(7) For the purposes of any provision of this Act which requires the determination of the age of a person by the court, his age shall be deemed to be that which it appears to the court to be after considering any available evidence."

27.– (1) In paragraph 2 of Schedule 1A to the 1973 Act (additional requirements in probation orders), for sub-paragraph (7) there shall be substituted the following sub-paragraph-

"(7) Instructions given by a probation officer under sub-paragraph (4) or (6) above shall, as far as practicable, be such as to avoid-

(a) any conflict with the offender's religious beliefs or with the requirements of any other community order (within the meaning of Part I of the Criminal Justice Act 1991) to which he may be subject; and

(b) any interference with the times, if any, at which he normally works or attends school or any other educational establishment."

(2) In paragraph 3 of that Schedule, for sub-paragraph (4) there shall be substituted the following sub-paragraph-

"(4) Instructions given by a probation officer under sub-paragraph (3) above shall, as far as practicable, be such as to avoid-

(a) any conflict with the offender's religious beliefs or with the requirements of any other community order (within the meaning of Part I of the (1991 c.53.)Criminal Justice Act 1991) to which he may be subject; and

(b) any interference with the times, if any, at which he normally works or attends school or any other educational establishment."

(3) In paragraph 5 of that Schedule, for the words "duly qualified medical practitioner", wherever they occur, there shall be substituted the words "registered medical practitioner".

(4) In that paragraph (both as amended by subsection (3) of section 38 of the 1997 Act and so far as that paragraph has effect without that amendment), in sub-paragraph (4), after the words "have been" there shall be inserted the words "or can be".

(5) In sub-paragraph (10) of that paragraph, before the definition of "chartered psychologist" there shall be inserted the following definition-

""registered medical practitioner" means a fully registered person within the meaning of the Medical Act 1983;".

(6) In paragraph 6 of that Schedule (both as amended by subsection (4) of section 38 of the 1997 Act and so far as that paragraph has effect without that amendment), in sub-paragraph (4), after the words "have been" there shall be inserted the words "or can be".

(7) Sub-paragraph (7) of that paragraph shall cease to have effect.

Magistrates' Courts Act 1980 (c.43)

28. In section 30(2)(a) of the 1980 Act (remand for medical examination), for the words "duly qualified medical practitioner" there shall be substituted the words "registered medical practitioner".

29.– (1) In subsection (2) of section 38 of the 1980 Act (committal for sentence on summary trial of offence triable either way), the words ", in accordance with section 56 of the Criminal Justice Act 1967," shall cease to have effect.

(2) After that subsection there shall be inserted the following subsection-

"(2A) Where the court commits a person under subsection (2) above, section 56 of the Criminal Justice Act 1967 (which enables a magistrates' court, where it commits a person under this section in respect of an offence, also to commit him to the Crown Court to be dealt with in respect of certain other offences) shall apply accordingly."

30.– (1) In subsection (2) of section 38A of the 1980 Act (committal for sentence on indication of guilty plea to offence triable either way), the words ", in accordance with section 56 of the Criminal Justice Act 1967," shall cease to have effect.

(2) In subsection (5) of that section, for the words "the court might have dealt with him" there shall be substituted the words "the magistrates' court could deal with him if it had just convicted him of the offence".

(3) After that subsection there shall be inserted the following subsection-

"(5A) Where the court commits a person under subsection (2) above, section 56 of the (1967 c.80.)Criminal Justice Act 1967 (which enables a magistrates' court, where it commits a person under this section in respect of an offence, also to commit him to the Crown Court to be dealt with in respect of certain other offences) shall apply accordingly."

31. In section 39(6)(b) of the 1980 Act (cases where magistrates' court may remit offender to another such court for sentence), for the words "section 34 or 36" there shall be substituted the words "section 34, 35 or 36".

32. In section 85(1)(a) of the 1980 Act (power to remit fine), for the words "section 74" there shall be substituted the words "section 77".

Criminal Justice Act 1982 (c.48)

33. In section 3(1) of the 1982 Act (restriction on imposing custodial sentences on persons under 21 not legally represented)-

(a) in paragraph (a), the words "under section 1A above" shall cease to have effect;

(b) in paragraph (c), for the words "section 8(2)" there shall be substituted the words "section 8(1) or (2)"; and

(c) in paragraph (d), for the words "section 53(2)" there shall be substituted the words "section 53(1) or (3)".

34.– (1) In subsection (3) of section 13 of the 1982 Act (conversion of sentence of detention in a young offender institution to sentence of imprisonment), for the words "section 15 below" there shall be substituted the words "section 65 of the Criminal Justice Act 1991 (supervision of young offenders after release)".

(2) In subsection (6) of that section, for the words "section 8(2)" there shall be substituted the words "section 8(1) or (2)".

35. In subsection (2) of section 16 of the 1982 Act (meaning of "attendance centre"), for the words from "of orders made" to the end there shall be substituted the words "of orders made under section 17 below."

36.– (1) In subsection (1) of section 17 of the 1982 Act (attendance centre orders), for the words "Subject to subsections (3) and (4) below," there shall be substituted the words "Where a person under 21 years of age is convicted by or before a court of an offence punishable with imprisonment (not being an offence the sentence for which is fixed by law or falls to be imposed under section 2(2), 3(2) or 4(2) of the Crime (Sentences) Act 1997), or".

(2) In that subsection, for paragraph (a) there shall be substituted the following paragraph-

"(a) would have power, but for section 1 above, to commit a person under 21 years of age to prison in default of payment of any sum of money or for failing to do or abstain from doing anything required to be done or left undone, or".

(3) In that subsection, in paragraph (b), for the words "any such person" there shall be substituted the words "a person under 21 years of age" and after that paragraph there shall be inserted the following paragraph-

"(bb) has power to deal with a person under 16 years of age under that Part of that Schedule for failure to comply with any of the requirements of a curfew order, or".

(4) After that subsection there shall be inserted the following subsection-

"(1A) For the purposes of subsection (1) above-

(a) the reference to an offence punishable with imprisonment shall be construed without regard to any prohibition or restriction imposed by or under any enactment on the imprisonment of young offenders; and

(b) a sentence falls to be imposed under section 2(2), 3(2) or 4(2) of the (1997 c.43.)Crime (Sentences) Act 1997 if it is required by that provision and the court is not of the opinion there mentioned."

(5) For subsection (8) of that section there shall be substituted the following subsection-

"(8) The times at which an offender is required to attend at an attendance centre shall, as far as practicable, be such as to avoid-

(a) any conflict with the offender's religious beliefs or with the requirements of any other community order (within the meaning of Part I of the Criminal Justice Act 1991) to which he may be subject; and

(b) any interference with the times, if any, at which he normally works or attends school or any other educational establishment."

37.– (1) In section 18 of the 1982 Act (discharge and variation of attendance centre orders), for subsection (4A) there shall be substituted the following subsections-

"(4A) Any power conferred by this section-

(a) on a magistrates' court to discharge an attendance centre order made by such a court, or

(b) on the Crown Court to discharge an attendance centre order made by the Crown Court,

includes power to deal with the offender, for the offence in respect of which the order was made, in any manner in which he could have been dealt with for that offence by the court which made the order if the order had not been made.

(4B)   A person sentenced by a magistrates' court under subsection (4A) above for an offence may appeal to the Crown Court against the sentence."

(2) Subsection (7) of that section shall cease to have effect.

(3) In that section, after subsection (9) there shall be added the following subsections-

"(10) Where an offender has been ordered to attend at an attendance centre in default of the payment of a sum of money or for such a failure or abstention as is mentioned in section 17(1)(a) above, subsection (4A) above shall have effect in relation to the order as if the words ", for the offence in respect of which the order was made," and "for that offence" were omitted.

(11) Where an attendance centre order has been made on appeal, for the purposes of this section it shall be deemed-

(a) if it was made on an appeal brought from a magistrates' court, to have been made by that magistrates' court;

(b) if it was made on an appeal brought from the Crown Court or from the criminal division of the Court of Appeal, to have been made by the Crown Court;

and subsection (4A) above shall have effect in relation to an attendance centre order made on appeal as if the words "if the order had not been made" were omitted."

38.– (1) In subsection (1) of section 19 of the 1982 Act (breaches of attendance centre orders or attendance centre rules), for the words "has been made" there shall be substituted the words "is in force".

(2) In subsection (5) of that section, after the word "failed" there shall be inserted the words "without reasonable excuse".

(3) After subsection (7) of that section there shall be added the following subsections-

"(8) Where an offender has been ordered to attend at an attendance centre in default of the payment of a sum of money or for such a failure or abstention as is mentioned in section 17(1)(a) above, subsections (3) and (5) above shall have effect in relation to the order as if the words ", for the offence in respect of which the order was made," and "for that offence" were omitted.

(9) Where an attendance centre order has been made on appeal, for the purposes of this section it shall be deemed-

(a) if it was made on an appeal brought from a magistrates' court, to have been made by that magistrates' court;

(b) if it was made on an appeal brought from the Crown Court or from the criminal division of the Court of Appeal, to have been made by the Crown Court;

and, in relation to an attendance centre order made on appeal, subsection (3)(a) above shall have effect as if the words "if the order had not been made" were omitted and subsection (5) above shall have effect as if the words "if it had not made the order" were omitted."

Criminal Justice Act 1988 (c.33)

39. Paragraph 40 of Schedule 15 to the Criminal Justice Act 1988 (minor and consequential amendments) shall cease to have effect.

Criminal Justice Act 1991 (c.53)

40. In section 11 of the 1991 Act (orders combining probation and community service), after subsection (1) there shall be inserted the following subsection-

"(1A) The reference in subsection (1) above to an offence punishable with imprisonment shall be construed without regard to any prohibition or restriction imposed by or under any enactment on the imprisonment of young offenders."

41.– (1) In subsection (5)(c) of section 12 of the 1991 Act (curfew orders), for the words "supervising officer" there shall be substituted the words "responsible officer".

(2) After subsection (6A) of that section there shall be inserted the following subsection-

"(6B) The court by which a curfew order is made shall give a copy of the order to the offender and to the person responsible for monitoring the offender's whereabouts during the curfew periods specified in the order."

(3) After subsection (7) of that section there shall be added the following subsection-

"(8) References in this section to the offender's being under the age of sixteen years are references to his being under that age on conviction."

42. In section 31(1) of the 1991 Act (interpretation of Part I), in paragraph (b) of the definition of "custodial sentence", for the words "section 53" there shall be substituted the words "section 53(3)".

43.– (1) In subsection (3) of section 40 of the 1991 Act (convictions during currency of original sentences), for the words from "for sentence" to the end there shall be substituted the words "to be dealt with under subsection (3A) below".

(2) After that subsection there shall be inserted the following subsections-

"(3A) Where a person is committed to the Crown Court under subsection (3) above, the Crown Court may order him to be returned to prison for the whole or any part of the period which-

(a) begins with the date of the order; and
(b) is equal in length to the period between the date on which the new offence was committed and the date mentioned in subsection (1) above.

(3B) Subsection (3)(b) above shall not be taken to confer on the magistrates' court a power to commit the person to the Crown Court for sentence for the new offence, but this is without prejudice to any such power conferred on the magistrates' court by any other enactment."

(3) In subsection (4) of that section, for the words "subsection (2)" there shall be substituted the words "subsection (2) or (3A)".

44. In each of subsections (3)(b) and (4)(a) of section 57 of the 1991 Act (responsibility of parent or guardian for financial penalties), for the words "section 35(4)(a)" there shall be substituted the words "section 35(4)".

45. In section 58 of the 1991 Act (binding over of parent or guardian), after subsection (8) there shall be added the following subsection-

"(9) For the purposes of this section-

(a) "guardian" has the same meaning as in the 1933 Act; and
(b) taking "care" of a person includes giving him protection and guidance and "control" includes discipline."

46.– (1) In paragraph 1 of Schedule 2 to the 1991 Act (enforcement etc. of community orders), after sub-paragraph (4) there shall be added the following sub-paragraph-

"(5) Where a probation order, community service order, combination order or curfew order has been made on appeal, for the purposes of this Schedule it shall be deemed-

(a) if it was made on an appeal brought from a magistrates' court, to have been made by a magistrates' court;

(b) if it was made on an appeal brought from the Crown Court or from the criminal division of the Court of Appeal, to have been made by the Crown Court."

(2) In each of paragraphs 3(1) and 4(1) of that Schedule, for paragraph (c) there shall be substituted the following paragraph-

"(c) where-
(i) the relevant order is a probation order and the offender is under the age of twenty-one years, or
(ii) the relevant order is a curfew order and the offender is under the age of sixteen years,

and the court has been notified as required by subsection (1) of section 17 of the 1982 Act, it may (subject to paragraph 6(6) below) make in respect of him an order under that section (attendance centre orders); or".

(3) In paragraph 4(1) of that Schedule-

(a) after the word "failed" there shall be inserted the words "without reasonable excuse"; and

(b) in paragraph (d), for the words "by or before the court" there shall be substituted the words "before the Crown Court".

(4) In paragraph 6 of that Schedule, in sub-paragraph (1), for the words "or (b)" there shall be substituted the words ", (b) or (c)".

(5) After sub-paragraph (3) of that paragraph there shall be inserted the following sub-paragraph-

"(3A) A community service order shall not be made under paragraph 3(1)(b) or 4(1)(b) above in respect of a person who is under the age of sixteen years."

(6) For sub-paragraph (5) of that paragraph there shall be substituted the following sub-paragraph-

"(5) Where the provisions of this Schedule have effect as mentioned in sub-paragraph (4) above in relation to a community service order under paragraph 3(1)(b) or 4(1)(b) above-

(a) the power conferred on the court by each of paragraphs 3(1)(d) and 4(1)(d) above and paragraph 7(2)(a)(ii) below to deal with the offender for the offence in respect of which the order was made shall be construed as a power to deal with the offender, for his failure to comply with the original order, in any manner in which the court could deal with him if that failure to comply had just been proved to the satisfaction of the court;

(b) the reference in paragraph 7(1)(b) below to the offence in respect of which the order was made shall be construed as a reference to the failure to comply in respect of which the order was made; and

(c) the power conferred on the court by paragraph 8(2)(b) below to deal with the offender for the offence in respect of which the order was made shall be construed as a power to deal with the offender, for his failure to comply with the original order, in any manner in which the court which made the original order could deal with him if that failure had just been proved to the satisfaction of that court;

and in this sub-paragraph "the original order" means the relevant order the failure to comply with whose requirements led to the making of the community service order under paragraph 3(1)(b) or 4(1)(b)."

(7) After sub-paragraph (5) of that paragraph there shall be added the following sub-paragraph-

"(6) The provisions of sections 17 to 19 of the 1982 Act (making, discharge, variation and breach of attendance centre order) shall apply for the purposes of paragraphs 3(1)(c) and 4(1)(c) above but as if there were omitted-

(a) subsection (13) of section 17;

(b) from subsection (4A) of section 18 and subsections (3) and (5) of section 19, the words ", for the offence in respect of which the order was made," and "for that offence"."

(8) After paragraph 6 of that Schedule there shall be inserted the following paragraph-

"**6A.**– (1) Where a relevant order was made by a magistrates' court in the case of an offender under 18 years of age in respect of an offence triable only on indictment in the case of an adult, any powers exercisable under paragraph 3(1)(d) above by that or any other court in respect of the offender after he has attained the age of 18 years shall be powers to do either or both of the following-

(a) to impose a fine not exceeding £5,000 for the offence in respect of which the order was made;

(b) to deal with the offender for that offence in any way in which a magistrates' court could deal with him if it had just convicted him of an offence punishable with imprisonment for a term not exceeding six months.

(2) In sub-paragraph (1)(b) above any reference to an offence punishable with imprisonment shall be construed without regard to any prohibition or restriction imposed by or under any enactment on the imprisonment of young offenders."

(9) In paragraph 7(5) of that Schedule, after the word "above" there shall be inserted the words "for an offence".

(10) In paragraph 8(2) of that Schedule, for paragraph (b) there shall be substituted the following paragraph-

"(b) revoke the order and deal with the offender, for the offence in respect of which the order was made, in any manner in which the court which made the order could deal with him if he had just been convicted of that offence by or before the court which made the order."

(11) After paragraph 8 of that Schedule there shall be inserted the following paragraph-

"**8A.**– (1) This paragraph applies where a probation order is in force in respect of any offender and on the application of the offender or the responsible officer it appears to a magistrates' court acting for the petty sessions area concerned that, having regard to circumstances which have arisen since the order was made, it would be in the interests of justice-

(a) for the probation order to be revoked; and
(b) for an order to be made under section 1A(1)(b) of the 1973 Act discharging the offender conditionally for the offence for which the probation order was made.

(2) No application may be made under paragraph 7 above for a probation order to be revoked and replaced with an order for conditional discharge under section 1A(1)(b) of the 1973 Act; but otherwise nothing in this paragraph shall affect the operation of paragraphs 7 and 8 above.

(3) Where this paragraph applies and the probation order was made by a magistrates' court-

(a) the magistrates' court dealing with the application may revoke the probation order and make an order under section 1A(1)(b) of the 1973 Act discharging the offender in respect of the offence for which the probation order was made, subject to the condition that he commits no offence during the period specified in the order under section 1A(1)(b); and
(b) the period specified in the order under section 1A(1)(b) shall be the period beginning with the making of that order and ending with the date when the probation period specified in the probation order would have ended.

(4) Where this paragraph applies and the probation order was made by the Crown Court, the magistrates' court may send the application to the Crown Court to be heard by that court, and if it does so shall also send to the Crown Court such particulars of the case as may be desirable.

(5) Where an application under this paragraph is heard by the Crown Court by virtue of sub-paragraph (4) above-

(a) the Crown Court may revoke the probation order and make an order under section 1A(1)(b) of the 1973 Act discharging the offender in respect of the offence for which the probation order was made, subject to the condition that he commits no offence during the period specified in the order under section 1A(1)(b); and

(b) the period specified in the order under section 1A(1)(b) shall be the period beginning with the making of that order and ending with the date when the probation period specified in the probation order would have ended.

(6) For the purposes of sub-paragraphs (3) and (5) above, subsection (1) of section 1A of the 1973 Act shall apply as if-

(a) for the words from the beginning to "may make an order either" there were substituted the words "Where paragraph 8A of Schedule 2 to the Criminal Justice Act 1991 applies, the court which under sub-paragraph (3) or (5) of that paragraph has power to dispose of the application may (subject to the provisions of that sub-paragraph) make an order in respect of the offender"; and

(b) paragraph (a) of that subsection were omitted.

(7) An application under this paragraph may be heard in the offender's absence if-

(a) the application is made by the responsible officer; and

(b) that officer produces to the court a statement by the offender that he understands the effect of an order for conditional discharge and consents to the making of the application;

and where the application is so heard section 1A(3) of the 1973 Act shall not apply.

(8) No application may be made under this paragraph while an appeal against the probation order is pending.

(9) Without prejudice to paragraph 11 below, on the making of an order under section 1A(1)(b) of the 1973 Act by virtue of this paragraph the court shall forthwith give copies of the order to the responsible officer, and the responsible officer shall give a copy to the offender.

(10) Each of sections 1(11), 2(9) and 66(4) of the Crime and Disorder Act 1998 (which prevent a court from making an order for conditional discharge in certain cases) shall have effect as if the reference to the court by or before which a person is convicted of an offence there mentioned included a reference to a court dealing with an application under this paragraph in respect of the offence."

(12) After paragraph 11 of that Schedule there shall be inserted the following paragraphs-

"11A. Paragraph 6A above shall apply for the purposes of paragraphs 7 and 8 above as it applies for the purposes of paragraph 3 above, but as if in paragraph 6A(1) for the words "powers exercisable under paragraph 3(1)(d) above" there were substituted the words "powers to deal with the offender which are exercisable under paragraph 7(2)(a)(ii) or 8(2)(b) below".

11B. Where under this Part of this Schedule a relevant order is revoked and replaced by an order for conditional discharge under section 1A(1)(b) of the 1973 Act and-

(a) the order for conditional discharge is not made in the circumstances mentioned in section 1B(9) of the 1973 Act (order made by magistrates' court in the case of an offender under eighteen in respect of offence triable only on indictment in the case of an adult), but

(b) the relevant order was made in those circumstances,

section 1B(9) of the 1973 Act shall apply as if the order for conditional discharge had been made in those circumstances."

Crime (Sentences) Act 1997 (c.43)

47. Section 1 of the 1997 Act (conditions relating to mandatory and minimum custodial sentences) shall cease to have effect.

48.– (1) In subsection (2) of section 3 of the 1997 Act (minimum of seven years for third class A drug trafficking offence)-

(a) for the words "specific circumstances" there shall be substituted the words "particular circumstances"; and

(b) for the words "the prescribed custodial sentence unjust" there shall be substituted the words "it unjust to do so".

(2) In subsection (3) of that section, for the words "specific circumstances" there shall be substituted the words "particular circumstances".

49.– (1) In subsection (2) of section 4 of the 1997 Act (minimum of three years for third domestic burglary)-

(a) for the words "specific circumstances" there shall be substituted the words "particular circumstances"; and

(b) for the words "the prescribed custodial sentence unjust" there shall be substituted the words "it unjust to do so".

(2) In subsection (3) of that section, for the words "specific circumstances" there shall be substituted the words "particular circumstances".

50.– (1) In subsection (2)(a) of section 35 of the 1997 Act (community sentences for fine defaulters), for the words "and (11)" there shall be substituted the words ", (10) and (11)". ·

(2) In subsection (5) of that section, paragraph (c) shall cease to have effect.

(3) In that subsection, the word "and" at the end of paragraph (d) shall cease to have effect and after paragraph (e) there shall be added the following paragraphs-

"(f) the reference in paragraph 7(1)(b) of that Schedule to the offence in respect of which the order was made shall be construed as a reference to the default in respect of which the order was made;

(g) the power conferred by paragraph 7(2)(a)(ii) of that Schedule to deal with an offender for the offence in respect of which the order was made shall be construed as a power to deal with the person in respect of whom the order was made for his default in paying the sum in question; and

(h) paragraph 8(2)(b) of that Schedule shall not apply."

(4) In subsection (7) of that section, for the words "section 12(5)" there shall be substituted the words "section 12(6)".

(5) In subsection (8) of that section, the word "and" at the end of paragraph (a) shall cease to have effect and after paragraph (b) there shall be added the following paragraphs-

"(c) the reference in paragraph 7(1)(b) of that Schedule to the offence in respect of which the order was made shall be construed as a reference to the default in respect of which the order was made;

(d) the power conferred by paragraph 7(2)(a)(ii) of that Schedule to deal with an offender for the offence in respect of which the order was made shall be construed as a power to deal with the person in respect of whom the order was made for his default in paying the sum in question; and

(e) paragraph 8(2)(b) of that Schedule shall not apply."

(6) In subsection (10) of that section, for the words "subsection (2)(b)" there shall be substituted the words "subsection (2)(a) or (b)".

51.– (1) In subsection (3) of section 37 of the 1997 Act (community sentences for persistent petty offenders)-

(a) in paragraph (a), for the words "(4) and (6)" there shall be substituted the words "(4), (5A) and (6)"; and

(b) in paragraph (b), for the words "(5) and (6)" there shall be substituted the words "(5), (5A) and (6)".

(2) For subsections (4) and (5) of that section there shall be substituted the following subsections-

"(4) In this section "community service order" has the same meaning as in the 1973 Act and-

(a) section 14(2) of that Act; and

(b) so far as applicable, the other provisions of that Act relating to community service orders and the provisions of Part I of the 1991 Act so relating,

shall have effect in relation to an order under subsection (3)(a) above as they have effect in relation to a community service order made under the 1973 Act in respect of an offender.

(5) In this section "curfew order" has the same meaning as in Part I of the 1991 Act and-

(a) section 12(6) of that Act; and

(b) so far as applicable, the other provisions of that Part relating to curfew orders,

shall have effect in relation to an order under subsection (3)(b) above as they have effect in relation to a curfew order made under that Act in respect of an offender.

(5A) A court shall not make an order under subsection (3)(a) or (b) above in respect of a person who on conviction is under 16."

52. In section 50 of the 1997 Act (disclosure of pre-sentence reports), after subsection (6) there shall be added the following subsection-

"(7) In this section "guardian" has the same meaning as in the 1933 Act."

53. In section 54 of the 1997 Act (general interpretation), after subsection (3) there shall be added the following subsection-

"(4) For the purposes of any provision of this Act which requires the determination of the age of a person by the court, his age shall be deemed to be that which it appears to the court to be after considering any available evidence."

54. In section 55(2) of the 1997 Act (interpretation of minor and consequential amendments), for the words "in any case where" (in both places where they occur) there shall be substituted the word "and".

Schedule 7
This schedule contains amendments to a number of Acts to consolidate enactments relating to the powers of courts to deal with offenders or defaulters.

SCHEDULE 8

MINOR AND CONSEQUENTIAL AMENDMENTS

Children and Young Persons Act 1933 (c.12)

1. In subsection (4A) of section 49 of the 1933 Act (restrictions on reports of proceedings), for paragraph (e) there shall be substituted the following paragraph-

"(e) where a detention and training order is made, the enforcement of any requirements imposed under section 76(6)(b) of the Crime and Disorder Act 1998."

2. In subsection (1A) of section 55 of the 1933 Act (power of court to order parent or guardian to pay fine imposed on child or young person), after paragraph (c) there shall be inserted the words "or

    (d) a court would impose a fine on a child or young person under section 77(3) of the Crime and Disorder Act 1998 (breach of requirements of supervision under detention and training order) or paragraph 3 of Schedule 5 to that Act (breach of requirements of reparation order or action plan order),".

3. After subsection (1) of section 56 of the 1933 Act (powers of other courts to remit young offenders to youth courts) there shall be inserted the following subsection-

    "(1A) References in subsection (1) above to an offender's being committed for trial include references to his being sent for trial under section 51 of the Crime and Disorder Act 1998."

4. In section 58 of that Act (power of Secretary of State to send certain young offenders to approved schools), for the words "subsection (2)", in both places where they occur, there shall be substituted the words "subsection (3)".

Administration of Justice (Miscellaneous Provisions) Act 1933 (c.36)

5.– (1) In subsection (2) of section 2 of the Administration of Justice (Miscellaneous Provisions) Act 1933 (procedure for indictment of offenders)-

    (a) after paragraph (ab) there shall be inserted the following paragraph-

    "(ac) the person charged has been sent for trial for the offence under section 51 (no committal proceedings for indictable-only offences) of the Crime and Disorder Act 1998 ("the 1998 Act"); or"; and

    (b) after paragraph (b) there shall be inserted the words "or
    (c) the bill is preferred under section 22B(3)(a) of the Prosecution of Offences Act 1985."

(2) After paragraph (iA) of the proviso to that subsection there shall be inserted the following paragraph-

    "(iB) in a case to which paragraph (ac) above applies, the bill of indictment may include, either in substitution for or in addition to any count charging an offence specified in the notice under section 51(7) of the 1998 Act, any counts founded on material which, in pursuance of regulations made under paragraph 1 of Schedule 3 to that Act, was served on the person charged, being counts which may be lawfully joined in the same indictment;".

Prison Act 1952 (c.52)

6. In subsection (1) of section 43 of the Prison Act 1952 (which enables certain institutions for young offenders to be provided and applies provisions of the Act to them), for paragraph (d) there shall be substituted the following paragraph-

"(d) secure training centres, that is to say places in which offenders in respect of whom detention and training orders have been made under section 73 of the Crime and Disorder Act 1998 may be detained and given training and education and prepared for their release."

7.– (1) In subsection (1) of section 49 of that Act (persons unlawfully at large), for the words from "imprisonment" to "secure training centre" there shall be substituted the words "imprisonment or custody for life or ordered to be detained in secure accommodation or in a young offenders institution".

(2) In subsection (2) of that section-

  (a) for the words from "imprisonment" to "secure training centre" there shall be substituted the words "imprisonment, or ordered to be detained in secure accommodation or in a young offenders institution"; and

  (b) for the words from "in a prison" to "secure training centre" there shall be substituted the words "in a prison or remand centre, in secure accommodation or in a young offenders institution".

(3) After subsection (4) of that section there shall be inserted the following subsection-

"(5) In this section "secure accommodation" means-

  . (a) a young offender institution;

  (b) a secure training centre; or

  (c) any other accommodation that is secure accommodation within the meaning given by section 75(7) of the Crime and Disorder Act 1998 (detention and training orders)."

Criminal Procedure (Attendance of Witnesses) Act 1965 (c.69)

8. In subsection (4) of section 2 of the Criminal Procedure (Attendance of Witnesses) Act 1965 (issue of witness summons on application to Crown Court), after the words "committed for trial" there shall be inserted the words ", or sent for trial under section 51 of the Crime and Disorder Act 1998,".

Criminal Justice Act 1967 (c.80)

9.– (1) In subsection (2) of section 56 of the Criminal Justice Act 1967 (committal for sentence for offences tried summarily)-

  (a) for the words "sections 37, 38 and 38A" there shall be substituted the words "sections 38 and 38A"; and

  (b) for the words "section 17(3) of the Crime (Sentences) Act 1997 (committal for breach of conditions of release supervision order)" there shall be substituted the words "section 40(3)(b) of the Criminal Justice Act 1991 (committal for sentence for offence committed during currency of original sentence)".

(2) Subsection (6) of that section shall cease to have effect.

10. In subsection (5) of section 67 of that Act (computation of sentences of imprisonment or detention passed in England and Wales)-

   (a) in paragraph (b), for the words "section 53(2)" there shall be substituted the words "section 53(3)"; and

   (b) paragraph (c) shall cease to have effect.

11. At the end of subsection (2) of section 104 of that Act (general provisions as to interpretation) there shall be inserted the words "if-

   (a) the sentences were passed on the same occasion; or

   (b) where they were passed on different occasions, the person has not been released under Part II of the (1991 c.53.)Criminal Justice Act 1991 at any time during the period beginning with the first and ending with the last of those occasions."

Criminal Appeal Act 1968 (c.19)

12. In subsection (2) of section 9 of the Criminal Appeal Act 1968 (appeal against sentence following conviction on indictment), after the words "for either way offence)" there shall be inserted the words "or paragraph 6 of Schedule 3 to the Crime and Disorder Act 1998 (power of Crown Court to deal with summary offence where person sent for trial for indictable-only offence)".

13.– (1) In subsection (2) of section 10 of that Act (appeal against sentence in other cases dealt with at Crown Court), the words "(other than a supervision order within the meaning of that Part)" shall cease to have effect.

(2) In subsection (3) of that section, after paragraph (c) there shall be inserted the following paragraph-

   "(cc) where the court makes such an order with regard to him as is mentioned in section 40(3A) of the Criminal Justice Act 1991."

Firearms Act 1968 (c.27)

14.– (1) In subsection (2) of section 21 of the Firearms Act 1968 (possession of firearms by persons previously convicted of crime), after the words "a secure training order" there shall be inserted the words "or a detention and training order".

(2) In subsection (2A) of that section, after paragraph (b) there shall be inserted the following paragraph-

   "(c) in the case of a person who has been subject to a detention and training order-
      (i) the date on which he is released from detention under the order;
      (ii) the date on which he is released from detention ordered under section 77 of the Crime and Disorder Act 1998; or
      (iii) the date of the half-way point of the term of the order,

   whichever is the later."

15. In subsection (1) of section 52 of that Act (forfeiture and disposal of firearms), for the words "secure training order" there shall be substituted the words "detention and training order".

Children and Young Persons Act 1969 (c.54)

16. In subsection (8) of section 7 of the 1969 Act (alterations in treatment of young offenders etc.), for the words from "person guilty" to "were begun" there shall be substituted the words "child or young person guilty of an offence".

17. In section 11 of the 1969 Act (supervision orders), for the words "a local authority designated by the order or of a probation officer" there shall be substituted the following paragraphs-

"(a) a local authority designated by the order;
(b) a probation officer; or
(c) a member of a youth offending team,"

18. Section 12D of the 1969 Act (duty of court to state in certain cases that requirement in place of custodial sentence) shall cease to have effect.

19. After subsection (3) of section 13 of the 1969 Act (selection of supervisor) there shall be inserted the following subsection-

"(4) Where a provision of a supervision order places a person under the supervision of a member of a youth offending team, the supervisor shall be a member of a team established by the local authority within whose area it appears to the court that the supervised person resides or will reside."

20.– (1) In subsection (8) of section 16 of the 1969 Act (provisions supplementary to section 15), after the words "under the preceding section" there shall be inserted the words "by a relevant court (within the meaning of that section)".

(2) Subsection (10) of that section shall cease to have effect.

21. After section 16A of the 1969 Act there shall be inserted the following section-

"16B.– (1) The provisions of section 12 of the Criminal Justice Act 1991 (curfew orders) shall apply for the purposes of section 15(3)(a) of this Act but as if-

(a) in subsection (1), for the words from the beginning to "before which he is convicted" there were substituted the words "Where a court considers it appropriate to make a curfew order in respect of any person in pursuance of section 15(3)(a) of the Children and Young Persons Act 1969, the court"; and
(b) in subsection (8), for the words "on conviction" there were substituted the words "on the date on which his failure to comply with a requirement included in the supervision order was proved to the court".

(2) Schedule 2 to the (1991 c.53.)Criminal Justice Act 1991 (enforcement etc. of community orders), so far as relating to curfew orders, shall also apply for the purposes of that section but as if-

(a) the power conferred on the magistrates' court by each of paragraphs 3(1)(d) and 7(2)(a)(ii) to deal with the offender for the offence in respect of which the order was made were a power to deal with the offender, for his failure to comply with a requirement included in the supervision order, in any manner in which the relevant court could deal with him for that failure to comply if it had just been proved to the satisfaction of that court;

(b) the power conferred on the Crown Court by paragraph 4(1)(d) to deal with the offender for the offence in respect of which the order was made were a power to deal with the offender, for his failure to comply with such a requirement, in any manner in which that court could deal with him for that failure to comply if it had just been proved to its satisfaction;

(c) the reference in paragraph 7(1)(b) to the offence in respect of which the order was made were a reference to the failure to comply in respect of which the curfew order was made; and

(d) the power conferred on the Crown Court by paragraph 8(2)(b) to deal with the offender for the offence in respect of which the order was made were a power to deal with the offender, for his failure to comply with a requirement included in the supervision order, in any manner in which the relevant court (if that order was made by a magistrates' court) or the Crown Court (if that order was made by the Crown Court) could deal with him for that failure to comply if it had just been proved to the satisfaction of that court.

(3) For the purposes of the provisions mentioned in subsection (2)(a) and (d) above, as applied by that subsection, if the supervision order is no longer in force the relevant court's powers shall be determined on the assumption that it is still in force.

(4) In this section "relevant court" has the same meaning as in section 15 above."

22. In subsection (14) of section 23 of the 1969 Act (remands and committals to local authority accommodation), paragraph (a) shall cease to have effect.

23. In subsection (1) of section 70 of the 1969 Act (interpretation), after the definition of "young person" there shall be inserted the following definition-

""youth offending team" means a team established under section 39 of the Crime and Disorder Act 1998."

Superannuation Act 1972 (c.11)

24. In Schedule 1 to the Superannuation Act 1972 (kinds of employment to which a scheme under section 1 of that Act may apply), at the end of the list of "Other Bodies" there shall be inserted the following entry-

"Youth Justice Board for England and Wales."

Powers of Criminal Courts Act 1973 (c.62)

25. After subsection (1) of section 1A of the 1973 Act (absolute and conditional discharge) there shall be inserted the following subsection-

"(1A) Subsection (1)(b) above has effect subject to section 66(4) of the Crime and Disorder Act 1998 (effect of reprimands and warnings)."

26.– (1) In subsection (1) of section 2 of the 1973 Act (probation orders), the words "by a probation officer" shall cease to have effect and for the words "the supervision of a probation officer" there shall be substituted the word "supervision".

(2) In subsection (2) of that section, for the words "a probation officer appointed for or assigned to that area" there shall be substituted the following paragraphs-

"(a) a probation officer appointed for or assigned to that area; or
(b) where the offender is under the age of 18 years when the order is made, a member of a youth offending team established by a local authority specified in the order."

(3) After that subsection there shall be inserted the following subsection-

"(2A) The local authority specified as mentioned in subsection (2)(b) above shall be the local authority within whose area it appears to the court that the offender resides or will reside."

(4) In subsection (4) of that section, for the words "the probation officer" there shall be substituted the words "the person".

(5) After that subsection there shall be inserted the following subsection-

"(4A) In the case of an offender under the age of 18 years, the reference in subsection (4) above to a probation officer includes a reference to a member of a youth offending team."

(6) In subsection (6) of that section-

(a) for the words "the probation officer" there shall be substituted the words "the person"; and
(b) for the words "that officer" there shall be substituted the words "that person".

27.– (1) In subsection (4) of section 14 of the 1973 Act (community service orders), for the words from "a probation officer" to the end there shall be substituted the following paragraphs-

"(a) a probation officer appointed for or assigned to the area for the time being specified in the order (whether under this subsection or by virtue of Part IV of Schedule 2 to the Criminal Justice Act 1991);
(b) a person appointed for the purposes of those provisions by the probation committee for that area; or

(c) in the case of an offender under the age of 18 years when the order is made, a member of a youth offending team established by a local authority for the time being specified in the order (whether under this subsection or by virtue of that Part)."

(2) After that subsection there shall be inserted the following subsection-

"(4A) The local authority specified as mentioned in subsection (4)(c) above shall be the local authority within whose area it appears to the court that the offender resides or will reside."

(3) After subsection (8) of that section there shall be inserted the following subsection-

"(9) In the case of an offender under the age of 18 years, references in subsections (2), (5)(c) or (6) above to a probation officer include references to a member of a youth offending team."

28. In subsection (2) of section 21 of the 1973 Act (restriction on imposing sentences of imprisonment etc. on persons not legally represented)-

(a) after the words "sentence or trial," there shall be inserted the words "or sent to that Court for trial under section 51 of the Crime and Disorder Act 1998,"; and
(b) for the words "which committed him" there shall be substituted the words "which committed or sent him".

29. In subsection (1)(b) of section 32 of the 1973 Act (enforcement etc. of fines imposed and recognizances forfeited by Crown Court), after the words "or dealt with" there shall be inserted the words ", or by which he was sent to that Court for trial under section 51 of the Crime and Disorder Act 1998".

30. After subsection (2) of section 23 of the 1973 Act (power of court on conviction of further offence to deal with suspended sentence) there shall be inserted the following subsection-

"(2A) The power to make an order under subsection (2) above has effect subject to section 102 of the Crime and Disorder Act 1998."

31. In section 42 of the 1973 Act (power of Crown Court on committal for sentence), subsection (2) shall cease to have effect.

32. In subsection (1) of section 46 of the 1973 Act (reports of probation officers), after the words "probation officer" there shall be inserted the words "or a member of a youth offending team".

33. In subsection (1) of section 57 of the 1973 Act (interpretation), after the definition of "suspended sentence" there shall be inserted the following definition-

""youth offending team" means a team established under section 39 of the Crime and Disorder Act 1998."

34.– (1) At the beginning of sub-paragraph (1) of paragraph 6 (requirements as to drug or alcohol dependency) of Schedule 1A to the 1973 Act there shall be inserted the words "Subject to sub-paragraph (1A) below,".

(2) After that sub-paragraph there shall be inserted the following sub-paragraph-

"(1A) If the court has been notified by the Secretary of State that arrangements for implementing orders under section 61 of the Crime and Disorder Act 1998 (drug treatment and testing orders) are available in the area proposed to be specified in the probation order, and the notice has not been withdrawn, this paragraph shall have effect as if the words "drugs or", in each place where they occur, were omitted."

(3) After that paragraph there shall be inserted the following paragraph-

"Interpretation

7. In the case of an offender under the age of 18 years, references in this Schedule to a probation officer include references to a member of a youth offending team."

Rehabilitation of Offenders Act 1974 (c.53)

35. After subsection (6) of section 5 of the Rehabilitation of Offenders Act 1974 (rehabilitation periods for particular sentences) there shall be inserted the following subsection-

"(6A) Where in respect of a conviction a detention and training order was made under section 73 of the Crime and Disorder Act 1998, the rehabilitation period applicable to the sentence shall be-

(a) in the case of a person aged fifteen years or over at the date of his conviction, five years if the order was, and three and a half years if the order was not, for a term exceeding six months;

(b) in the case of a person aged under fifteen years at the date of his conviction, a period beginning with that date and ending one year after the date on which the order ceases to have effect.

36. In subsection (2) of section 7 of that Act (limitations on rehabilitation under Act etc.), after paragraph (b) there shall be inserted the following paragraph-

"(bb) in any proceedings on an application for a sex offender order under section 2 or, as the case may be, 20 of the Crime and Disorder Act 1998 or in any appeal against the making of such an order;".

Bail Act 1976 (c.63)

37. After subsection (8A) of section 3 of the Bail Act 1976 (general provisions) there shall be inserted the following subsection-

"(8B)   Subsection (8) above applies where a court has sent a person on bail to the Crown Court for trial under section 51 of the Crime and Disorder Act 1998 as it applies where a court has committed a person on bail to the Crown Court for trial."

38. In paragraph 8(1) of Schedule 1 to that Act (persons entitled to bail: supplementary provisions), after the words "subsection (6)(d)" there shall be inserted the words "or (e)".

Magistrates' Courts Act 1980 (c.43)

39. In subsection (3) of section 11 of the 1980 Act (certain sentences and orders not to be made in absence of accused), for the words "secure training order" there shall be substituted the words "detention and training order".

40.– (1) In subsection (1)(a) of section 24 of the 1980 Act (summary trial of information against child or young person for indictable offence), for the words "that subsection" there shall be substituted the words "subsection (3) of that section".

(2) In subsection (2) of that section, for the words from "that other offence" to the end there shall be substituted the words "the charges for both offences could be joined in the same indictment".

41. Section 37 of the 1980 Act (committal to Crown Court with a view to greater term of detention in a young offender institution) shall cease to have effect.

42. In subsection (1) of section 65 of the 1980 Act (meaning of "family proceedings"), after paragraph (p) there shall be inserted the following paragraph-

"(q) sections 11 and 12 of the Crime and Disorder Act 1998;".

43. In subsection (2) of section 108 of the 1980 Act (right of appeal to the Crown Court), the words "a probation order or" shall cease to have effect.

44. In subsection (4)(c) of section 125 of the 1980 Act (warrants)-

   (a) the word "and" at the end of sub-paragraph (ii) shall cease to have effect;
   (b) in sub-paragraph (iii), for the words "or 97 above" there shall be substituted the words ", 97 or 97A above; and"; and
   (c) after that sub-paragraph there shall be inserted the following sub-paragraph-
   "(iv) paragraph 4 of Schedule 3 to the Crime and Disorder Act 1998."

45. In section 126 of the 1980 Act (execution of certain warrants outside England and Wales)-

   (a) the word "and" at the end of paragraph (c) shall cease to have effect;
   (b) after that paragraph there shall be inserted the following paragraph-

"(cc) warrants of arrest issued under section 97A above;"; and

(c) after paragraph (d) there shall be inserted the words "; and

(e) warrants of arrest issued under paragraph 4 of Schedule 3 to the Crime and Disorder Act 1998."

46. At the beginning of subsection (1) of section 133 of the 1980 Act (consecutive terms of imprisonment) there shall be inserted the words "Subject to section 102 of the Crime and Disorder Act 1998,".

Supreme Court Act 1981 (c.54)

47. After subsection (1) of section 47 of the Supreme Court Act 1981 (sentences and other orders of Crown Court when dealing with offenders) there shall be inserted the following subsection-

"(1A) The power to give a direction under subsection (1) above has effect subject to section 102 of the Crime and Disorder Act 1998."

48. In subsection (1)(a) of section 81 of the Supreme Court Act 1981 (bail), after the words "Criminal Justice Act 1987" there shall be inserted the words "or who has been sent in custody to the Crown Court for trial under section 51 of the Crime and Disorder Act 1998".

Criminal Justice Act 1982 (c.48)

49. In subsection (2) of section 1 of the 1982 Act (general restriction on custodial sentences), for the words from "remanded in custody" to the end there shall be substituted the following paragraphs-

"(a) remanded in custody;
(b) committed in custody for trial or sentence; or
(c) sent in custody for trial under section 51 of the Crime and Disorder Act 1998."

50.– (1) In subsection (1) of section 1A of the 1982 Act (detention in a young offender institution), for the words "not less than 15 years of age" there shall be substituted the words "not less than 18 years of age".

(2) In subsection (3) of that section, for the words "the minimum period applicable to the offender under subsection (4A) below" there shall be substituted the words "21 days".

(3) In subsection (4) of that section, for the words "the minimum period applicable" there shall be substituted the words "21 days".

(4) Subsection (4A) of that section shall cease to have effect.

(5) At the beginning of subsection (6) of that section there shall be inserted the words "Subject to section 102 of the Crime and Disorder Act 1998,"

51. In subsection (2) of section 1C of the 1982 Act (accommodation of offenders sentenced to detention in a young offender institution), the words "but if he is under 18 at the time of the direction, only for a temporary purpose" shall cease to have effect.

52.– (1) In subsection (1) of section 3 of the 1982 Act (restriction on certain sentences where offender not legally represented), for paragraph (e) there shall be substituted the following paragraph-

"(e) make a detention and training order,".

(2) In subsection (2) of that section-

(a) after the words "sentence or trial," there shall be inserted the words "or sent to that Court for trial under section 51 of the Crime and Disorder Act 1998,"; and

(b) for the words "which committed him" there shall be substituted the words "which committed or sent him".

53.– (1) In subsection (3)(a) of section 19 of the 1982 Act (breaches of attendance centre orders or attendance centre rules), the words "revoke it and" shall cease to have effect.

(2) In subsection (5) of that section, the words "revoke the attendance centre order and" shall cease to have effect.

(3) In subsection (5A) of that section, for paragraph (b) there shall be substituted the following paragraph-

"(b) in the case of an offender who has wilfully and persistently failed to comply with those requirements, may impose a custodial sentence notwithstanding anything in section 1(2) of the Criminal Justice Act 1991."

(4) After that subsection there shall be inserted the following subsection-

"(5B) Where a court deals with an offender under subsection (3)(a) or (5) above, it shall revoke the attendance centre order if it is still in force."

Mental Health Act 1983 (c.20)

54. In subsection (8) of section 37 of the Mental Health Act 1983 (powers of courts to order hospital admission or guardianship), for the words from "pass sentence of imprisonment" to "in respect of the offender" there shall be inserted the following paragraphs-

"(a) pass a sentence of imprisonment, impose a fine or make a community order (within the meaning of Part I of the Criminal Justice Act 1991) in respect of the offence; or

(b) make an order under section 58 of that Act (binding over of parent or guardian) in respect of the offender,".

Mental Health (Scotland) Act 1984 (c.36)

55.– (1) In subsection (8A) of section 74 of the Mental Health (Scotland) Act 1984 (effect of certain directions), for the words "the Crime and Punishment (Scotland) Act 1997" there shall be substituted the words "Part I of the Prisoners and Criminal Proceedings (Scotland) Act 1993".

(2) The amendment made by sub-paragraph (1) above shall be deemed to have had effect from 1 January 1998.

Repatriation of Prisoners Act 1984 (c.47)

56. In subsection (4)(b) of section 2 (transfer of prisoners out of United Kingdom) of the Repatriation of Prisoners Act 1984, for sub-paragraph (i) there shall be substituted the following sub-paragraph-

> "(i) released on licence under section 33(1)(b), (2) or (3), 33A(2), 34A(3) or 35(1) of the (1991 c.53.)Criminal Justice Act 1991 or section 28(5) or 29(1) of the Crime (Sentences) Act 1997;".

57. In subsection (9) of section 3 of that Act (transfer of prisoners into United Kingdom)-

(a) for the words "section 48 of the (1991 c.53.)Criminal Justice Act 1991 (discretionary life prisoners transferred to England and Wales)" there shall be substituted the words "section 33 of the (1997 c.43.)Crime (Sentences) Act 1997 (life prisoner transferred to England and Wales)"; and

(b) for the words "section 34 of that Act (duty of Secretary of State to release discretionary life prisoners)" there shall be substituted the words "section 28 of that Act (duty to release certain life prisoners)".

58.– (1) Paragraph 2 of the Schedule to that Act as it has effect, and is deemed always to have had effect, by virtue of paragraph 2 of Schedule 2 to the 1997 Act shall be amended as follows.

(2) In sub-paragraph (4), for the definition of "the enactments relating to release on licence" there shall be substituted the following definition-

> ""the enactments relating to release on licence" means sections 33(1)(b), (2) and (3), 33A(2), 34A(3), 35(1) and 37(1) and (2) of the Criminal Justice Act 1991 and section 28(5) and (7) of the Crime (Sentences) Act 1997;".

59.– (1) Paragraph 2 of the Schedule to that Act (operation of certain enactments in relation to the prisoner) as it has effect by virtue of paragraph 3 of Schedule 2 to the 1997 Act-

(a) shall have effect in relation to all prisoners repatriated to England and Wales after the commencement of Schedule 2; and

(b) as it so has effect, shall be amended as follows.

(2) In sub-paragraph (2), for the words "34(3) and (5) and 35(1) of the (1991 c.53.)Criminal Justice Act 1991" there shall be substituted the words "35(1) of the Criminal Justice Act 1991 and section 28(5) and (7) of the (1997 c.43.)Crime (Sentences) Act 1997".

(3) In sub-paragraph (4), for the definition of "the enactments relating to release on licence" there shall be substituted the following definition-

""the enactments relating to release on licence" means sections 33(1)(b), (2) and (3), 33A(2), 34A(3), 35(1) and 37(1) and (2) of the (1991 c.53.)Criminal Justice Act 1991 and section 28(5) and (7) of the (1997 c.43.)Crime (Sentences) Act 1997;".

60. For paragraph 3 of the Schedule to that Act there shall be substituted the following paragraph-

"Life imprisonment

3. Where the relevant provisions include provision equivalent to a sentence in relation to which subsection (1) of section 29 of the (1997 c.43.)Crime (Sentences) Act 1997 (power to release certain life prisoners etc.) applies, that subsection shall have effect as if the reference to consultation with the trial judge if available were omitted."

Police and Criminal Evidence Act 1984 (c.60)

61. After subsection (4) of section 27 of the 1984 Act (fingerprinting of certain offenders and recording of offences) there shall be inserted the following subsection-

"(4A) In subsection (4) above "conviction" includes-

(a) a caution within the meaning of Part V of the Police Act 1997; and
(b) a reprimand or warning given under section 65 of the Crime and Disorder Act 1998."

62. After section 47 of the 1984 Act there shall be inserted the following section-

"**47A.** Where a person has been charged with an offence at a police station, any requirement imposed under this Part for the person to appear or be brought before a magistrates' court shall be taken to be satisfied if the person appears or is brought before the clerk to the justices for a petty sessions area in order for the clerk to conduct a hearing under section 50 of the Crime and Disorder Act 1998 (early administrative hearings)."

Prosecution of Offences Act 1985 (c.23)

63. In subsection (2) of section 23 of the 1985 Act (discontinuance of proceedings), after paragraph (b) there shall be inserted the following paragraph-

"(c) in the case of any offence, any stage of the proceedings after the accused has been sent for trial under section 51 of the Crime and Disorder Act 1998 (no committal proceedings for indictable-only and related offences)."

64. After that section there shall be inserted the following section-

"**23A.–** (1) This section applies where-

(a) the Director of Public Prosecutions, or a public authority (within the meaning of section 17 of this Act), has the conduct of proceedings for an offence; and
(b) the accused has been sent for trial under section 51 of the Crime and Disorder Act 1998 for the offence.

(2) Where, at any time before the indictment is preferred, the Director or authority gives notice under this section to the Crown Court sitting at the place specified in the notice under section 51(7) of the Crime and Disorder Act 1998 that he or it does not want the proceedings to continue, they shall be discontinued with effect from the giving of that notice.

(3) The Director or authority shall, in any notice given under subsection (2) above, give reasons for not wanting the proceedings to continue.

(4) On giving any notice under subsection (2) above the Director or authority shall inform the accused of the notice; but the Director or authority shall not be obliged to give the accused any indication of his reasons for not wanting the proceedings to continue.

(5) The discontinuance of any proceedings by virtue of this section shall not prevent the institution of fresh proceedings in respect of the same offence."

Criminal Justice Act 1987 (c.38)

65. After subsection (3) of section 4 of the Criminal Justice Act 1987 (notices of transfer in serious fraud cases) there shall be inserted the following subsection-

"(4) This section and sections 5 and 6 below shall not apply in any case in which section 51 of the Crime and Disorder Act 1998 (no committal proceedings for indictable-only offences) applies."

Criminal Justice Act 1988 (c.33)

66. In subsection (1) of section 40 of the Criminal Justice Act 1988 (power to join in indictment count for common assault etc.), at the end there shall be inserted the words "or are disclosed by material which, in pursuance of regulations made under paragraph 1 of Schedule 3 to the Crime and Disorder Act 1998 (procedure where person sent for trial under section 51), has been served on the person charged".

Legal Aid Act 1988 (c.34)

67.– (1) In subsection (4) of section 20 of the Legal Aid Act 1988 (competent authorities to grant representation under Part V), after paragraph (a) there shall be inserted the following paragraph-

"(aa) which sends a person for trial under section 51 of the Crime and Disorder Act 1998 (no committal proceedings for indictable-only offences),".

(2) After subsection (5) of that section there shall be inserted the following subsection-

"(5A) A magistrates' court which has a duty or a power to send a person for trial under section 51 of the Crime and Disorder Act 1998 is also competent, before discharging that duty or (as the case may be) deciding whether to exercise that power, as respects any proceedings before the Crown Court on the person's trial."

(3) In subsection (3)(a) of section 21 of that Act (availability of representation under Part V), after the word "committed" there shall be inserted the words "or sent".

(4) In subsection (4) of that section, after the word "commits" there shall be inserted the words "or sends".

Children Act 1989 (c.41)

68. In subsection (4) of section 8 of the 1989 Act (which defines "family proceedings"), after paragraph (h) there shall be inserted the following paragraph-

"(i) sections 11 and 12 of the Crime and Disorder Act 1998."

69. In subsection (3) of section 47 of the 1989 Act (local authority's duty to investigate), after the words "this Act" there shall be inserted the words "or section 11 of the Crime and Disorder Act 1998 (child safety orders)".

Prisons (Scotland) Act 1989 (c.45)

70.– (1) Section 16 of the Prisons (Scotland) Act 1989 (discharge of prisoners) which, notwithstanding its repeal by the Prisoners and Criminal Proceedings (Scotland) Act 1993, is an "existing provision" for the purposes of Schedule 6 to that Act of 1993, shall for those purposes be amended as follows.

(2) In subsection (1), for the words "or Sunday" there shall be substituted the words "Sunday or public holiday".

(3) At the end there shall be inserted the following subsection-

"(3) For the purposes of this section "public holiday" means any day on which, in the opinion of the Secretary of State, public offices or other facilities likely to be of use to the prisoner in the area in which he is likely to be following his discharge from prison will be closed."

71. In section 39 of that Act (rules for the management of prisons)-

    (a) in subsection (7)-

        (i) at the beginning there shall be inserted the words "Subject to subsection (7A) below,";

        (ii) for the words "a short-term or long-term prisoner within the meaning of" there shall be substituted the words "any person who is, or is treated as, a long-term or short-term prisoner for the purposes of any provision of"; and

        (iii) the words from "and the foregoing" to the end shall cease to have effect; and

    (b) after that subsection there shall be inserted the following subsections-

"(7A) Additional days shall not be awarded under rules made under subsection (7) above in respect of a sentence where the prisoner has at any time been released on licence, in relation to that sentence, under Part I of the Prisoners and Criminal Proceedings (Scotland) Act 1993; and any reference to a sentence in such rules shall be construed in accordance with section 27(5) of that Act.

(7B) In the application of subsection (7) above to a prisoner subject to an extended sentence within the meaning of section 210A of the 1995 Act, the reference to his sentence shall be construed as a reference to the custodial term of that extended sentence."

Criminal Justice Act 1991 (c.53)

72. For subsection (3) of section 1 of the 1991 Act (restrictions on imposing custodial sentences) there shall be substituted the following subsection-

"(3) Nothing in subsection (2) above shall prevent the court from passing a custodial sentence on the offender if he fails to express his willingness to comply with-

(a) a requirement which is proposed by the court to be included in a probation order or supervision order and which requires an expression of such willingness; or

(b) a requirement which is proposed by the court to be included in a drug treatment and testing order or an order under section 61(6) of the Crime and Disorder Act 1998."

73. In subsection (5)(a) of section 3 of the 1991 Act (procedural requirements for custodial sentences), for the words "a probation officer or by a social worker of a local authority social services department" there shall be substituted the following sub-paragraphs-

    "(i) a probation officer;

    (ii) a social worker of a local authority social services department; or

    (iii) where the offender is under the age of 18 years, a member of a youth offending team;".

74. In subsection (4) of section 6 of the 1991 Act (restrictions on imposing community sentences)-

    (a) after paragraph (a) there shall be inserted the following paragraph-
        "(aa) a drug treatment and testing order;";

    (b) the word "and" immediately following paragraph (e) shall cease to have effect; and

    (c) after paragraph (f) there shall be inserted the following paragraph-
        "(g) an action plan order."

75. In subsection (3) of section 7 of the 1991 Act (procedural requirements for community sentences), after paragraph (a) there shall be inserted the following paragraph-

    "(aa) a drug treatment and testing order;".

76. In subsection (1) of section 11 of the 1991 Act (combination orders), for the words "the supervision of a probation officer" there shall be substituted the word "supervision".

77. In subsection (3) of section 15 of the 1991 Act (regulation of community orders)-

    (a) in paragraph (a), after the words "probation officer" there shall be inserted the words "or member of a youth offending team"; and

    (b) after that paragraph there shall be inserted the following paragraph-
        "(aa) in relation to an offender who is subject to a drug treatment and testing order, the probation officer responsible for his supervision;".

78. In subsection (1) of section 31 of the 1991 Act (interpretation of Part I)-

    (a) immediately before the definition of "attendance centre order" there shall be inserted the following definition-
        ""action plan order" means an order under section 69 of the Crime and Disorder Act 1998;";

    (b) in the definition of "custodial sentence", in paragraph (b), after the word "age," there shall be inserted the words "a detention and training order," and the words "or a secure training order under section 1 of the Criminal Justice and Public Order Act 1994" shall cease to have effect; and

    (c) after that definition there shall be inserted the following definitions-
        ""detention and training order" has the meaning given by section 73(3) of the Crime and Disorder Act 1998;
        "drug treatment and testing order" means an order under section 61 of that Act;".

79.– (1) In subsection (1)(b) of section 32 of the 1991 Act (Parole Board), for the words "the functions conferred by Part II of the Crime (Sentences) Act 1997 ("Part II")" there shall be substituted the words "the functions conferred by this Part in respect of long-term and short-term prisoners and by Chapter II of Part II of the Crime (Sentences) Act 1997 ("Chapter II") in respect of life prisoners within the meaning of that Chapter".

(2) In subsections (3), (4) and (6) of that section, for the words "Part II" there shall be substituted the words "this Part or Chapter II".

80.– (1) In subsection (3) of section 33 of the 1991 Act (duty to release short-term and long-term prisoners)-

(a) in paragraph (a), for the words "subsection (1)(b) or (2) above or section 35 or 36(1) below" there shall be substituted the words "this Part"; and

(b) in paragraph (b), for the words "38(2) or 39(1)" there shall be substituted the words "39(1) or (2)".

(2) After that subsection there shall be inserted the following subsection-

"(3A) In the case of a prisoner to whom section 44A below applies, it shall be the duty of the Secretary of State to release him on licence at the end of the extension period (within the meaning of section 58 of the Crime and Disorder Act 1998)."

(3) Subsection (4) of that section shall cease to have effect.

81. After that section there shall be inserted the following section-

"**33A.–** (1) As soon as a prisoner-

(a) whose sentence is for a term of less than twelve months; and

(b) who has been released on licence under section 34A(3) or 36(1) below and recalled to prison under section 38A(1) or 39(1) or (2) below,

would (but for his release) have served one-half of his sentence, it shall be the duty of the Secretary of State to release him unconditionally.

(2) As soon as a prisoner-

(a) whose sentence is for a term of twelve months or more; and

(b) who has been released on licence under section 34A(3) below and recalled to prison under section 38A(1) below,

would (but for his release) have served one-half of his sentence, it shall be the duty of the Secretary of State to release him on licence.

(3) In the case of a prisoner who-

(a) has been released on licence under this Part and recalled to prison under section 39(1) or (2) below; and

(b) has been subsequently released on licence under section 33(3) or (3A) above and recalled to prison under section 39(1) or (2) below,

section 33(3) above shall have effect as if for the words "three-quarters" there were substituted the words "the whole" and the words "on licence" were omitted."

82. In subsection (1) of section 36 of the 1991 Act (power to release prisoners on compassionate grounds), for word "prisoner" there shall be substituted the words "short-term or long-term prisoner".

83.– (1) In subsection (1) of section 37 of the 1991 Act (duration and conditions of licences)-

  (a) for the words "subsection (2)" there shall be substituted the words "subsections (1A), (1B) and (2)"; and
  (b) the words "any suspension under section 38(2) below or, as the case may be," shall cease to have effect.

(2) After subsection (1A) of that section there shall be inserted the following subsection-

  "(1B) Where a prisoner whose sentence is for a term of twelve months or more is released on licence under section 33A(2) or 34A(3) above, subsection (1) above shall have effect as if for the reference to three-quarters of his sentence there were substituted a reference to the difference between-

  (a) that proportion of his sentence; and
  (b) the duration of the curfew condition to which he is or was subject."

(3) In subsection (2) of that section, for the words "section 36(1) above" there shall be substituted the words "section 34A(3) or 36(1) above".

(4) In subsection (4) of that section-

  (a) after the words "a licence" there shall be inserted the words "under this Part"; and
  (b) the words "(which shall include on his release conditions as to his supervision by a probation officer)" shall cease to have effect.

(5) After that subsection there shall be inserted the following subsection-

  "(4A) The conditions so specified may in the case of a person released on licence under section 34A above whose sentence is for a term of less than twelve months, and shall in any other case, include on the person's release conditions as to his supervision by-

  (a) a probation officer appointed for or assigned to the petty sessions area within which the person resides for the time being; or
  (b) where the person is under the age of 18 years, a member of a youth offending team established by the local authority within whose area the person resides for the time being."

(6) For subsection (5) of that section there shall be substituted the following subsection-

"(5) The Secretary of State shall not include on release, or subsequently insert, a condition in the licence of a long-term prisoner, or vary or cancel any such condition, except after consultation with the Board."

84. After subsection (5) of section 39 of the 1991 Act (recall of prisoners while on licence) there shall be inserted the following subsection-

"(5A) In the case of a prisoner to whom section 44A below applies, subsections (4)(b) and (5) of that section apply in place of subsection (5) above."

85. After subsection (4) of section 40 of the 1991 Act (convictions during currency of original sentences) there shall be inserted the following subsections-

"(5) Where the new offence is found to have been committed over a period of two or more days, or at some time during a period of two or more days, it shall be taken for the purposes of this section to have been committed on the last of those days.

(6) For the purposes of any enactment conferring rights of appeal in criminal cases, any such order as is mentioned in subsection (2) or (3A) above made with regard to any person shall be treated as a sentence passed on him for the offence for which the sentence referred to in subsection (1) above was passed."

86.– (1) For subsections (1) and (2) of section 41 of the 1991 Act (remand time to count towards time served) there shall be substituted the following subsections-

"(1) Where a person is sentenced to imprisonment for a term in respect of an offence, this section applies to him if the court directs under section 9 of the Crime (Sentences) Act 1997 that the number of days for which he was remanded in custody in connection with-

(a) the offence; or
(b) any other offence the charge for which was founded on the same facts or evidence,

shall count as time served by him as part of the sentence.

(2) For the purpose of determining for the purposes of this Part whether a person to whom this section applies-

(a) has served, or would (but for his release) have served, a particular proportion of his sentence; or
(b) has served a particular period,

the number of days specified in the direction shall, subject to subsections (3) and (4) below, be treated as having been served by him as part of that sentence or period."

(2) After subsection (3) of that section there shall be inserted the following subsection-

"(4) Where the period for which a licence granted under section 33A(2), 34A(3) or 36(1) above to a short-term prisoner remains in force cannot exceed one-quarter of his sentence, nothing in subsection (2) above shall have the effect of reducing that period."

87.– (1) In subsection (3) of section 43 of the 1991 Act (young offenders), for the words "subsections (1)" there shall be substituted the words "subsection (1)".

(2) In subsection (5) of that section, for the words "section 37(4)" there shall be substituted the words "section 37(4A)".

88.– (1) In subsection (1) of section 45 of the 1991 Act (fine defaulters and contemnors), for the words "except sections 35 and 40" there shall be substituted the words "except sections 33A, 34A, 35 and 40".

(2) In subsection (3) of that section-

  (a) for the words "subsections (1) to (4)" there shall be substituted the words "subsections (1) to (3)"; and

  (b) for the words "section 38(2) or 39(1)" there shall be substituted the words "section 39(1) or (2)".

(3) In subsection (4) of that section-

  (a) the words "any suspension under section 38(2) below; or" shall cease to have effect; and

  (b) for the words "section 39(1)" there shall be substituted the words "section 39(1) or (2)".

89. In subsection (2) of section 46 of the 1991 Act (persons liable to removal from the United Kingdom), for the words from "section 37(4)" to the end there shall be substituted the words "section 37 above shall have effect as if subsection (4A) were omitted".

90. For subsection (2) of section 47 of the 1991 Act (persons extradited to the United Kingdom) there shall be substituted the following subsection-

"(2) In the case of an extradited prisoner, section 9 of the Crime (Sentences) Act 1997 (crediting of periods of remand in custody) shall have effect as if the days for which he was kept in custody while awaiting extradition were days for which he was remanded in custody in connection with the offence, or any other offence the charge for which was founded on the same facts or evidence."

91. In section 50 of the 1991 Act (transfer by order of certain functions to Board), for subsection (3) (including that subsection as applied by any order under subsection (1) of that section) there shall be substituted the following subsection-

"(3) In section 37 above, in subsection (5) for the words "after consultation with the Board" there shall be substituted the words "in accordance with recommendations of the Board", and subsection (6) shall be omitted."

92. In subsection (4) of section 51 of the 1991 Act (interpretation of Part II)-

(a) for the words "Subsections (2) and (3)" there shall be substituted the words "Subsection (3)"; and
(b) for the words "as they apply" there shall be substituted the words "as it applies".

93. After subsection (7) of section 53 of the 1991 Act (notices of transfer in certain cases involving children) there shall be inserted the following subsection-

"(8) This section shall not apply in any case in which section 51 of the Crime and Disorder Act 1998 (no committal proceedings for indictable-only offences) applies."

94.– (1) In subsection (1) of section 65 of the 1991 Act (supervision of young offenders after release), for the words from "a probation officer" to the end there shall be substituted the following paragraphs-

"(a) a probation officer;
(b) a social worker of a local authority social services department; or
(c) in the case of a person under the age of 18 years on his release, a member of a youth offending team."

(2) After that subsection there shall be inserted the following subsections-

"(1A) Where the supervision is to be provided by a probation officer, the probation officer shall be an officer appointed for or assigned to the petty sessions area within which the offender resides for the time being.

(1B) Where the supervision is to be provided by-

(a) a social worker of a local authority social services department; or
(b) a member of a youth offending team,

the social worker or member shall be a social worker of, or a member of a youth offending team established by, the local authority within whose area the offender resides for the time being."

95. In subsection (1) of section 99 of the 1991 Act (general interpretation), after the definition of "young person" there shall be inserted the following definition-

""youth offending team" means a team established under section 39 of the Crime and Disorder Act 1998."

96.– (1) After sub-paragraph (5) of paragraph 1 of Schedule 2 to the 1991 Act (enforcement etc. of community orders) there shall be inserted the following sub-paragraph-

"(6) Where a drug treatment and testing order has been made on an appeal brought from the Crown Court, or from the criminal division of the Court of Appeal, for the purposes of this Schedule it shall be deemed to have been made by the Crown Court."

(2) In sub-paragraph (1)(d) of paragraph 3 of that Schedule, the words "revoke the order and" shall cease to have effect.

(3) After sub-paragraph (2) of that paragraph there shall be inserted the following sub-paragraph-

"(2A) Where a magistrates' court deals with an offender under sub-paragraph (1)(d) above, it shall revoke the relevant order if it is still in force."

(4) In sub-paragraph (1)(d) of paragraph 4 of that Schedule, the words "revoke the order and" shall cease to have effect.

(5) After sub-paragraph (2) of that paragraph there shall be inserted the following sub-paragraph-

"(2A) Where the Crown Court deals with an offender under sub-paragraph (1)(d) above, it shall revoke the relevant order if it is still in force."

(6) After paragraph 12(4) of that Schedule there shall be inserted the following sub-paragraphs-

"(5) Where-

(a) the court amends a probation order or community service order under this paragraph;
(b) a local authority is specified in the order in accordance with section 2(2)(b) or 14(4)(c) of the 1973 Act; and
(c) the change, or proposed change, of residence also is or would be a change of residence from the area of that authority to the area of another such authority,

the court shall further amend the order by substituting the other authority for the authority specified in the order.

(6) In sub-paragraph (5) above

"local authority" has the meaning given by section 42 of the Crime and Disorder Act 1998, and references to the area of a local authority shall be construed in accordance with that section."

(7) In paragraph 17(1) of that Schedule, the words from "and the court shall not" to the end shall cease to have effect.

97. In paragraph 1(2) of Schedule 5 to the 1991 Act (Parole Board: supplementary provisions), for the words "its functions under Part II of this Act" there shall be substituted the following paragraphs-

"(a) its functions under this Part in respect of long-term and short-term prisoners; and

(b) its functions under Chapter II of Part II of the Crime (Sentences) Act 1997 in respect of life prisoners within the meaning of that Chapter".

Prisoners and Criminal Proceedings (Scotland) Act 1993 (c.9)

98.– (1) In subsection (1) of section 1 of the 1993 Act (release of short-term, long-term and life prisoners), at the beginning there shall be inserted the words "Subject to section 26A(4) of this Act,".

(2) In subsection (2) of that section, at the end there shall be added the words "unless he has before that time been so released, in relation to that sentence, under any provision of this Act".

(3) After subsection (3) of that section there shall be inserted the following subsection-

"(3A) Subsections (1) to (3) above are subject to section 1A of this Act."

99.– (1) After subsection (1) of section 4 of the 1993 Act (persons detained under the Mental Health (Scotland) Act 1984) there shall be inserted the following subsection-

"(1A) This Part of this Act shall apply to a person conveyed to and detained in a hospital pursuant to a hospital direction under section 59A of the 1995 Act as if, while so detained, he was serving the sentence of imprisonment imposed on him at the time at which that direction was made."

(2) The amendment made by sub-paragraph (1) above shall be deemed to have had effect from 1 January 1998.

100. In section 5 of the 1993 Act (fine defaulters and persons in contempt of court)-

(a) in subsection (1), for the words "and (3)" there shall be substituted the words "to (4)"; and

(b) after subsection (3) there shall be inserted the following subsection-

"(4) Where a person has had imposed on him two or more terms of imprisonment or detention mentioned in subsection (1)(a) or (b) above, sections 1A and 27(5) of this Act shall apply to those terms as if they were terms of imprisonment."

101. In section 7 of the 1993 Act (children detained in solemn proceedings)-

(a) in subsection (1)(b), at the end there shall be added the words "unless he has before that time been so released, in relation to that sentence, under any provision of this Act";

(b) after that subsection there shall be inserted the following subsections-

"(2A) This subsection applies where a child detained under section 208 of the 1995 Act is sentenced, while so detained, to a determinate term of detention in a young offenders institution or imprisonment and, by virtue of section 27(5) of this Act, such terms of detention or imprisonment are treated as single term.

(2B) In a case where subsection (2A) applies and the single term mentioned in that subsection is less than four years, the provisions of this section shall apply.

(2C) In a case where subsection (2A) applies and the single term mentioned in that subsection is of four or more years-

(a) section 6 of this Act shall apply to him as if the single term were an equivalent sentence of detention in a young offenders institution, if that term is served in such an institution; and

(b) the provisions of this Act shall apply to him as if the single term were an equivalent sentence of imprisonment, if that term is served in a remand centre or a prison.";

(c) after subsection (4) there shall be inserted the following subsection-

"(4A) Where an order under subsection (3) above is made, the making of the order shall, if there is in force a licence relating to the person in respect of whom the order is made, have the effect of revoking that licence."; and

(d) in subsection (5), after the word "construed" there shall be inserted the words "and sections 1A and 27 shall apply".

102. In section 11 of the 1993 Act (duration of licences), subsections (3)(b) and (4) shall cease to have effect.

103. In section 14 of the 1993 Act (supervised release of short-term prisoners), subsections (2) and (3) shall cease to have effect.

104.– (1) In subsection (1) of section 16 of the 1993 Act (orders for return to prison after commission of further offence), after the word "released" there shall be inserted the words "at any time".

(2) In paragraph (a) of subsection (7) of that section, after the word "shall" there shall be inserted the words ", if the licence is in force when the order is made,".

(3) Paragraph (b) of that subsection shall cease to have effect.

105. In section 17 of the 1993 Act (revocation of licence), after subsection (4) there shall be inserted the following subsection-

"(4A) Where the case of a prisoner to whom section 3A of this Act applies is referred to the Parole Board under subsection (3) above, subsection (4) of that section shall apply to that prisoner in place of subsection (4) above."

106. In section 20 of the 1993 Act (Parole Board for Scotland), at the end of subsection (4) there shall be inserted the words-

> "and rules under this section may make different provision for different classes of prisoner."

107. After subsection (7) of section 27 of the 1993 Act (interpretation) there shall be inserted the following subsection-

> "(8) For the purposes of this section "public holiday" means any day on which, in the opinion of the Secretary of State, public offices or other facilities likely to be of use to the prisoner in the area in which he is likely to be following his discharge from prison will be closed."

108. In Schedule 6 to the 1993 Act (transitional provisions), after paragraph 6C there shall be inserted the following paragraph-

> "**6D.** Where a prisoner released on licence is treated by virtue of the provisions of this or any other enactment as a prisoner whose licence was granted under section 2(4) of this Act, the validity of his licence shall not be affected by the absence in the licence of such a condition as is specified in section 12(2) of this Act."

Probation Service Act 1993 (c.47)

109. In subsection (1)(dd) of section 4 of the (1993 c.47.)Probation Service Act 1993 (functions of probation committee), for the words "a secure training order (within the meaning of section 1 of the Criminal Justice and Public Order Act 1994)" there shall be substituted the words "a detention and training order (within the meaning of section 73 of the Crime and Disorder Act 1998)".

110.– (1) In subsection (1) of section 17 of that Act (probation committee expenditure), for the words "(5) and (5A)" there shall be substituted the words "and (5)".

(2) Subsection (5A) of that section shall cease to have effect.

Criminal Justice and Public Order Act 1994 (c.33)

111. In subsection (3) of section 12 of the 1994 Act (escort arrangements and officers), after the words "secure training orders" there shall be inserted the words "or detention and training orders".

112. In paragraph 4 of Schedule 1 to the 1994 Act (escort arrangements: England and Wales), in the definition of "the offender", after the words "section 1 of this Act" there shall be inserted the words "or detention and training under section 73 of the Crime and Disorder Act 1998".

113.– (1) In sub-paragraph (1) of paragraph 3 of Schedule 2 to the 1994 Act (certification of custody officers: England and Wales)-

(a) in paragraph (b), for the words "person in charge" there shall be substituted the word "monitor"; and

(b) in paragraph (c), for the words "person in charge" there shall be substituted the word "governor".

(2) In sub-paragraph (2) of that paragraph, for the words "or person in charge" there shall be substituted the words ", monitor or governor".

Drug Trafficking Act 1994 (c.37)

114. In subsection (7) of section 2 of the Drug Trafficking Act 1994 (confiscation orders), paragraph (a) shall cease to have effect.

Proceeds of Crime (Scotland) Act 1995 (c.43)

115. At the end of section 18 of the Proceeds of Crime (Scotland) Act 1995 (order to make material available) there shall be added the following subsection-

"(12)   In this section "constable" includes a person commissioned by the Commissioners of Customs and Excise."

116. In subsection (6) of section 19 of that Act (authority for search)-

(a) for the words "subsection (10)" there shall be substituted the words "subsections (10) and (12)"; and

(b) for the words "it applies" there shall be substituted the words "they apply".

Criminal Procedure (Scotland) Act 1995 (c.46)

117.– (1) For section 18(3) of the 1995 Act (prints and samples) there shall be substituted the following subsection-

"(3) Subject to subsection (4) below, all record of any relevant physical data taken from or provided by a person under subsection (2) above, all samples taken under subsection (6) below and all information derived from such samples shall be destroyed as soon as possible following a decision not to institute criminal proceedings against the person or on the conclusion of such proceedings otherwise than with a conviction or an order under section 246(3) of this Act."

(2) The amendment made by sub-paragraph (1) above shall be deemed to have had effect from 1 August 1997.

118. In subsection (3) of section 49 of the 1995 Act (references to children's hearings), in paragraph (b), after the words "the sheriff" there shall be inserted the words "or district".

119.   In section 106(1)(bb) of the 1995 Act (appeals against automatic sentences), which is prospectively inserted by section 18(1) of the Crime and Punishment (Scotland) Act 1997, for the words "205B(3) or 209(1A)" there shall be substituted the words "or 205B(3)".

120.   In section 108A of the 1995 Act (prosecutor's right of appeal against refusal to impose automatic sentence), which is prospectively inserted by section 18(2) of the (1997 c.48.)Crime and Punishment (Scotland) Act 1997, for the words "205B(3) or 209(1A)" there shall be substituted the words "or 205B(3)".

121.   In section 118(4A) of the 1995 Act (disposal of appeals), which is prospectively inserted by section 18(5) of the (1997 c.48.)Crime and Punishment (Scotland) Act 1997, in paragraph (c), sub-paragraph (iii) shall cease to have effect.

122.   In section 167 of the 1995 Act (findings and sentences in summary proceedings), in subsection (7), at the beginning there shall be inserted the words "Subject to section 204A of this Act,".

123.   In subsection (5C) of section 175 of the 1995 Act (right of appeal in summary proceedings), the words "paragraph (a) of" shall be omitted.

124.   In subsection (1) of section 307 of the 1995 Act (interpretation), in the definition of "officer of law"-

(a) after paragraph (b) there shall be inserted the following paragraph-
   "(ba) any person commissioned by the Commissioners of Customs and Excise;"; and
(b) in paragraph (e), for the words "class or persons" there shall be substituted the words "class of persons".

Criminal Procedure and Investigations Act 1996 (c.25)

125.   In subsection (2) of section 1 of the Criminal Procedure and Investigations Act 1996 (application of Part I of that Act)-

(a) after paragraph (c) there shall be inserted the following paragraph-
   "(cc) a person is charged with an offence for which he is sent for trial under section 51 (no committal proceedings for indictable-only offences) of the Crime and Disorder Act 1998,"; and
(b) at the end there shall be inserted the words "or
   (f) a bill of indictment charging a person with an indictable offence is preferred under section 22B(3)(a) of the Prosecution of Offences Act 1985."

126.   In section 5 of that Act (compulsory disclosure by accused), after subsection (3) there shall be inserted the following subsection-

"(3A) Where this Part applies by virtue of section 1(2)(cc), this section does not apply unless-

(a) copies of the documents containing the evidence have been served on the accused under regulations made under paragraph 1 of Schedule 3 to the Crime and Disorder Act 1998; and

(b) a copy of the notice under subsection (7) of section 51 of that Act has been served on him under that subsection."

127. In subsection (1) of section 13 of that Act (time limits: transitional)-

(a) after the words "section 1(2)(b) or (c)," there shall be inserted the words-
"(cc) the accused is sent for trial under section 51 of the Crime and Disorder Act 1998 (where this Part applies by virtue of section 1(2)(cc)),"; and

(b) after the words "section 1(2)(e)" there shall be inserted the words "or (f)".

128. In subsection (1)(a) of section 28 of that Act (introduction to Part III), after the words "committed for trial" there shall be inserted the words ", or sent for trial under section 51 of the Crime and Disorder Act 1998,".

129. In subsection (1) of section 39 of that Act (meaning of pre-trial hearing), after the words "committed for trial for the offence concerned" there shall be inserted the words ", after the accused has been sent for trial for the offence under section 51 of the Crime and Disorder Act 1998,".

Crime (Sentences) Act 1997 (c.43)

130.- (1) In subsection (3) of section 28 of the 1997 Act (duty to release certain life prisoners), after paragraph (b) there shall be inserted the words "and

(c) the provisions of this section as compared with those of sections 33(2) and 35(1) of the Criminal Justice Act 1991 ("the 1991 Act")".

(2) In subsection (7) of that section, in paragraph (c), for the words from "the time when" to the end there shall be substituted the words "he has served one-half of that sentence".

131.- (1) In subsection (2) of section 31 of the 1997 Act (duration and conditions of licences), the words "(which shall include on his release conditions as to his supervision by a probation officer)" shall cease to have effect.

(2) After that subsection there shall be inserted the following subsection-

"(2A) The conditions so specified shall include on the prisoner's release conditions as to his supervision by-

(a) a probation officer appointed for or assigned to the petty sessions area within which the prisoner resides for the time being;

(b) where the prisoner is under the age of 22, a social worker of the social services department of the local authority within whose area the prisoner resides for the time being; or

(c) where the prisoner is under the age of 18, a member of a youth offending team established by that local authority under section 39 of the Crime and Disorder Act 1998."

(3) In subsection (6) of that section, for the words "section 24(2) above" there shall be substituted the words "section 46(3) of the 1991 Act", and for the words "the words in parentheses" there shall be substituted the words "subsection (2A) above".

132.– (1) In subsection (1) of section 35 of the 1997 Act (fine defaulters: general), for the words "the 1980 Act" there shall be substituted the words "the Magistrates' Courts Act 1980 ("the 1980 Act")".

(2) In subsection (5)(e) of that section, for the words "paragraph 3(2)(a)" there shall be substituted the words "sub-paragraphs (2)(a) and (2A) of paragraph 3".

(3) In subsection (8) of that section-

(a) in paragraph (a), the words "to revoke the order and deal with an offender for the offence in respect of which the order was made" shall cease to have effect; and

(b) in paragraph (b), for the words "paragraph 3(2)(a)" there shall be substituted the words "sub-paragraphs (2)(a) and (2A) of paragraph 3".

133. In section 54 of the 1997 Act (general interpretation), subsection (2) shall cease to have effect.

134. Subsection (5)(b) of section 57 of the 1997 Act (short title, commencement and extent) shall have effect as if the reference to the Channel Islands included a reference to the Isle of Man.

135.– (1) Schedule 1 to the 1997 Act (transfer of prisoners within the British Islands) shall be amended as follows.

(2) In sub-paragraph (3) of paragraph 6-

(a) after paragraph (a) there shall be inserted the following paragraph-
"(aa) in relation to a person who is supervised in pursuance of a detention and training order, being ordered to be detained for any failure to comply with requirements under section 76(6)(b) of the Crime and Disorder Act 1998;"; and

(b) in paragraph (b), for the words "recalled to prison under the licence" there shall be substituted the words "recalled or returned to prison".

(3) In paragraph 8-

    (a) in sub-paragraph (2), for the words from "sections 10" to "27 of this Act" there shall be substituted the words "sections 33 to 39, 41 to 46 and 65 of the 1991 Act, paragraphs 8, 10 to 13 and 19 of Schedule 12 to that Act and sections 75 to 77 of the Crime and Disorder Act 1998";

    (b) in sub-paragraph (4), for the words from "sections 16" to "27 of this Act" there shall be substituted the words "sections 37 to 39, 43 to 46 and 65 of the 1991 Act, paragraphs 8, 10 to 13 and 19 of Schedule 12 to that Act and sections 76 and 77 of the Crime and Disorder Act 1998";

    (c) in sub-paragraph (5), after the words "Any provision of" there shall be inserted the words "Part II of the 1991 Act or"; and

    (d) after sub-paragraph (5) there shall be inserted the following sub-paragraphs-"

(6) Section 41 of the 1991 Act, as applied by sub-paragraph (2) or (4) above, shall have effect as if section 67 of the Criminal Justice Act 1967 (computation of sentences of imprisonment passed in England and Wales) or, as the case may require, section 9 of this Act extended to Scotland.

(7) Section 65(7)(b) of the 1991 Act, as applied by sub-paragraph (2) or (4) above, shall have effect as if the reference to a young offender institution were a reference to a young offenders institution."

(4) In paragraph 9-

    (a) in sub-paragraph (1), paragraph (a) and, in paragraph (b), the words "to that and" shall cease to have effect;

    (b) in sub-paragraph (2), for the words from "sections 10" to "27 of this Act" there shall be substituted the words "sections 33 to 46 and 65 of the 1991 Act, paragraphs 8, 10 to 13 and 19 of Schedule 12 to that Act and sections 75 to 77 of the Crime and Disorder Act 1998";

    (c) in sub-paragraph (4), for the words from "section 16" to "27 of this Act" there shall be substituted the words "sections 37 to 40A, 43 to 46 and 65 of the 1991 Act, paragraphs 8, 10 to 13 and 19 of Schedule 12 to that Act and sections 76 and 77 of the Crime and Disorder Act 1998";

    (d) sub-paragraph (5) shall cease to have effect;

    (e) in sub-paragraph (6), after the words "Any provision of" there shall be inserted the words "Part II of the 1991 Act or"; and

    (f) after sub-paragraph (6) there shall be inserted the following sub-paragraphs-

"(7)   Section 41 of the 1991 Act, as applied by sub-paragraph (2) or (4) above, shall have effect as if section 67 of the (1967 c.80.)Criminal Justice Act 1967 or, as the case may require, section 9 of this Act extended to Northern Ireland.

(8) Section 65(7)(b) of the 1991 Act, as applied by sub-paragraph (1), (2) or (4) above, shall have effect as if the reference to a young offender institution were a reference to a young offenders centre."

(5) In paragraph 10-

    (a) in sub-paragraph (2)(a)-

        (i) for the words from "sections" to ""1997 Act")" there shall be substituted the words "sections 1, 1A, 3, 3A, 5, 6(1)(a), 7, 9, 11 to 13, 15 to 21, 26A and 27 of, and Schedules 2 and 6 to, the Prisoners and Criminal Proceedings (Scotland) Act 1993 ("the 1993 Act")"; and

        (ii) after the word "3," there shall be inserted words "6(1)(b)(i) and (iii)";

    (b) in sub-paragraph (2)(b), for the words "sub-paragraphs (3) and (4)" there shall be substituted the words "sub-paragraph (3)";

    (c) sub-paragraph (4) shall cease to have effect;

    (d) in sub-paragraph (5)(a), for the words from "sections 15" to "37 of the 1997 Act" there shall be substituted the words "sections 1A, 2(4), 3A, 11 to 13, 15 to 21, 26A and 27 of, and Schedules 2 and 6 to, the 1993 Act";

    (e) for sub-paragraph (6)(b) there shall be substituted the following sub-paragraph-

        "(b) in the said sub-paragraph (2) the reference to section 6(1)(b)(i) of the 1993 Act is a reference to that provision so far as it relates to a person sentenced under section 205(3) of the Criminal Procedure (Scotland) Act 1995."; and

    (f) for sub-paragraph (7) there shall be substituted the following sub-paragraph-

"(7)   Any provision of Part I of the 1993 Act which is applied by sub-paragraph (2) or (5) above shall have effect (as so applied) as if any reference to a chief social work officer were a reference to a chief social worker of a local authority social services department."

(6) In paragraph 11-

    (a) in sub-paragraph (2)(a)-

        (i) for the words from "sections" to "1997 Act")" there shall be substituted the words "sections 1, 1A, 3, 3A, 5, 6(1)(a), 7, 9, 11 to 13, 15 to 21, 26A and 27 of, and Schedules 2 and 6 to, the 1993 Act"; and

        (ii) after the word "3," there shall be inserted the words "6(1)(b)(i) and (iii),";

    (b) in sub-paragraph (4)(a), for the words from "sections 15" to "37 of the 1997 Act" there shall be substituted the words "sections 1A, 3A, 11 to 13, 15 to 21, 26A and 27 of, and Schedules 2 and 6 to, the 1993 Act";

    (c) in sub-paragraph (5), for the words "Sub-paragraph (5)" there shall be substituted the words "Sub-paragraph (6)"; and

    (d) in sub-paragraph (6), the words "or Part III of the 1997 Act" shall cease to have effect and, in the Table, for the entry relating to the expression "young offenders institution" there shall be substituted the following entry-

"Probation officer appointed for or assigned to such petty sessions area

Probation Officer appointed by the Probation Board for Northern Ireland"

(7) In sub-paragraph (5) of paragraph 12, in the Table, the entry relating to the expression "Prison rules" shall cease to have effect.

(8) In sub-paragraph (5) of paragraph 13, in the Table, the entry relating to the expression "Prison rules" shall cease to have effect.

(9) In sub-paragraph (1)(a) of paragraph 17 (prisoners unlawfully at large), after the words "section 49(1)" there shall be inserted the words "and (5)".

(10)   In sub-paragraph (1) of paragraph 20, in the definition of "supervision", after the word "purpose" there shall be inserted the words "or a detention and training order".

136.   In Schedule 2 to the 1997 Act (repatriation of prisoners to the British Islands), paragraphs 4 and 8 are hereby repealed.

137.   In Schedule 4 to the 1997 Act (minor and consequential amendments), the following provisions are hereby repealed, namely-

(a) in paragraph 6, sub-paragraph (1)(b);
(b) paragraphs 9 and 11; and
(c) in paragraph 12, sub-paragraph (4).

138.– (1) In Schedule 5 to the 1997 Act (transitional provisions and savings), paragraphs 1 to 4 and 6 are hereby repealed and the following provisions shall cease to have effect, namely-

(a) paragraph 5(2);
(b) paragraphs 8, 9(1) and 10(1);
(c) in paragraph 11, sub-paragraph (1), in sub-paragraph (2)(c), the words "or Part III of the 1997 Act" and, in sub-paragraph (3), the words from the beginning to "1995; and"; and
(d) in paragraph 12, sub-paragraph (1) and, in sub-paragraph (2)(c), the words "or Part III of the 1997 Act".

(2) In paragraph 11(2) of that Schedule-

(a) in paragraph (a)-
(i) for the words from "sections 15" to "1997 Act" there shall be substituted the words "sections 1, 1A, 3, 3A, 5, 6(1)(a), 7, 9, 11 to 13, 15 to 21, 26A and 27 of, and Schedules 2 and 6 to, the Prisoners and Criminal Proceedings (Scotland) Act 1993 ("the 1993 Act")"; and
(ii) for the words "the 1989 Act" there shall be substituted the words "the Prisons (Scotland) Act 1989 ("the 1989 Act")"; and
(b) in paragraph (b), for the words from "sections 15" to "1997 Act" there shall be substituted the words "sections 1A, 2(4), 3A, 11 to 13, 15 to 21, 26A and 27 of, and Schedules 2 and 6 to, the 1993 Act".

(3) In paragraph 12(2) of that Schedule-

    (a) in paragraph (a)-

        (i) for the words from "sections 15" to "1997 Act" there shall be substituted the words "sections 1, 1A, 3, 3A, 5, 6(1)(a), 7, 9, 11 to 13, 15 to 21, 26A and 27 of, and Schedules 2 and 6 to, the (1993 c.9.)Prisoners and Criminal Proceedings (Scotland) Act ("the 1993 Act")"; and

        (ii) for the words "the 1989 Act" there shall be substituted the (1989 c.45.)words "the Prisons (Scotland) Act 1989 ("the 1989 Act")"; and

    (b) in paragraph (b), for the words from "sections 15" to "1997 Act" there shall be substituted the words "sections 1A, 2(4), 3A, 11 to 13, 15 to 21, 26A and 27 of, and Schedules 2 and 6 to, the 1993 Act".

139.   In Schedule 6 to the 1997 Act (repeals), the entries relating to sections 33 to 51 and 65 of the 1991 Act are hereby repealed.

Crime and Punishment (Scotland) Act 1997 (c.48)

140.   Section 4 of the Crime and Punishment (Scotland) Act 1997 (supervised release orders) is hereby repealed.

141.– (1) In Schedule 1 to that Act (minor and consequential amendments), the following provisions are hereby repealed, namely-

    (a) paragraphs 1, 9(7), 10(2)(a), 13(3) and 21(3); and

    (b) in paragraph 14, sub-paragraphs (2)(a), (3)(e), (4) to (7), (9), (10)(a), (11)(b), (12), (13) to (15) and (17).

(2) In paragraph 14 of that Schedule, for sub-paragraph (16) there shall be substituted the following sub-paragraph-

    "(16)   In section 27(1) (interpretation), in the definition of "supervised release order" the words "(as inserted by section 14 of this Act)" shall cease to have effect."

142.   Schedule 2 to that Act (transitional provisions) is hereby repealed.

143.– (1) Schedule 3 to that Act (repeals) shall be amended in accordance with this paragraph.

(2) In the entry relating to the Prisons (Scotland) Act 1989, in the third column, the words "In section 39, subsection (7)" are hereby repealed.

(3) In the entry relating to the Prisoners and Criminal Proceedings (Scotland) Act 1993-

    (a) the words relating to sections 1, 3(2), 5, 6(1), 7, 9, 12(3), 16, 17(1), 20, 24, and Schedule 1;

(b) in the words relating to section 14, the words "and in subsection (4), the words "short-term"";

(c) in the words relating to 27(1)-

    (i) the words "the definitions of "short term prisoner" and "long-term prisoner" and";

    (ii) in the words relating to the definition of "supervised release order" the words "and the words from "but" to the end"; and

(d) the words relating to section 27(2), (3), (5) and (6),

are hereby repealed.

(4) In the entry relating to the Criminal Procedure (Scotland) Act 1995, in the third column, the words relating to section 44 are hereby repealed.

Sex Offenders Act 1997 (c.51)

144. In subsection (1)(a) of section 4 of the Sex Offenders Act 1997 (young sex offenders), after the word "under" there shall be inserted the words "a detention and training order or".

Schedule 8
This schedule deals with minor and consequential amendments.

SCHEDULE 9

TRANSITIONAL PROVISIONS AND SAVINGS

Presumption of incapacity

1. Nothing in section 34 of this Act shall apply in relation to anything done before the commencement of that section.

Effect of child's silence at trial

2. Nothing in section 35 of this Act shall apply where the offence was committed before the commencement of that section.

Sexual or violent offenders: extended sentences

3. Section 58 of this Act does not apply where the sexual or violent offence was committed before the commencement of that section.

Drug treatment and testing orders

4. Section 61 of this Act does not apply in relation to an offence committed before the commencement of that section.

Young offenders: cautions

5.– (1) Any caution given to a child or young person before the commencement of section 65 of this Act shall be treated for the purposes of subsections (2) and (4) of that section as a reprimand.

(2) Any second or subsequent caution so given shall be treated for the purposes of paragraphs (a) and (b) of subsection (3) of that section as a warning.

Abolition of secure training orders

6. In relation to any time before the commencement of subsection (7) of section 73 of this Act, section 9A of the 1997 Act shall have effect as if after subsection (1) there were inserted the following subsection-

"(1A) Section 9 above applies to periods of detention which offenders are liable to serve under secure training orders as it applies to sentences of imprisonment."

Sentencing guidelines

7.– (1) Section 80 of this Act does not apply by virtue of subsection (1)(a) of that section in any case where the Court is seised of the appeal before the commencement of that section.

(2) In this paragraph "the Court" and "seised" have the same meanings as in that section.

Confiscation orders on committal for sentence

8. Section 83 of this Act does not apply where the offence was committed before the commencement of that section.

Football spectators: failure to comply with reporting duty

9. Section 84 of this Act does not apply where the offence was committed before the commencement of that section.

Power to release short-term prisoners on licence

10.– (1) Section 99 of this Act does not apply in relation to a prisoner who, immediately before the commencement of that section, has served one or more days more than the requisite period for the term of his sentence.

(2) In this paragraph "the requisite period" has the same meaning as in section 34A of the 1991 Act (which is inserted by section 99 of this Act).

Early release: two or more sentences

11.– (1) Where the terms of two or more sentences passed before the commencement of section 101 of this Act have been treated, by virtue of section 51(2) of the 1991 Act, as a single term for the purposes of Part II of that Act, they shall continue to be so treated after that commencement.

(2) Subject to sub-paragraph (1) above, section 101 of this Act applies where one or more of the sentences concerned were passed after that commencement.

Recall to prison of short-term prisoners

12.– (1) Sub-paragraphs (2) to (7) below have effect in relation to any prisoner whose sentence, or any part of whose sentence, was imposed for an offence committed before the commencement of section 103 of this Act.

(2) The following provisions of this Act do not apply, namely-

   (a) section 103;
   (b) paragraphs 83(1)(b) and 88(3)(a) of Schedule 8 to this Act and section 119 so far as relating to those paragraphs; and
   (c) section 120(2) and Schedule 10 so far as relating to the repeal of section 38 of the 1991 Act and the repeals in sections 37(1) and 45(4) of that Act.

(3) Section 33 of the 1991 Act has effect as if, in subsection (3)(b) (as amended by paragraph 80(1) of Schedule 8 to this Act), for the words "section 39(1) or (2)" there were substituted the words "section 38(2) or 39(1) or (2)".

(4) Section 33A of the 1991 Act (as inserted by paragraph 81 of Schedule 8 to this Act) has effect as if-

   (a) in subsection (1), for the words "section 38A(1) or 39(1) or (2)" there were substituted the words "section 38(2) or 38A(1)"; and
   (b) in subsection (3), for the words "section 39(1) or (2)", in both places where they occur, there were substituted the words "section 38(2)".

(5) Section 34A of the 1991 Act (as inserted by section 99 of this Act) has effect as if, in subsection (2)(g), for the words "section 39(1) or (2)" there were substituted the words "section 38(2)".

(6) Section 40A of the 1991 Act (as inserted by section 105 of this Act) has effect as if, in subsection (1), for the word "39" there were substituted the word "38".

(7) Section 44 of the 1991 Act (as substituted by section 59 of this Act) has effect as if-

   (a) in subsections (3) and (4), after the words "subject to" there were inserted the words "any suspension under section 38(2) above or, as the case may be,"; and
   (b) in subsection (7), for the words "sections 37(5) and 39(1) and (2)" there were substituted the words "section 37(5), 38(2) and 39(1) and (2)".

(8) Section 45 of the 1991 Act has effect as if, in subsection (3) (as amended by paragraph 88(2) of Schedule 8 to this Act), for the words "section 39(1) or (2)" there were substituted the words "section 38(2) or 39(1) or (2)".

(9) For the purposes of this paragraph and paragraph 13 below, consecutive sentences, or sentences that are wholly or partly concurrent, shall be treated as parts of a single sentence.

Release on licence following recall to prison

13. Section 104 of this Act does not apply in relation to a prisoner whose sentence, or any part of whose sentence, was imposed for an offence committed before the commencement of that section.

Release on licence following return to prison

14.– (1) Section 105 of this Act does not apply where the new offence was committed before the commencement of that section.

(2) In this paragraph "the new offence" has the same meaning as in section 40 of the 1991 Act.

Remand time: two or more sentences

15.– (1) Where the terms of two or more sentences passed before the commencement of paragraph 11 of Schedule 8 to this Act have been treated, by virtue of section 104(2) of the Criminal Justice Act 1967, as a single term for the purposes of section 67 of that Act, they shall continue to be so treated after that commencement.

(2) Subject to sub-paragraph (1) above, paragraph 11 of Schedule 8 to this Act applies where one or more of the sentences concerned were passed after that commencement.

Schedule 9
This schedule deals with transitional provisions and savings.

SCHEDULE 10

Repeals

Chapter	Short title	Extent of repeal
30 Geo 3 c.48.	Treason Act 1790.	The whole Act.
36 Geo 3 c.7.	Treason Act 1795.	The whole Act.
36 Geo 3 c.31.	Treason by Women Act (Ireland) 1976	The whole Act.
57 Geo 3 c.6.	Treason Act 1817.	The whole Act.
11 & 12 Vict c.12.	Treason Felony Act 1848.	Section 2.
21 & 22 Geo 5 c.24.	Sentence of Death (Expectant Mothers) Act 1933.	The whole Act.
23 Geo 5 c.12.	Children and Young Persons Act 1933.	In section 47(2), the words from the beginning to "court; and". In Schedule 2, in paragraph 15(a), the word "shall", in the second place where it occurs, and, in paragraph 17, the words "or, if a metropolitan stipendiary magistrate, may sit alone".
1945 c.15 (N.I.).	Criminal Justice Act (Northern Ireland) 1945.	Sections 32 and 33.
1967 c.80.	Criminal Justice Act 1967.	In section 56, subsections (3), (6) and (13). Section 67(5)(c).
1968 c.19.	Criminal Appeal Act 1968.	In section 10(2), the words "(other than a supervision order within the meaning of that Part)".
1969 c.54.	Children and Young Persons Act 1969.	Section 12D. Section 13(2). In section 16, subsection (10) and, in subsection (11), the words "seventeen or". Section 23(14)(a).

Chapter	Short title	Extent of repeal
1969 c.54. – *Contd.*	Children and Young Persons Act 1969. – *Contd.*	In section 34, in subsection (1), paragraph (a) and, in paragraph (c), the words "7(7), 7(8),". Section 69(5). In Schedule 6, the entries relating to sections 55, 56(1) and 59(1) of the Children and Young Persons Act 1933.
1972 c.71.	Criminal Justice Act 1972.	Section 49.
1973 c.62.	Powers of Criminal Courts Act 1973.	In section 1, in subsections (8)(b) and (8A) the words "37 or". Section 1B(10). In section 1C(1), paragraph (b) and the word "and" immediately preceding it. In section 2(1), the words "by a probation officer" and the words from "For the purposes" to "available evidence". Section 11. Section 14(8). In section 31, in subsection (3A), the words "Subject to subsections (3B) and (3C) below,", subsections (3B) and (3C), in subsection (4), the words "4 or" and, in subsection (6), the words "about committal by a magistrates' court to the Crown Court". Section 32(5). Section 42(2). In Schedule 1A, paragraph 6(7). In Schedule 5, paragraph 35.
1976 c.63.	Bail Act 1976.	In section 3(5), the words "If it appears that he is unlikely to remain in Great Britain until the time appointed for him to surrender to custody".

Chapter	Short title	Extent of repeal
1980 c.43.	Magistrates' Courts Courts Act 1980.	Section 37. In sections 38(2) and 38A(2), the words ", in accordance with section 56 of the Criminal Justice Act 1967,". In section 108(2), the words "a probation order or". In section 125(4)(c), the word "and" at the end of sub-paragraph (ii). In section 126, the word "and" at the end of paragraph (c). In Schedule 7, paragraph 120(b).
1982 c.48.	Criminal Justice Act 1982.	Section 1A(4A). Section 1B. In section 1C(2), the words "but if he is under 18 at the time of the direction, only for a temporary purpose". In section 3(1)(a), the words "under section 1A above". Section 18(7). In section 19, in subsection (3)(a), the words "revoke it and" and, in subsection (5), the words "revoke the attendance centre order and". Section 66(3). In Schedule 14, paragraph 28.
1987 c.42.	Family Law Reform Act 1987.	Section 8(1). In Schedule 2, paragraph 26.
1988 c.33.	Criminal Justice Act 1988.	Section 69(2). In Schedule 15, paragraph 40.
1989 c.45.	Prisons (Scotland) Act 1989.	In section 39(7), the words from "and the foregoing" to the end.
1991 c.53.	Criminal Justice Act 1991.	In section 6(4), the word "and" immediately following paragraph (e).

Chapter	Short title	Extent of repeal
1991 c.53. – *Contd.*	Criminal Justice Act 1991. – *Contd.*	In section 31(1), in the definition of "custodial sentence", in paragraph (b), the words "or a secure training order under section 1 of the Criminal Justice and Public Order Act 1994".
		Section 33(4). In section 37, in subsection (1), the words "any suspension under section 38(2) below or, as the case may be," and, in subsection (4), the words "(which shall include on his release conditions as to his supervision by a probation officer)". Section 38. In section 45(4), the words "any suspension under section 38(2) below; or". In section 61(1), paragraph (b) and the word "or" immediately preceding that paragraph. Section 62. In Schedule 2, in paragraphs 3(1)(d) and 4(1)(d), the words "revoke the order and" and, in paragraph 17(1), the words from "and the court" to the end. In Schedule 11, paragraphs 10, 11 and 14. In Schedule 12, paragraph 17(3).
1993 c.9.	Prisoners and Criminal Proceedings (Scotland) Act 1993.	Section 11(3)(b) and (4). Section 14(2) and (3). Section 16(7)(b). In paragraph 6B(1) of Schedule 6, the word "and" after head (a).
1993 c.47.	Probation Service Act 1993.	Section 17(5A).

Chapter	Short title	Extent of repeal
1994 c.33.	Criminal Justice and Public Order Act 1994.	Sections 1 to 4. Section 20. In section 35, in subsection (1), the words "who has attained the age of fourteen years" and subsection (6). Section 130(4). In Schedule 10, paragraph 42.
1994 c.37.	Drug Trafficking Act 1994.	Section 2(7)(a).
1995 c.46.	Criminal Procedure (Scotland) Act 1995.	Section 118(4A)(c)(iii). In section 175(5C), the words "paragraph (a) of". In section 209(1), the words "not less than twelve months but".
1997 c.43.	Crime (Sentences) Act 1997.	Section 1. Section 8. Sections 10 to 27. In section 31(2), the words "(which shall include on his release conditions as to his supervision by a probation officer)". In section 35, in subsection (5), paragraph (c) and the word "and" at the end of paragraph (d), and in subsection (8), in paragraph (a), the words "to revoke the order and deal with an offender for the offence in respect of which the order was made" and the word "and" at the end of that paragraph. Section 43(4). Section 54(2). In Schedule 1, in paragraph 9(1), paragraph (a) and, in paragraph (b), the words "to that and", paragraph 9(5), paragraph 10(4), in paragraph 11(6), the words "or Part III of the 1997 Act", in paragraph

Chapter	Short title	Extent of repeal
1997 c.43. – *Contd.*	Crime (Sentences) Act 1997. – *Contd.*	12(5), in the Table, the entry relating to the expression "prison rules" and, in paragraph 13(5), in the Table, the entry relating to the expression "prison rules". In Schedule 2, paragraphs 4 and 8. In Schedule 4, paragraph (1)(b), paragraphs 9 and 11 and paragraph 12(4). In Schedule 5, paragraphs 1 to 4, paragraph 5(2), paragraph 6, paragraph 8, paragraph 9(1), paragraph 10(1), in paragraph 11, sub-paragraph (1), in sub-paragraph (2)(c), the words "or Part III of the 1997 Act" and, in sub-paragraph (3), the words from the beginning to "1995; and", and in paragraph 12, sub-paragraph (1) and, in sub-paragraph (2)(c), the words "or Part III of the 1997 Act". In Schedule 6, the entries relating to sections 33 to 51 and 65 of the Criminal Justice Act 1991.
1997 c.48.	Crime and Punishment (Scotland) Act 1997.	Section 4. Chapter I of Part III. In Schedule 1, paragraph 1, paragraph 9(7), paragraph 10(2)(a), paragraph 13(3), in paragraph 14, sub-paragraphs (2)(a), (3)(e), (4) to (7), (9), (10)(a), (11)(b), (12), (13) to (15) and (17), and paragraph 21(3). Schedule 2. In Schedule 3, in the entry relating to the Prisons (Scotland) Act 1989, the words

Chapter	Short title	Extent of repeal
1997 c.48. – *Contd.*	Crime and Punishment (Scotland) Act 1997. – *Contd.*	"In section 39, subsection (7)", in the entry relating to the Prisoners and Criminal Proceedings (Scotland) Act 1993, the words relating to sections 1, 3(2), 5, 6(1), 7, 9, 12(3), 16, 17(1), 20, 24, 27(2), (3), (5) and (6) and Schedule 1, in the words relating to section 14, the words "and, in subsection (4), the words "short-term"", in the words relating to section 27(1), the words "the definitions of "short term prisoner" and "long-term prisoner" and" and "and the words from "but" to the end" and, in the entry relating to the Criminal Procedure (Scotland) Act 1995, the words relating to section 44.
1997 c.50.	Police Act 1997.	In section 94(4), the word "and" immediately preceding paragraph (c).

Schedule 10
This schedule deals with repeals.

Index

detention and training orders 94–5
drug treatment and testing orders
74–7, 161–4, 169–72
parenting orders 15, 26
reparation orders 82–4, 165–9
probation orders, drug treatment and
testing orders 116–17
Probation Service Act 1993 124–5, 218,
234
Proceeds of Crime (Scotland) Act 1995
219
proof
anti-social behaviour orders 7, 32
child safety orders 19, 20
sex-offender orders 9
Prosecution of Offences Act 1985 53–8,
65–6, 205–6, 220
Protection from Harassment Act 1997
41–2
Public Order Act 1986 23, 40–1
public place, definition 23, 25

racial group, definition 37–8, 44, 118–19
racially-aggravated offences 37–44
assault 38–9
conviction 38–43, 44, 118–19
criminal damage 39–40
definition 37–8, 43, 118–19
harassment 40–4
public order 40–1
Scotland 43–4, 118–19
sentencing guidelines 100, 119
rape 68, 104
see also sexual offenders
reasonable cause
anti-social behaviour orders 6, 7–8, 28,
31–2
sex-offender orders 9–10, 10
recall, prisoners 124–5, 127–8, 210–12,
229–30
recognizance, surety 67–8
regulations 136, 148
Rehabilitation of Offenders Act 1974 200
rehabilitation programmes 80–1
release 129–30, 204–5, 210–12, 216–18

see also licences
consecutive sentences 125–7
curfew conditions 123–5
detention and training orders 93–4,
96–7
early release 125–7, 129–35, 229
life sentences 126–7, 131–2, 205
re-released prisoners 71–2, 107–8,
128–9, 230
short-term prisoners 122–9, 210,
216–18, 228
unconditional release 128
relevant authority, definition 5, 52, 136
relevant date, sex-offender orders 8, 10,
11, 29
relevant officer, definition 104
relevant period, definition 13–14
religious beliefs 175
action plan orders 85
child safety orders 20–1
parenting orders 17
reparation orders 82–3
remand 65, 230
see also custody
15/16-year-old males 120–2
crediting periods 129–30, 212
young persons 119–22
reparation orders
breaches 165–6
discharge 164–5
young offenders 81–4, 164–9
Repatriation of Prisoners Act 1984 141,
204–5
repeals 139, 141, 231–7
reporting restrictions 150–1
reports, crime and disorder 13–14
reprimands
sex-offender orders 11
young offenders 78–81, 205, 228
re-released prisoners 71–2, 107–8, 128–9,
230
see also release
requisite period, definition 123
responsible officers, definition 15, 19
retention, seizure of items 35–7, 142–4

Index compiled by Terry Halliday, *Indexing Specialists*, Hove.